Separation and Divorce

SEPARATION AND DIVORCE

A Canadian Woman's Survival Guide

NANCY GIBSON

Hurtig Publishers
Edmonton

Copyright © 1986 by Nancy Gibson

All rights reserved. No part of this book may be reproduced or transmitted in any form by any means, electronic, electrical, mechanical, chemical, optical, or otherwise, including photocopying and recording, or by any information storage or retrieval system, without written permission from the publisher, except for brief passages quoted by a reviewer in a newspaper or magazine.

Hurtig Publishers Ltd.
10560–105 Street
Edmonton, Alberta
Canada T5H 2W7

Canadian Cataloguing in Publication Data

Gibson, Nancy.
 Separation and divorce

 ISBN 0-88830-306-8

 1. Divorced women — Canada — Life skills guides. 2. Separation (Psychology) 3. Single women — Canada — Life skills guides. I. Title.
HQ838.G52 1986   646.7'8   C86-091293-0

Cover Design: Tad Aronowicz
Cover Photo: Casimir Bart
Typesetting: Attic Typesetting Inc.

Printed and bound in Canada

To Mary Jane, Rena, and "the women"
and of course, to John

Some women will see their reflection in these pages because they have been my friends; others may find traces of their past here because I have heard their stories from mutual friends; most women will find themselves somewhere in these pages because so many of our experiences are universal.

Contents

Preface and Acknowledgements/1

Introduction — **The Mythological Marriage**/4

        Emotional Conflict/5

        Myths You Have Lived With/8

        References/11

Chapter I — **The Final Stage of a Failing Marriage**/12

        Communication/14

        Counselling/16

        Reconciliation?/19

        References/25

Chapter II — **The Grieving Process: It's All Right to Cry**/26

        Denial/27

        Anger/30

        Bargaining/32

        Depression/33

        Strategies for Coping With Depression/35

        Acceptance/42

        Changing Living Patterns/43

        Your Parents/45

        The Old and the New — In-Laws/47

        Relating to Your Ex/50

        Self-assessment/52

        References/57

Chapter III — **Kids and Divorce**/58

        Telling the Children/58

        Custody/61

        Child Care/62

        Mom, the Rescuer/72

                Kids as Pawns/75
                The Fantasy of the Absent Parent/77
                Manipulation of and by Children/79
                Grandparents/82
                Dealing With Outsiders/83
                Kids as Intermediaries/84
                Advantages of Divorce for Kids/85
                Keeping in Touch With Your Children/85
                References/91

Chapter IV — **The Law**/92
                Identifying the Alternatives/92
                Choosing a Lawyer/95
                The Initial Interview/96
                The Legal Process of Divorce/99
                Your Divorce Trial/100
                Alimony and Maintenance/101
                The New Divorce Act, 1985/107
                Solutions/114
                Property/114
                Marriage Contracts/116
                Courts and Their Levels/116
                Affidavits, Restraining Orders, Ex Parte Orders, and Other Legal Delicacies/118
                Out-of-Town, Interprovincial, and International Divorces/121
                Informal Marriages, or Common-Law Relationships/122
                Curves and Redundancies You Should Know About/123
                References/125

Chapter V — **Budgeting and Finances**/127
　　Interim Protection/127
　　Step One: Establishing How Much/128
　　Step Two: Budget and Records/128
　　Step Three: Adjusting Your Budget to Fit Your
　　　　Income/132
　　Step Four: Banking/141
　　Cash or Charge?/141
　　Planning for the Future/142
　　Bills That Will Surprise You!/142
　　You're Not in It Alone/143
　　Insurance/143
　　Retirement/144
　　Establishing a Credit Rating/144
　　Income Tax/145
　　How Much Is in the Pot?/147
　　References/147

Chapter VI — **Change and Serenity**/148
　　Changing Social Values/149
　　Changing Personal Values/150
　　Flashbacks/151
　　Becoming Responsible/155
　　Back to Work/167
　　Alternatives to Full-time Employment/182
　　References/187

Chapter VII — **Dating and Remarriage**/188
　　Rebound/188
　　Beginning to Date/189
　　Gossip/191
　　Practice Relationships/193

Sex/194
Self-acceptance/195
Love Affairs/196
Sex by Default/197
An Affair With a Married Man/199
Dating and Children/200
Telling Your Parents/202
Permanent Relationships/202
References/207

Epilogue/208

Note re **Appendices**/209

Appendix I—**Forms From the Old Divorce Act**/210

Appendix II—**Forms From the New Divorce Act,** 1985/233

Preface and Acknowledgements

The friendship of four women has produced this book. Although I did the actual writing, this book is also a product of the co-operation, ideas, and support of Ann Mackie, Louise Gaunce, and Doreen Davies. The first draft was written in the winter of 1982/83 in Spain, far from the other three women. It was modified in early 1986 to reflect the new divorce legislation which permits a one-year separation as a ground for divorce. The final responsibility for this book is, of course, my own.

When the idea for this book was born, three of us were remarried; only Ann was living alone (or as alone as you can get with four kids). This book was the result of Ann's request for help from her friends during the tough first months following the end of her marriage. Ann and I had been friends since we were both sixteen, having met at our first job, as summer nurses' aides at the Winnipeg General Hospital. The friendship persisted through the years despite the separation of time and distance. Knowing that I had already experienced a divorce, Ann called in June of 1980, suggesting a weekend visit in Saskatoon (half-way between our home cities). She needed time away to talk and think about the dramatic changes occurring in her life.

By the end of a weekend marathon of talking, laughing, and crying, Ann felt more confident about returning home to embark upon life as a single parent. I, too, was enriched and energized from the hours of sharing experiences and emotions. But it was Ann who remarked that every woman should have the support of another woman, who is herself divorced, at such a time.

After a lot of thought and some long long-distance phone-calls, we decided to meet again in Saskatoon, each bringing another woman who had experienced a divorce, had children, and was interested in the idea of a book. The first meeting in August 1980 was followed by several other weekends over the next couple of years in which we put our ideas, experiences, and advice for other women on cassette tapes. The tapes were a major resource for this book, though I have drawn widely from other women, other books, and my family. These tapes were painstakingly transcribed by Marion Saffran, who also typed an early draft of the book. I am grateful for her assistance and encouragement all along the way.

Why a book? Many women are deeply affected by divorce, and do not have the self-confidence or desire to reach out for help from a friend or a support group. My adjustment to life on my own was a long and tortuous procedure. I was ashamed and afraid that my friends would reject me. Though Ann's adjustment was no shorter in many respects, her loneliness and pain were lessened somewhat by the constant assurance of support from Louise, Doreen, and me. Many women who "go it alone" for various reasons may still seek out a book that provides both useful facts and advice and the reassurance of shared experiences.

There are many books about divorce on the market, handbooks for do-it-yourself divorce, collections of case studies, sociological analyses of causes and effects, and biographical and fictional accounts. This book is unusual in that it offers a combination of information and reassurance: concrete information for realistic planning for career, finances, and children, as well as tangible advice for getting a divorce and reassurance that there are many acceptable ways of dealing with the problem. The book is designed to teach the reader how to become self-sufficient emotionally and economically, and above all, how to become self-confident.

This book is intended to help other women work their way through the difficult stages of separation and divorce. It is a collection of specific information, techniques, and suggestions. It is directed toward women who are contemplating the end of a marriage or who have recently experienced this. Men will also find some sections useful—for example, those on selecting a lawyer, and budgeting.

The actual legal steps involved in ending a marriage are thoroughly discussed, as are their implications. For this chapter I owe Penny Bent, my friend, my sister-in-law and my lawyer, a debt of gratitude. Her careful reading and editing of the legal material have helped to ensure that the advice offered to readers is accurate. Any errors or misinterpretations are my own responsibility.

Equally as important as the informational passages are the companion passages, where reactions of women to the various stages of divorce are set forth in the form of quotations. There are some points within this book where no generalization seems quite adequate. In such cases the varying points of view or attitudes may be reflected in the clusters of anonymous quotes. They are anonymous because it is sometimes easier to be honest about very personal things this way. The quotes are taken from many women, and are a device that I have used to include the experiences and perspectives of other people. Often there is no single right answer to a problem, but instead a variety of alternatives from which to choose. I have tried to offer as many as possible within these pages.

With the right information and the knowledge that others have also been in the same position with the same feelings, the reader can dust off her self-confidence, work through the process of divorce, and get on with living.

After all, not everyone has a divorcee for a best friend.

INTRODUCTION

The Mythological Marriage

Self-confidence can only exist with self-knowledge and self-acceptance, or, put another way, self-confidence comes from knowing why you do most of the important things in your life; from liking yourself most days; and from being able to laugh at yourself on the off days. It is not perfection that you should be seeking, but the ability to be honest with yourself and others, even if it has been a long time since you really examined your own motivations and reactions.

The ending of a marriage often forces such a self-examination, since you are suddenly confronted with a failure of large proportions. Although divorce is much more common an event than it used to be, it is still an admission of failure on the part of two people to coexist within the accepted family structure of our society, marriage. Yet the declaration of the end of a marriage may be a healthy sign that one or both members of the couple is able to face the situation with honesty. It is very difficult to be honest and objective when a central pattern in your life is being altered irrevocably. Your emotions are in a turmoil and your self-confidence is often at a low ebb just when you need it most. Now is the time when you should honestly—and fairly—assess your own personality, and your goals as a single person.

But how can you do this when you are so full of anger or sadness or fear or self-recrimination? The thread that runs through this book is that you can learn to develop some confidence in yourself as a person who can competently solve the many problems that arise from ending a marriage. You may already have many of the skills necessary for independent living, or you may need to polish up some skills that haven't been used for a long time.

> *"If I could have picked up a book and read about the experiences of other women like myself, it would have helped me to see that what I was going through was predictable."*

"I gain strength from knowing that this has happened to others, and that the stages of pain and grieving are normal and will pass."

Our society values the institution of marriage very highly. We are taught our roles as husband and wife very early in our childhood, from the examples of our elders, the stories we are told, and the games we play. Television, which dominates the waking hours of many pre-school children, strongly reinforces the model of the middle-class, urban, nuclear family, not only in programming but especially in advertising. Our educational system also reinforces the two-parent family model with distinctive roles for husband and wife, father and mother. Boys and girls tend to study different subjects in school in preparation for their adult roles. Boys tend to study more industrial arts, mathematics, and sciences, while girls lean toward the arts, humanities, home economics, and secretarial courses.

There are exceptions to these stereotypes, of course. With at least one of every three marriages ending in divorce, more and more children are growing up in non-traditional families with single parents or step-parents. Television programming is beginning to reflect some of these alternatives as well, but it is still strongly reinforcing the status quo.

EMOTIONAL CONFLICT

Flying in the face of social tradition by ending a marriage causes deep-seated personality conflict, even in those of us who see ourselves as radicals. Divorce is a negation of all of our years of programming by society, though many people never consciously recognize the impact that this has. Contravening society's value system causes internal tension within each individual, and in some cases a degree of ostracism (or punishment) on the part of family and friends.

Conflict also arises from the drastic change that divorce imposes upon the mental environment of the individual. The process of becoming "married" is gradual, and affects many aspects of our personality. Linking your identity with another person takes time and effort (remember?), and the end result is a sense of "coupledom." You feel and behave married. In the case of most women, the process is signalled by a name change, adopting the surname of the husband. Just as adjusting to being married is a process, divorce must also be recognized as a process, the process of undoing the married self-image, and replacing it with something else.

Because society values the "married" image more highly than the "divorced" image, this conflict occurs on both an impersonal (often subconscious) and a personal level. The key to experiencing divorce successfully is to recognize it as a process rather than an event. There are many skills and techniques required to navigate yourself and your family through the process of divorce and the establishment of a new personal identity.

Conflict also arises because of the blame/guilt scenarios that our legal tradition imposes. Although technically, in many places, one person still has to divorce the other in court, the idea of a no-fault divorce, or more correctly, shared responsibility for the failure of the relationship, is now taking hold, recognizing that divorce usually occurs because of irreconcilable differences in the personal value systems of *two* individuals. We all make choices for our own behaviour based upon our past experiences. Major differences in these choices can lead to conflict, and unresolved conflict to divorce.

The process of divorce involves recognition of the sources of conflict within the marriage. By examining the values reflected by the behaviour of your recent mate you get a sense of your own value system. It is important to learn to distinguish between your own values and those imposed upon you by society and your recent mate. Re-examine your values and sift through them.

The tension you feel about these internal conflicts will often express itself indirectly, in physical or emotional symptoms rather than at a conscious level. Various new aches and pains may develop, sleep patterns may be disturbed, and behaviour may be altered because of decrease in self-assurance in dealing with other people. Sometimes this conflict is expressed through a decrease in physical coordination. Many women go through a time of being "accident prone." This can be fairly mild, simply a propensity for bumping into furniture and door frames, or it can be at a much more serious level, leading to car accidents.

> *"I am a careful driver, but I had three accidents during the first year I was on my own. The first accidents of my life—and they were all avoidable, if I had been paying more attention at the time!"*

> *"I got my very first speeding tickets—two of them—in the first month after my divorce. Driving the same roads I had always driven!"*

Recognize these symptoms for what they are and begin to look at your value system.

As you begin to take a serious look at yourself, you will find that there are many layers of external values covering over and interweaving with your own value system. At the end of a marriage you are often very vulnerable, believing that your central values have been rejected or are at least incompatible with someone else's. Your ability to operate within your value system comes into question, as does the validity of the system itself. Perhaps the real solution is not a judgement of your own values, but a need to examine them more closely. Perhaps you have been working under an externally imposed system even more than you think. Perhaps you have been living within an artificial value system that combines your own girlhood dreams of a happy marriage, your parents' objectives as they brought you up, your husband's expectations of a wife, and society's model of the ideal marriage, all brought to you in living colour on your television set. All of us are motivated by external values and role models to some extent, and the result, for many people, is a mythological image of what a marriage should be.

> *"The image of what he wants me to be and what I think I should be and what society thinks I should be—I'll never measure up."*

> *"It's a formula for failure: you're second best all the way. It's so discouraging, because even when I have done my best, I don't measure up. It's a terrible burden."*

> *"There are so many pressures from society about the beauty of youth, and we all know from picking up magazines how we are supposed to dress. Unfortunately, those clothes don't look that way on me."*

> *"And we do it to the men, too, I guess, to some extent. We want him to be bright, young and successful."*

> *"And we do it to our kids."*

> *"Everyone lays expectations on the people close to them. What is important is to recognize and understand what they are."*

> *"To learn to recognize the expectations of the mythological marriage in myself and others is a life-long process for me."*

MYTHS YOU HAVE LIVED WITH

The first step in escaping from the constricting expectations of society is to trace some of your attitudes back to their origins. Many of your standards are remnants of customs or ideals of previous generations, and have stayed on as myths in our own generation. Society is conservative. Myths tend to reinforce the status quo, the values of the majority. They tend to be behind the times, and are retained and displayed long after they have become irrelevant because of our predilection for glorifying the past. Myths can, however, be examined objectively, and like bad dreams, when they are put into words, may even seem funny in the light of day.

THE GOOD WIFE AND MOTHER

One myth is of the "good wife and mother." This is tightly bound up with Western religion, in which the valuing of meekness and humility emphasizes giving to others and putting yourself last. A good wife always puts herself last, and a good mother does the same, continually denying her own feelings, unless they are positive, nurturing, and selfless.

At first glance this is a difficult model to criticize. However, striving for such self-denial and humility is insidious. It prevents the possibility of a good relationship within a marriage in our generation, in that you cannot share your whole self. You often must deny so much more than you can share, and this is dishonest. You cannot have a truly intimate, deep relationship unless you do share your deeper feelings, both negative and positive. This is not to say that honesty should occur in a relationship at the price of consideration, but only that women are beginning to believe that they have a right to be themselves, and many believe that it is realistic to expect acceptance of this kind of sharing of self within a marriage. Neither is this to say that all feelings should be shared all the time with someone who feels the same way, or who completely understands. Not only is this unrealistic and unattainable, but it could lead to a highly refined form of shared neuroticism, unless such seriousness was leavened with laughter.

And that is how you look at a myth: you take it out and turn it over and over in your mind. See how it has affected you. Did you subconsciously set unrealistic goals for yourself? Did you accept the unsuitable goals of someone else without consciously examining them in the light of your own value system? Before you reject a myth out of hand, look again: are there some ideas that should be retained? Some values that should be kept as part of the up-to-date package that you will keep, after the sorting through?

THE VICTORIAN HANGOVER

Another myth to examine is really a package, a collection of connected ideas, derived from a previous era—the Victorian Hangover. The proper Victorian wife was submissive to her autocratic husband, wore tight corsets to create the illusion of youth and an hourglass figure, couldn't show even her ankles in public, submitted to her husband's sexual favours with distaste and silent suffering, and was "indisposed" or had "the vapours" once a month. The mythology of the Victorian middle class held that babies were found under cabbage leaves in the garden. Daughters were given no preparation for the sexual aspects of marriage because women didn't talk about sex, other than to warn their daughters to be brave and to be good wives (close your eyes and think of England). This heritage of ideas and values is only a few generations removed from us, and its effect is still profound.

> *"There was a mirror in the front hall of my grandfather's house, just above the telephone. I spent every summer there as a teenager with him. Often when I was on the phone I would unconsciously be looking into the mirror, playing with my hair. My grandfather would become angry when he saw me doing this and would tell me to stop looking at myself, stop primping, stop being vain."*

Overcoming the Victorian Hangover was one of the main objectives of the early twentieth century feminists. They were seeking a balanced set of ideas, full freedom for women in all aspects of life. And yet over and over again we discover that freedom cannot be given to any woman. She can be shown some of its components, but she must make the final selection herself.

THE PERFECT MARRIAGE

Another myth is that of "the perfect marriage." Many of us are brought up on fairy tales and Walt Disney movies and have strong romantic views of what love and marriage should be like. These socially instilled values are unrealistic and do not provide practical preparation. The content of children's reading is changing, however.

"At first I bitterly resented the current popular books my children were reading, which appeared to be scaled down soap opera scripts, full of divorced parents and unhappy kids. But then I realized that such books were providing my kids with a much more practical set of expectations than my fairy tales ever could. And deep down, I wish for them some pain and sadness as well as happiness, and those old fairy tales never continued past the wedding day, anyway. Somehow I doubt that Snow White or Cinderella ever divorced the Prince. However, a student of history will tell you that Princes always had mistresses. It makes me wonder about the 'happily ever after'."

There are many dangers inherent in the myth of the perfect marriage, but one is the tendency to try to create a facade, a covering for the marriage that hides any unhappiness, and almost succeeds in convincing everyone that everything is always all right, that this is indeed a happy marriage. The tragedy is that outsiders are usually convinced and are blithely unaware that they could help until it is too late. The need to protect the facade of the perfect marriage increases loneliness within a disintegrating marriage by insulating the couple from honest outside friendships.

Here again, the argument must be balanced by a qualification: it is not necessary to discuss the intimate details of your marital relationship with others all the time, but it is helpful to have an understanding and loyal friend or two who know you well enough to be acquainted with your true goals and feelings, and who can support you from time to time in the various painful situations that arise as life goes on. Such a friend will likely be someone other than your mother because a mother will tend to reinforce many of the behaviour patterns that you are trying to change. Patterns of behaviour are passed on from parent to child at a very deep level. Unhealthy patterns of expressing anger are learned by observation at a very young age and are very hard to change even when the child has become an adult.

THE CLEAN SLATE

Another myth is that of "the clean slate," or that we can start a relationship all over again, a new beginning. This, of course, is impossible, because we carry with us the accumulated experience of the past. The idea is very attractive, however, especially if a reconciliation is being considered, but a new start can only be made if all the patterns of the marriage can be assessed and some of them changed.

THE BROKEN HOME

Another myth which will be dealt with here only briefly is that of the "broken home." We know now that a broken home isn't enough to cause a child to become a juvenile delinquent, just as the presence of both parents is not enough to prevent it. Even the term "broken home" is out-dated now, as we see children from such homes behaving as competent and responsible adults. Distantly related to this myth is the image of the "gay divorcee"—the woman who is completely free, dresses beautifully, is always very alluring and fascinating, and has an air of mystery about her. She is also a threat to other peoples' husbands, a bit of a vamp. Most of us are too busy juggling job, kids, housework, day care, babysitters, and community activities to be anything other than a bit slap-happy from time to time!

As you examine these myths, much of their power over you will vanish. Once you are aware of the fact that you are being subconsciously influenced by outdated values which do not match those that you are actively trying to strengthen, it is much easier to assess the impact of such myths on your personality—and to limit it. In other words, it is recognition of their deeper influence on you that will help you to gain control of the myths perpetuated by our society.

References

Barfoot, Joan, *Dancing in the Dark*. Scarborough: Avon Books, 1982.
A novel which demonstrates the emptiness of the "perfect" marriage, with the housewife trying to live out the stereotype.

Dowling, Colette, *The Cinderella Complex: Women's Hidden Fear of Independence*. New York: Summit Books, 1981.
An examination of the need that women have to be looked after, to have someone else make their decisions for them. The author suggests techniques for overcoming this strong social pressure by understanding the dynamics of dependence, and actively seeking freedom and independence.

CHAPTER ONE

The Final Stage of a Failing Marriage

"My overwhelming thought, as it became clearer and clearer in my mind that the marriage was going to end, was fear: fear about my inability to manage financially, fear for the effect it would have on the children, fear for my parents and in-laws and the rest of my family and friends. Where would I find the strength to hold myself together and still pull them all through it, too?"

Fear and panic. These feelings often accompany the realization that the marriage really is going to end. Nevertheless, this conscious recognition that the relationship is beyond repair and that a new life must be faced is the beginning of the long road to a successful existence as a single person.

There is seldom a single, clear-cut cause for the end of a marriage, although it is so easy to blame it on one spouse's love affair, or overwork, or lack of interest in the family. Usually, however, the real reasons are much deeper, and may not even be recognized until much later. Perhaps identifying the cause isn't so important at the time of realization that the marriage is ending, since searching for a reason requires a level of objectivity which may be beyond your capability under the stress of impending separation. Maybe it is enough, for the present, to accept the fact of the marriage's end and to leave worrying about the reasons for it until you are a little further away from the situation in time. Or, if seeking the reason is important to you, you might be wise to do so with the assistance of a counsellor or psychiatrist in order to avoid the danger of putting all the blame on yourself— or on him.

As well as fear and panic, there is often the feeling of having been rejected or abandoned, or both. Although this feeling is most likely to be paramount if "he" left, and especially if you feel that he is involved with someone else, this rejection is potentially your most serious enemy. If you dwell on it too long, it will erode your last shred of self-confidence, prolong your adjustment period, and generally make life miserable for you and those around you for a long time.

It is important to realize that the end of a marriage is an admission that you have *both* been unable to create a satisfactory relationship, that the reasons for this are complicated, and that if there is blame, it *must* be shared. Further, you must come to grips with the fact that the only person who can pull you through this difficult time is—you. Friends and relatives can help so much with their love, reassurance, and support, but only you can do the thinking and the adjusting.

Others may need a little guidance from you before they can be really helpful. If you are not careful, your friends and relatives will be happy to help you lay all the blame at the feet of your husband. It is important for you and for them to recognize that it is no one's fault— or everyone's fault—and that taking sides, although tempting, is not very helpful. There is often a great deal of anger and pain that must be experienced, but these emotions can become exaggerated and prolonged by too many "blame the ex" sessions with your friends. A serious effort at enforced neutrality speeds you on to a level of objectivity, which will help you get on with the process of accepting the end of the relationship.

The ending of a marriage is not a sudden thing, although the recognition of it and the actual separation of the couple make it seem so. Some couples may have been aware of their problems and attempted to confront them; others may have been trying desperately to hide them from themselves and from others. Still others may not have been consciously aware that they had problems at all until one or the other partner drifted into an affair, or simply woke up one morning and wanted out. Even this apparently sudden decision is usually based on a slowly dawning awareness of differences in values, goals, or general view of life. Sometimes the gradual decrease in communication in a marriage is so insidious that it goes unrecognized until it seems to have created a gulf too wide to bridge, or until the essential trust of one another with serious thoughts and feelings is gone, or until the interest in each other is dead. So many things can go wrong within a relationship; sometimes these things can be recognized in time and repaired, often enriching the relationship in the process, but separation occurs when one or both people believe that the relationship is beyond the point of repair.

COMMUNICATION

Communication within a marriage—or any other relationship—is never perfect, in that no two people see any situation in exactly the same way. If you ever want to test this, select a special event from the past, and some evening when three or four of the participants in the past event are in your living room, ask each of them to describe it. You will be astonished to find that people could interpret the same situation in such dramatically different ways. (A word of caution—such reminiscences can degenerate into arguments.) You will all find it hard to believe that you were all present at the same event. And most important, you will be surprised at how little of each person's scenario coincides with your own.

Within a marriage, in the day-to-day business of communicating, discrepancies in how each person understands given situations are normal. Often the misunderstandings go unnoticed, as each person assumes that the other's perception is congruent, or at least similar enough that agreement can be taken for granted. This assumption works well as a modus operandi—no one wants to spend the time or energy checking out these perceptions all the time. Trouble arises only when there is apparent agreement, but wide perceptual differences that are not acknowledged in time. Here we have the discussion: "I thought you said..." "That's not what I said at all. What I said was...." "No, you didn't. You said...." "Well, what I meant was...." And so on.

In the 1960s, when the study of behaviour potential and the psychology of groups became popular, Carl Rogers, a psychologist, became very interested in potential barriers to communication. One of his suggestions was to check your assumptions by repeating what you understand from someone else's statement, thereby validating it. This technique has its uses in many situations and should be employed if there is any doubt on an important issue in order to avoid potential trouble. It can also be over-used ad nauseam, if people get into the habit of peppering their conversation with: "What I hear you saying is...." Checking validity by repeating the essence of a statement is one example of a technique for improving communication within a marriage. If lack of communication is one of the major problems underlying a potential separation, the reasons for this problem should be examined long enough to determine whether it is irreparable. Perhaps you both need to learn some communication skills, or to dust off some skills you haven't bothered to use lately. Maybe you have lost the knack of really listening to each other, and you will both benefit from some sessions on communication, if not for the present relationship, at least for the future. It is still important that you develop your communication skills, but not necessarily within this relationship.

One of the great things that has come out of the perhaps overdone attitude of the 1960s to "tell it like it is" is the new accent on honesty in relationships. The years of publicity and publications about sensitivity training, T-groups, and group therapy made us all more aware of the importance of communicating what we feel. The residual effect is a stronger knowledge of the importance of honesty in any relationship, particularly in marriage and child-raising. The overstatement of the 1960s that insisted that every emotion in every interpersonal transaction should be carefully dissected and analyzed has been modified. We now think that the ability to examine interpersonal transactions is an important and useful skill for everyone to master, but that the emphasis should be moved from compulsory honesty to considerate honesty, from compulsory confrontation to the more complex idea of consideration as well as honesty in all interpersonal communication. No longer do we insist that conversations be riddled with questions about how each person feels about what he or she is hearing.

Instead, we expect a certain honesty coupled with subtlety and wisdom. For example, even if you feel angry or hurt about what someone has just said to you, perhaps now is not the time to discuss your reaction. Perhaps tempers are close to the boiling point, or there are other people present to whom such a discussion would be annoying or offensive. Or perhaps you should look a little deeper into what was said, and realize that the person did not mean to hurt you and in fact is unaware that he or she did. If this is so, it may not be necessary at all to ever point out your feelings, unless hurting you in this way is a continuing habit.

What is being offered in this discussion is not a simple formula for communication, such as many faddish, do-it-yourself books and even training organizations offer. Rather, it is the more complex notion of honesty tempered with common-sense, self-confidence, and consideration for the other person or people involved in your own day-to-day relationships. Interpersonal communications are very complex: there are so many perspectives, such as what you actually said, what tone of voice you actually used, what you think you said, and how you think you said it, what the other person heard you say, how this was integrated with the other person's perception of you, and what each of you wish you had said. If each verbal transaction was analyzed according to the potential interpretations, little real communication would take place. However, once you have the ability to analyze a conversation in this way, you are able to be much more sensitive, and much more honest, without much effort at all. So read books on communication techniques, take training courses, attend group sessions if you are interested, and then put what you learn into the context of your own life, not idealistically (which is often selfishly or snobbishly), but pragmatically. From all experiences in life, we should derive what is relevant to our own lives, rather than try to bend our own lives to fit someone else's model.

COUNSELLING

It is very difficult to sort out the conflicting emotions inherent in ending a marriage, and to make all the necessary decisions and plans involved in preparing for single life. Often advice from others can be helpful. Counselling usually begins with trusted relatives or close friends, old family friends, or religious advisors and leaders. It may be useful to have a few sessions with an objective outsider, someone who is trained to help you sift through the events and emotions in a more objective way than you can manage when you are in the middle of it all. Most communities offer marriage counselling, separation counselling, and counselling for your children if and when it is needed.

Many people harbour the misconception that a counsellor will try to put the marriage back together again, even though the partners have agreed to divorce. Although this may be true of some counsellors, many are now also proficient in the field of separation counselling, or in helping you to work through the stages of ending a marriage in a reasonable and fair way, while also providing support to one or both members of the couple.

The selection of a counsellor is an important step and should involve some care. Certainly, references from friends or professionals are useful, but remember, you are looking for more than just a professional counsellor. You must first decide what sort of assistance you are seeking. Is it personal counselling, so that you can decide whether or not you really do want to end the relationship? Is it joint counselling for both of you, to heal the relationship? Is it joint or separate counselling for advice on ending the marriage? Is it family counselling to help children as well as the adults to adjust to the new situation of separation? Is it counselling for each child on an individual basis to provide an objective outsider to whom they can talk about their concerns regarding their parents' separation? Do you want long-term counselling to help you sort out your thoughts and feelings and pain, or is it short-term, task-oriented advice that you are after?

Some people go through the whole process of separation and divorce without any outside assistance. Until recently, as part of the Victorian Hangover, asking for help from any outsider, be it a psychiatrist or a friend, was thought to be a sign of weakness and thus avoided by many who might well have benefited from such sessions. Increasingly, however, seeking advice in such a situation is seen as a sign of maturity, of dealing realistically with a serious problem. A good counsellor often provides psychological short-cuts through the forest of conflicting emotions and motivations.

A counsellor can help you in a variety of ways: teaching you techniques to change long-standing behaviour habits, helping you to develop a degree of objectivity in assessing your own personality and skills, and helping you to establish yourself as an independent person. A counsellor can also serve as a safety valve, someone who will listen to your point of view at a time when you are experiencing a great deal of stress and may not be thinking as clearly as you would like. Somehow, talking to an outsider often defuses the anger and the pain. Expressing your feelings in a safe setting where you can't lose face with your partner or a friend helps you to learn to listen to yourself. Such an opportunity to talk things out with someone who not only understands but is trained to help you to regain your self-confidence and to help you make the best decisions for yourself and your family can be extremely helpful.

Although it may be difficult to take the first step of finding a counsellor and then making yourself attend that first session, that same session is often followed by an enormous sense of relief; finally, someone really is there to help you. The assurance of future sessions as required means that you know that there will always be another opportunity for you to vent your feelings, deal with the pain and the grieving, and move on to the next stage in your life.

SELECTING A COUNSELLOR

Before you select a counsellor, you should have some idea of what you hope to achieve with counselling. It may be any of the things suggested above or a combination of them. There are many sources of counsellors. Your government social services agency or mental health officer, a friend who has been through a divorce, a friend who works in the field of psychology or counselling, your family doctor, and your local public health clinic are all potential sources of counsellors' names. Once you have a name, call the local social services registry and make sure that the person is licensed to practice and is reputable within the professional organization. Find out as much as you can about the person's approach and type of case experience, and then make your first appointment. This first appointment is always difficult, because you must go over all the things that have happened in at least enough detail for the counsellor to become familiar with you and your situation. At the same time, however, you must check for biases and attitudes in the counsellor that may not fit with your personality. You are looking for someone whom you can respect, and whose advice you will consider seriously even if it is sometimes quite different from your own ideas. You want someone who has enough experience to understand your point of view. For example, an older woman might have some difficulty taking advice from a twenty-two-year-old counsellor who has never been married. And yet such people may be sufficiently removed from your situation to provide additional objectivity, and their training may well have prepared them to be very competent counsellors. Some women prefer their counsellors to also be women. Some seek a counsellor who has also experienced a divorce. Neither of these qualities is a guarantee against bias; any man or a woman has a set of experiences and values which colours his or her perspective. A person who has been previously divorced may or may not have worked out all his or her own personal problems. In the final analysis, what is important is that you like each other and that the counsellor appears to have attained a level of personal maturity which permits recognition and compensation for the inevitable biases.

Discuss the issue of confidentiality with your counsellor during the first session. With whom does the counsellor discuss cases? What kind of notes are taken on each session? Where are they filed, who has access to them, and how long are they kept? Make sure that you are satisfied with the level of confidentiality, but remember, too, that the counsellor should have adequate access to other professionals for consultation on any professional matter.

The cost of counselling may be a significant factor. Sometimes counselling is covered by government or other health insurance plans. Make sure you understand the arrangements for payment before you begin your counselling sessions. Often in our strange society, the expensive psychiatrist is cheaper than a social worker or lay counsellor, since the psychiatrist is more likely to be covered by your medical insurance plan. But even if you must pay for counselling, it may indeed be money well spent.

> *"Not everybody needs a professional counsellor; but friends often get caught taking sides."*

> *"I found it was better for each of us to go to separate counsellors for awhile. Since the counsellors worked in the same office, we were able to have joint sessions later on to work out problems in arranging the separation, but I was not willing to share a counsellor with my spouse; I needed the counsellor to be there for me, to understand me as a separate person and to help me to do the same."*

> *"You need someone who can look at you as an individual, someone who can look at you objectively and maybe help you to see how you are hurting yourself. It can help you to change some of your own patterns of behaviour."*

> *"And remember that you didn't marry the counsellor; if it isn't working out, find another one."*

As well as emotional and psychological counselling there are other kinds of counselling which might help you as you make the transition to life on your own. Legal counselling will be discussed at length later on, as will financial counselling. If at all possible, use these resources to ascertain what your situation really is before you separate.

RECONCILIATION?

The possibility of patching up or rebuilding the marriage must be fully considered by both partners, if possible. At this stage the idea of beginning again can become terribly attractive, both in view of the unknown situation of separation and divorce and in view of the years invested in the marriage. It is difficult to think objectively about a reconciliation; emotions may instead vacillate between anger and the desire to hang on to the dream of a happy marriage. "He said, 'Come back. I want you to quit work and have a baby.' Gosh, it was tempting!"

The potential for changing the marital situation must be weighed against the attractive myth of a clean slate. Beginning again involves changing many habitual patterns within the relationship. It requires a dedicated effort on the part of both partners and likely some outside counselling. Under these circumstances, reconciliations are often successful after a temporary separation and lead to enriched and happy marriages.

You lose nothing in the eyes of the law should the attempted reconciliation fail, but this should be confirmed by your lawyer. In Canada you are permitted up to ninety days' reconciliation (all at once or in small test amounts) without legally interrupting the continuum of the full year of separation which establishes ground for a divorce. Such a reconciliation does not invalidate other grounds; in other words, you can still say that the reconciliation period did not constitute forgiveness for adultery.

The most important prerequisite for a reconciliation to succeed, or to leave a minimum of damage in its wake in the event of failure, is confidence in yourself. During the time in which you have been living apart, you must have developed a sense of yourself, a sense of what is essential and important in you, the essence of which you do not want to compromise under any circumstances. Only with such self-knowledge can you develop your own self-confidence, and only with this can you honestly work on the relationship. If you are still so full of pain or resentment that you cannot be fair to your husband, or so full of guilt and remorse that you cannot stand up to him, the old patterns will continue. In reconciliation you are both trying to strengthen—or develop anew—two very important elements: trust and respect for each other. The importance of these two qualities in any relationship cannot be overstated; and yet they may be especially fragile under the strain of a reconciliation. You will fail each other many times, falling short of your own and each other's expectations, and you must have the self-confidence to take such failures with a grain of salt, and try again. The ability to laugh at yourself and to laugh together at your mistakes as you work at the relationship, will go a long way to reduce the tension.

There are many patterns for reconciliation, and they vary widely from one situation to another, depending on the presence of children and their ages, jobs, finances, and other factors. Some people try to establish an entirely new relationship by beginning with dating each other again. The danger to be avoided here is that the unrealistic fantasies of falling in love all over again will cloud your ability to contribute honestly to the relationship and to recognize your partner's efforts. An even riskier way to have a trial reconciliation is a weekend away together, or a trip. The shorter the time, the higher the tension is likely to be. There are advantages to being away in a new place, unaffected by the pressures of everyday living, but be careful not to make your expectations unrealistic. And even if you do have a wonderful time together, make sure that you test the relationship under everyday circumstances before you make the final decision to live together again.

When you do decide to try living together again, avoid making impossible promises to yourself or to your partner. Recognize that there are some patterns of behaviour that you are both trying to change, and be patient and not too critical. Make sure that you give each other and yourselves credit when even a little change occurs: nothing encourages improvement and change like recognition and appreciation.

CHANGING BEHAVIOUR PATTERNS

Remember that both of you already have images of each other that will be hard to change. For example, if you have always been more submissive than your husband and he made most of the decisions in the marriage, he will find it difficult to see you as the capable and competent decision-maker that you are trying to become. He may have difficulty learning to share decision-making and power over financial matters. In the stereotypical marriage, such patterns are hard to change, and even when progress is made, it may not be immediately evident.

Determining what your new role will be within the marriage is a difficult but often rewarding exercise. Often the renewed relationship calls for a redistribution of household tasks in a more equitable fashion. This should be undertaken in a systematic way to minimize the potential for tension and animosity. This entails listing the various jobs within the household, including all the record-keeping, banking, housework, and child-care tasks. Once this list is made, an equitable distribution of tasks can be developed. Making the list can be fun. On a Saturday morning, each of you should take pencil and paper and a large cup of coffee into separate rooms and list everything that you do throughout the year related to the home. This should include outside work, errands, and car maintenance, too. When the lists are finished, calculate the amount of time spent on each task per week. Then trade lists with each other and go off alone again to review the other person's list. Read it carefully. You will find lots of things that you didn't realize you each did and lots of things that take much more time than you thought they did. There may be things that you can add which the other person forgot or takes for granted. Just the process of making the list is often very revealing, especially once the times are attached. For example, the woman may spend half an hour a week cleaning the toilets, while the man spends an equal amount of time on income tax, averaged over the year. (In our house these tasks are viewed with equal disgust!) The couple may then decide that the pattern of assignment of such tasks should stay the same, or should be traded or alternated from time to time. What such a task breakdown does is give each person a very realistic idea of how much time is being contributed to the maintenance of the household.

Once you have read over each other's lists, put the two together, and then divide the tasks. The criteria that guide your division of labour are up to you. You may feel that you should share equally in the nasty ones, and alternate, or you may decide to retain past patterns of distribution. You may choose to trade tasks so that each can become proficient in some of the important ones such as banking, budgeting, record-keeping, figuring out the income tax, and grocery-shopping. Or you may decide that such tasks should be distributed according to past experience or expertise. You may even wish to use the task distribution to alter the stereotypical roles within the marriage, assigning traditional female tasks such as cooking, shopping, and laundry to the male partner, and household repairs, budgeting, and car maintenance to the female.

Whatever way you choose to divide the list, the important thing is that both people are convinced that the distribution is equitable and fair. Then follows a potentially tense time of readjustment. Tact is required as you watch your mate fumble through a task that you could do better and faster. In time you will both become proficient at your new responsibilities. Beware of sabotaging your new system by too much criticism of each other's beginning efforts. You might also guard against feelings of jealousy or competitiveness when you find that your mate can do so-called "female" tasks as well as or better than you. It takes a fair amount of maturity for a woman to credit her husband with doing all the cooking for the family—and better than she could do herself!

THE ANYTHING BOOK

Exercises such as task lists are useful tools in building and strengthening or rebuilding any relationship because they lend a sense of objectivity to the process. Another such exercise is expressing yourself in writing, even if you are not used to doing so. The safest way to write is for your eyes only. A few years ago there was a profusion of what were called "anything books" on the market. These are attractively designed hardcover books of empty pages. Any notebook will also serve as an anything book. It is merely a vehicle for learning to express—and assess—yourself more objectively. What you must bear in mind is that you are writing for yourself only—not to show your spouse or anyone else. This ensures a higher level of honesty, since you are not trying to justify or defend your thoughts or feelings to anyone but yourself. And then begin trying to write about a situation or a feeling or a worry, or whatever you choose. When you have finished, put it away for a day or two, then pull it out again and read it carefully. Look for signs of dishonesty—places where you were unfair in your interpretation of the situation you are describing, unfair to either yourself or someone else, or both.

You can develop this habit of writing for yourself and use it to express your anger in a harmless way, to sort out alternatives in a difficult situation, or to learn to recognize the patterns of your own behaviour. As you become more proficient in expressing yourself honestly in writing to yourself, this will affect and improve your ability to be honest in face-to-face communication with others.

At times you may choose to try to express yourself to your partner in writing. But be sure that you don't simply fire off an emotional invective that makes you feel better, and your spouse feel much worse, when there might be a better way to deal with the situation. By all means write such letters, but sleep on them before you decide to deliver them. You'll throw most such letters away the next day, but you still feel better for having given vent to your thoughts on paper.

The final bit of advice regarding reconciliation is to make sure that whatever changes you may try to make in yourself are changes that you really want to make, and that they do not deny or undermine what you have identified as your essential qualities, or your core. Changes which are made simply to please someone else may lack sincerity, breed resentment, and prevent the development of an honest relationship.

> *"He says he desperately wants to come back, and yet there is a part of me that says that I have fought and struggled with this thing, and I have come to like some of the aspects of being on my own and what I am now. How realistic is it to turn around and begin work on the relationship again? Is it possible? Is it going to be worth the effort?"*

> *"I am so afraid of being hurt again, and of putting the children through it all again if he walks away. I am so afraid of going through the whole effort of faith, hope, trial—and failure—what if it all dissolves again?"*

> *"I fear being rejected again. To put myself in that vulnerable position again seems crazy."*

> *"I am struggling now with a new identity for myself. Is it possible to have this identity within that marriage relationship? I never felt really listened to, understood, really accepted for me. But he is sending a lot of love my way; maybe...?"*

> *"We will try to look closely at ourselves and each other, maybe even list our differences so that we can try to look at them objectively. We must identify the important differences, differences in values and basic assumptions so that we can learn to understand each other."*

This chapter began with a discussion of some of the methods that exist for trying to save a marriage. Some of these methods can also be adapted to help you to face the end of the relationship—especially counselling and putting your thoughts down on paper. The rest of this book is concerned with the adjustment to living on your own after the marriage has ended. This is indeed a new beginning, although it will take time for you to experience the various and often painful stages of adjustment. It is a matter of learning to accept the past, to let it go and focus on living now.

References

Bach, George and Peter Wyden, *The Intimate Enemy*. Toronto: Avon, 1968.

This book provides useful insights into techniques and behaviour patterns characteristic of marital disagreements. It provides a basis for changing dangerous or unhealthy patterns of fighting.

Triere, Lynette and Richard Peacock, *Learning to Leave*. New York: Warner Books, 1982.

CHAPTER TWO

The Grieving Process: It's All Right to Cry

This chapter is about the normal process of grieving, and the pain and sadness that follow the recognition that a marriage has ended. Patterns of adjustment vary; some women have done much of their grieving before the actual separation. Others go through a time of depression, either just before or just after the separation, or both. The fact of a separation and impending divorce is jarring to everyone, and this extends to children, relatives, and friends. Whatever your particular pattern of adjustment turns out to be, you can help yourself through much of it by recognizing that your reactions and emotional confusion are likely quite normal, and that the feelings will pass with time. Understanding some of the stages and expecting a certain sequence will help you to help both yourself and those around you through a difficult adjustment.

The grieving which takes place after separation or divorce is a normal and fairly predictable process. It can take a year or more to work through it. In this chapter I have borrowed heavily from the research of Dr. Elizabeth Kübler-Ross, in which she identifies the stages that people experience in adjusting to the finality of death. The principles which she identifies have much wider implications, however, and can be used to explain the stages of grief and mourning in almost any situation of loss, including the end of a marriage. Understanding that the stages of grieving are a normal process which takes time is reassuring. As well as this assurance of normalcy, knowing what the various stages are will help you to guard against the possibility of getting stuck along the way. Grieving for any loss, whether of a person through death, divorce, or distance, as when children grow up and leave home, or even for a place which is no longer accessible, is a normal part of living and adapting to inevitable change.

DENIAL

Some women continue to run their lives as if their husbands were still coming home at night, or were just away for a little while. Their decisions continue to be based upon the value system of a husband, and no progress is made toward independence. Often, during this stage, a woman avoids telling her children or her relatives and friends the truth of the situation. This is because she has not yet been able to face it herself. Denial, the first stage of grieving, is the refusal to accept the reality of what is happening. With separation or divorce, this stage is expressed by various kinds of pretense. If this stage lasts too long, the situation becomes emotionally dangerous.

Denial is expressed in many familiar ways. Examples are the woman who explains that her husband is away on an extended business trip, but will come home as soon as this phase of his important career is over; the woman who rationalizes that the separation is temporary—"We just needed a break from each other." Such women will argue that these situations are healthy, and do not signify any change in the marriage. (And of course, occasionally this is true.) But in a strained marriage, such separations, unless accompanied by efforts on the part of both partners to seriously assess their patterns of living together, will lead to more separations and a divorce. Denial and rationalization, although they serve to protect us from the hurt at first, can prevent us from dealing constructively with a real situation.

A pattern of self-delusion can become a habit which prevents any further personal development. The extreme case is that of a woman who, even years after the divorce, still speaks incessantly of "my husband," and lives in a strange mixture of the past and the incomplete present; incomplete, because every action and event in the present is received and thought of and discussed in terms of the absent husband. Even though her husband may be remarried and have established a new family, she still calls him regularly to run errands for her or to do her household repairs and advise her. She is unable to let go of her image of herself as "wife," and thus is unable to develop an independent life of her own. Her reality is an illusion that causes awkwardness and embarrassment to those around her.

As well as the danger of an arrest in personal growth, prolonged denial necessitates a high level of pretense, or game-playing, on the part of your family and friends. Friends don't quite know how to react to your frequent comments and reminders of your husband. For them, life has moved on, and they are at a loss to know how to react to the references to what has become a fictional relationship. Usually, friends sense that this pattern of behaviour is unhealthy, but they don't quite know how to change the subject. Often it is impossible, anyway: conversation reverts right back to "he would be so angry if he could see me now," or, "you sound just like my husband," or, "my husband likes this restaurant, too." Any one of these remarks is harmless, but a woman whose speech is peppered with such observations is stalled at the stage of denial.

Women who go through this were usually quite submissive during the marriage. Their identities were strongly related to their husbands and they are unable to create a separate identity even though all the external trappings are in place. The fact that the marriage has ended is evident to everyone else, and yet those close to such women feel a sort of pity and are reluctant to point out the real situation. The self-delusion of the woman thus threatens the honesty and integrity of the very support that will help her to recover from her loss.

RESISTANCE TO CHANGE

Denial, as we have seen earlier, is a normal part of the grieving process and must be recognized as such. But denial should soon be followed by confrontation of the truth of the situation. This is often a hard step to take because denial is complicated by the common human characteristic of resistance to change. The normal patterns of family and social life are sustained, preserving outward appearances and permitting the couple to hold onto the belief that things are okay.

Such resistance to change creates its own problems of stress; maintaining a façade of "normalcy" takes a lot of emotional energy, and it also cuts you off from the support that friends and relatives might offer if they knew the truth.

Still, people are more comfortable in a familiar situation—even a bad marriage—than they are facing the unknown future of divorce. People often remain in bad marriages for many years because their resistance to acknowledging a changed situation prevents them from either seeking counselling or ending the marriage. So often friends and relatives are astonished to hear of the "sudden" end of such a marriage. Because both members of the couple were denying the reality of the break-down of the marriage, no one knew that there were even serious problems. Sometimes friends react with resentment, because they feel that they have been deceived, and that they were not trusted enough to be told the truth. They do not understand the strength and the dynamics of resistance to change, and its corollary, denial.

An increasingly public example of this resistance to change at its most extreme is the case of the battered wife. She will return repeatedly to a degrading and often dangerous situation, rather than cope with change. She will insist that things aren't really all that bad, even when her body shows obvious signs of beatings. She is afraid of the present situation, but even more so of the unknown future if she leaves. Sometimes she believes that her life is in danger if she leaves, that he will find her and the children wherever they go. There is help for such women now, in nearly every community. The police are aware of women's shelters, safe houses established to keep such families until alternative plans can be made.

Denial and resistance to change, then, are normal. The patterns of denial and consequent habitual superficiality can, however, become ingrained. What is not normal is prolonging these reactions to the point where they prevent adaptation to a new situation.

DENIAL ON THE PART OF FRIENDS

Another form of denial occurs sometimes on the part of friends of the couple. Their reluctance to see the friendship circle altered causes them to deny the reality of the separation. They continue to invite you out socially as a couple, or they may invite you each separately, but continue to treat you as half of a married couple. Other friends may indicate their denial by telling you every detail of your absent spouse's life by telephone or in person. Such people must be helped to face the real situation so that you can get on with redesigning your image as a single person. Most friends will accept the situation when confronted politely; a few must be reluctantly dropped for awhile.

SELECTIVE MEMORY LOSS

Another phenomenon that can occur, which also reflects a form of denial, is a temporary loss of memory. This can take several forms. For example, one woman lost the ability to recall details of events during her marriage, including her children's babyhood. This was particularly upsetting, since she couldn't answer their questions about what they did when they were small. This state persisted for a couple of years, and then after the divorce, as the marriage and its dissolution became things of the past, her memory of those years returned. The subconscious often operates to protect the individual from pain, and a selective memory is an example of this.

Harsh as it may sound, the sooner that the end of the marriage is recognized for what it is—final—the better. This is not to say that the decision should be made overnight. You must be sure in your own mind that there is no possibility of continuing the marriage before you go on with the next step. The realization will not likely come as a flash to you one day; you will have to work at it, think about it, and sort through your own feelings until you are reasonably sure. You don't even have to be entirely sure every day, because many of us waver from time to time on the occasional off-day. There will be relapses when you are filled with doubt, and seriously consider returning to the marriage. At such times talk to an unbiased friend who will help you to examine your feelings for signs of self-delusion. Is this just more denial, or is it possible that a reconciliation might work? If it is just a momentary relapse, get back on track and get on with your life.

The ending of a marriage is indeed a loss, regardless of who initiated the ending of the relationship itself. Both members of the couple, as well as children, relatives, and close friends, will feel a sense of loss and an accompanying sorrow for the end of a marriage, even if it was not a particularly good relationship.

ANGER

After denial the next stage in the grieving process is anger, and it is very cleansing and healthy. It is sometimes quite a shock to a woman who sees herself as gentle and controlled when the repressed anger of many years comes to the surface.

This stage of anger, of asking "Why me?," is a good sign, though it may not appear so at first. It is far better that all the pent-up feelings of hurt and sorrow and resentment be acknowledged and expressed. Kept inside, they may inhibit later relationships. For example, women who say they hate men may have failed to deal with their anger and resentment with one particular man.

Anger should be recognized and expressed one way or another. Repressed anger leads to all manner of neuroses, as any psychiatrist will tell you. Not that you should necessarily shout, throw dishes at the wall, or kick the cat; nevertheless, you should permit yourself to acknowledge the very natural feelings of disappointment, injustice, and so on. Once you recognize these feelings, you will be able to recover from them.

Acknowledging anger means expressing it in some way. This may be simply permitting yourself to spend time alone reviewing the events of the marriage which give rise to anger. Often the anger has just been delayed, stored away, and is surprisingly strong even years later. Perhaps it was not expressed adequately at the time of the event, or it was not expressed at all because of habit, training, or fear.

Sometimes a quiet review by yourself is not enough. There is a chance that you become stuck in a circle of anger, reviewing the same events over and over again, and being overwhelmed by your own anger. You may want to vent your anger in a discussion with a friend, or with a counsellor. It is usually counterproductive to attempt to vent it with your ex-spouse. Neither of you can be objective about the marriage at this stage, and such discussions tend to reinforce the dissension that already exists. Remind yourself that you have left the marriage behind and that what is important is that you learn to cope with your feelings on your own.

Your anger about past events can be disproportionate to the event itself. In times of stress the mind tends to use a variety of defence mechanisms to reduce the impact of a painful event. One such mechanism is projection, the process whereby anger toward one person or event can be directed at another. For example, your anger at the end of a marriage can be fairly complex. It is linked with a disappointment in yourself and fear of the future. Both of these emotions are difficult to acknowledge, and so they are often expressed as anger at the ex-spouse, and consequently the anger may be disproportionate. Sometimes, however, anger is directed at whoever is near, and this is usually the child or children, who are also experiencing their own grief and confusion. It is important that such a transference of anger be recognized as soon as possible for the good of the family unit, and certainly for the well-being of the children.

The anger, disappointment, and fear are also experienced by your children and are of a different quality because the children also perceive themselves as powerless. What happens to them is entirely dependent upon their parents. Powerlessness also leads to anger and frustration, which are often reflected in children's behaviour during the period of indecision and readjustment.

Like adult behaviour, children's anger may seem to be expressed inappropriately. Kids may fight with each other more than usual and misbehave at school, rather than risk expressing their feelings to their parents, whose actions are responsible for their confusion. If children do not express their anger, but instead withdraw, as many do, the parents should make sure that an opportunity is provided for the children to express their feelings either directly or with the help of a counsellor.

Favourite teachers should also be made aware of the personal pressures affecting the children at the time. They may offer support and understanding, as well as useful observations in the children's social behaviour. It is much healthier for a child to be permitted to openly acknowledge the impending divorce early. The myth that family problems should remain in the family is dangerous here. Often the most useful support for a child is that of another child who has already experienced parental divorce.

The strong anger that children may express toward their parents at this time should be received with as much patience and forbearance as you can muster, and the understanding that it is a necessary part of their own grieving process.

BARGAINING

The next stage on the list is bargaining, or making deals. If only you get back together or if only the marriage works out, you promise to be a good wife, to give him more freedom, to stop nagging, to have another baby, to hide your occasional depressions, to never again lose your temper, and all manner of self-effacing (and impossible-to-keep) assurances. In turn, he will promise to come home on time every night, take you out to dinner every week, stay home on weekends, never bring work home from the office, and spend more time with the children.

All of this sounds very tempting, especially when coupled with the insecurity of your new life without him. However, if no deep changes have taken place in either of you, the promises are empty dreams, impossible to keep because the old patterns will reimpose themselves all too soon. Without time to think and without outside counselling, a broken relationship is unlikely to heal itself.

The stage of bargaining, or desperate promises to yourself or to your husband, is more an attempt to ward off the inevitable end than it is a real willingness to patch up the marriage. It is difficult to distinguish a valid effort from a desperate promise, but the key lies in the honest pursuit of change. A relationship cannot change itself, nor can the good intentions of one person change it. Both people must be prepared to make an honest appraisal of themselves and each other before destructive behaviour patterns can be recognized and overcome. This process is much slower and more complex than promising good behaviour for the reward of a patched-up marriage. The patching is just on the surface and can't last. The facile promises of the bargaining stage must be seen for what they are: a stay of execution. They may indeed open the door to a valid reconciliation, but the commitment will have to become serious and honest, on both sides.

DEPRESSION

Once it is obvious that the bargaining period has failed, the next stage is a deep depression, as the inevitability of the end of the relationship is fully realized. This is a very dark and lonely time, when only the negative aspects of separation and divorce are considered. But it is a very necessary part of the healing process.

The deep sadness may be expressed by frequent crying without warning. It can be awkward and embarrassing. You may be walking down the aisle in the supermarket, and suddenly you are overwhelmed with tears, looking at a tin of food you both like; or during a perfectly innocuous conversation with a friend you suddenly find yourself crying uncontrollably. You may have decided to go to a movie with a friend, and the love scene does it this time. It can happen anywhere. You can be talking to your children, reading a book, or watching television, and the tears come. Unexpected triggers are everywhere.

Try as you may, you cannot stop this from happening, and it can be embarrassing to you and to others. The unexpected tears can cause inconvenience, but they can also be worrisome because you seem to have so little control over your own emotions. Once you realize that this happens to many people, and that it is temporary, you can begin to accept it. In time the intervals between sob sessions become longer and longer. There is a real pleasure on the day that you discover that you have only used up two tissues, and you have stopped crying. That is when you begin to realize that you are indeed regaining control over your emotions.

There are a few things that you can do to help yourself through this awkward time. Since you are unable to predict when these crying sessions will take place, and equally unable to avoid all the things that might trigger them, you must always carry lots of tissues and a make-up kit for repairs, if you wear make-up. The older you are, the more residual damage there is to your appearance after crying. You may need to buy some especially good cover-up make-up for the shadows and bags which are in evidence under your eyes after a good cry. Sunglasses are another great cover-up, unless it happens to be midnight. Cold water or even ice cubes can help to control the facial puffiness. Another thing that helps is a container of eye drops in your purse. Any of the ones that constrict the blood vessels and make your eyes look clear again, instead of bloodshot, will do. And finally, you can learn to lessen the embarrassment for yourself and anyone else who happens to be with you when you lose control for a minute. Try to treat it casually, and your friends will likely try to do the same. A comment like, "Here come the waterworks again," will help smooth things over.

> *"The uncontrollable crying changed to uncontrollable laughter for me one day. One day, about a year and a half after the separation, I began to laugh, and then I laughed and laughed until I became a little hysterical. It was a little embarrassing, since I was at a meeting at the time, but I remember the marvellous feeling of relief that swept over me as I realized that I could laugh again."*

ABSENTMINDEDNESS

In times of acute stress, as well as depression, another kind of memory loss can occur. For awhile you aren't as good as usual at remembering things from one minute to the next. You lose the thread of your sentences, and you forget where you put things. You find yourself standing at the fridge with the door open, but can't remember what you wanted to get. Some of this happens as you get older, but it is often exaggerated with sustained emotional stress and depression. This, too, is temporary, but may last for several months. All you can do is write things down. Carry a diary with you, and write down all appointments, grocery lists, birthdays, and so on. Then keep the book with you at all times in the same place: your purse or briefcase, or the kitchen counter. Don't trust anything to your memory while it is unreliable, and don't lose your diary!

As a footnote to this discussion about uncontrollable emotions, we must recognize that there are many people who respond to emotional tension in just the opposite way: they are unable to express their pain and sadness, unable to cry. They feel wooden inside. Perhaps "frozen" is a better word. This, too, is likely a temporary state but should be watched carefully. Such people are more prone to avoiding the necessary confrontation and acceptance of their sadness. People whose emotions are obvious are frequently reminded of their need to deal with the changed situation; people who hide their feelings from others and sometimes even from themselves can postpone conscious reassessment and adjustment indefinitely. Alternatively, a temporary freezing of emotions may be a godsend, freeing you to cope with the things at hand for awhile until enough time has passed so that you can deal more objectively with the new situation. In any case, what is important is that ultimately, in whatever way you choose, you do have a serious look at your feelings and attitudes and adjust them to suit your newfound single existence.

STRATEGIES FOR COPING WITH DEPRESSION

MOOD-CHANGING DRUGS

Both the tears and the quirks of memory can be taken in stride to some extent, and they will pass; but here is a word of warning. You must use your common sense, and if any of these things, the depression and crying, the memory loss, or any other change in your emotional control, last for too long or become too severe, see a doctor. The doctor may well decide to give you a drug to even out your mood swings, or decrease your emotional repertoire for awhile. Such medicines, taken with care, can be very helpful; a period in which your emotions are somewhat controlled gives you a chance to develop new patterns of behaviour, or develop techniques for controlling your erratic feelings. Obviously, all chemicals which alter your normal responses are inherently dangerous, and some can foster physical or psychological dependencies, or both. Responsible use of such drugs, like seeing a psychiatrist, is no longer frowned upon by society, and much of the guilt that used to go along with taking advantage of chemical assistance no longer exists. Only use drugs under the supervision of your doctor, and then be sure that you take full advantage of the improvement in your mental health. Make good use of the "chemical vacation" from your depression.

EXERCISES AND RELAXATION

There are other ways to help yourself overcome the effects of tension and stress, and fill in some of the hours that you might otherwise spend brooding. Some of these techniques will be useful long after you have recovered from the depression. One is to sign yourself up for a series of exercise classes. Physical exercise can help you to cope with emotional stress by relieving the inevitable muscle tension, and balancing emotional fatigue with physical tiredness. Exercise classes may also teach relaxation techniques which can help when you are wide awake and miserable at two o'clock in the morning. An exercise program also gives you a sense of health, and reassurance that you are able to prevent this crisis from causing too much damage to your physical well-being.

It is possible to overdo exercising, to begin to use it as a technique of escape which protects you from confronting the pain of your situation by taking up all your time and energy. Even exercise, if it becomes an avoidance technique for too long, can be harmful. Perhaps a healthy plan would be to exercise after you have spent time thinking and planning your next stage of life, when you really do deserve a break from intellectual things.

Learning—or relearning—to relax is an important part of coping with emotional pain and depression. Think carefully about the things that make you relax. A hot bath? A long walk? Reading a light magazine article? A game of solitaire? A jig-saw puzzle? Watching a television program or going to a movie? (Be careful in your selection of these—perhaps you should avoid the love stories.) A glass of wine? The last has the potential for abuse that other drugs have, and this is not the time to increase your alcohol consumption; as with everything, moderation and common sense are recommended. The point of relaxing activities is to change your mood and to shift your concentration to another subject that is not laden with emotional impact. Some communities also have courses in relaxation techniques. There should be some time each day that is scheduled for relaxing, whether a short period in the afternoon or just before bed or both.

FRIENDS AND RELATIVES

This stage of the grieving process is more smoothly achieved if you have a reliable support system. Friends can be a great source of support and comfort at the time of separation, although continuing friendships from the marriage may involve some rethinking. Close female friends from youth or even from during the marriage usually accept the fact of the separation quickly and can be an important source of emotional support. You should, however, recognize that your circumstances affect them somewhat as well. The ending of your marriage may cause them to pause and reconsider their own marriages. Some may feel grateful that their relationship is stronger and that their marriage is secure; others may be close to considering a separation of their own and your example will either strengthen their resolve or make them feel less secure. Some might even subconsciously see you as a threat to their husband because you are suddenly single and available. Some friends may, in their own thinking about your divorce, blame you (or your spouse), and this taking sides can be awkward for both of you. It is sometimes difficult for you to help a friend to sort out her feelings about your separation when you haven't yet done this for yourself. Your anger and resentment toward your mate may temporarily colour both your perspectives and limit your objectivity. Your friend may feel obliged to take your side and defend your anger. She can do this temporarily, and she can likely do it in a way that is accepting of your feelings, helping you to express your anger without judging your mate too strongly.

You may sense a bit of tension from some of your friends which you can't exactly trace. Usually this passes, but it arises from their attempts to think through your changed situation and to adjust to it. If they are mature, and if you help them a bit, they will cope with their own feelings of disappointment and sadness.

Other friends may reserve judgement of your mate. Do not interpret this as a rejection of you or your anger. Remember, your friend doesn't have the same turmoil of mixed emotions that you do, and is in a better position to be objective.

There are other types of friendships which suffer more damage with a separation—those with couples with whom you both went out on a Friday night, or you played bridge, or you went to college, or who live next door. Your separation breaks up this convenient unit. The other couple may feel that they should support one or the other of you, or they may try to remain neutral. They may even divide their loyalty, and the wife will support the woman in the separation, and the husband the man.

It is sometimes awkward, and you may choose to declare a moratorium on some of these friendships until you have had time to work out your own adjustment. The risk in temporarily freezing friendships is that you might find the friends altered, or you may find that after you have become adjusted to your new life, you no longer have much in common with them. Some friends will be outgrown as you change, anyway. This, of course, depends upon how much you change and how quickly. If you decide to take a holiday from various friendships, be fair to the people, and explain to them that you need time alone to think things through, and that you will call them again in a month or two, when you can. Though it is difficult for a friend to accept not being needed in what appears to be a time of stress, most of them will accept your decision, and quietly support you in absentia, waiting to accept the new you on your own terms.

You may find it necessary to deal with some relatives in a similar fashion. It may be too painful to see certain in-laws until you are more sure of yourself as a single parent. Some of your own relatives may have difficulty accepting your separation and you may be unable to help them until you have had a little more time to think.

If you do choose to declare a moratorium on various parts of your previous life while you reassess your feelings, be sure that you don't unwittingly become too isolated. For some women who have always felt a vague sense of disloyalty which prevents them from discussing personal things outside the family, accepting help from friends is difficult, if not impossible. It is very important for the newly separated woman to be able to recognize when she needs help, and to have the sense and courage to learn to ask for it, to recognize when it is genuinely being offered, and to accept it graciously.

Sometimes, however, rather than seeking isolation some women run from friend to friend seeking support and reassurance, needing to tell their side of the story over and over again. This reaction is a form of being stuck somewhere between the denial and the anger stages. It will last until the woman is able to begin to assess her own behaviour and to learn to be by herself. Most friends will simply accept the story with little or no comment, or will agree with the version presented by such a woman. Occasionally a wise friend will risk a little more, and tell you that it is time to stop dwelling on your break-up. Here again, as with so many other things, it is a question of balance. It is healthy to talk about the feelings and emotions which arise with separation, but it is not healthy to allow such talking to prevent a serious self-assessment.

It is almost impossible for a person who is experiencing her own emotional turmoil and is in such need of support to be aware of the effect she is having on others. You are usually unaware of your repetition, and your friends' consequent boredom. In your great need to justify your position to your friends, and thus to yourself, you fail to realize that you have hit a block. By not taking time to think by yourself, or to really listen to any of the advice your friends may have, you are preventing yourself from growing. Sooner or later you simply have to decide that you have spent enough time on this stage, and that it is time to move on.

For awhile you may be unable to accept advice because of your own defensiveness and insecurity. What you must eventually come to realize is that your separation is not nearly as important to other people as it is to you. To you it is all-consuming, sapping your strength and preventing you from thinking of anything else. Because of the shock of adjustment, you are overwhelmed by a strange variety of emotions, all of them strong. Friends are usually much more accepting of your situation than you are; they have seen many other marriages break up, and for them it is not the unique, central experience that it is for you. Their lives move on, and although they may be concerned for you, they do not spend every waking moment thinking about you. They are, therefore, in a position to be considerably more objective than you are, and their advice should occasionally be sought, even if you cannot agree with it in the end. The concern and advice of genuinely interested friends may set your thinking on a better path or trigger a new perspective in your own mind.

Taking stock of yourself is the most important thing you can do at this juncture in your life, and if it means that you may lose a few friends, or outgrow a few others, then it may be a reasonable price to pay in the long run. Such losses will be balanced by new friends who will not be chosen in concert with your ex-husband.

Once you are on your own, you can strengthen and deepen friendships with women. There is little time in many marriages for close female friends, unless they happen to fit into the couple's activities; even then, much of the time together is spent as a foursome, with little opportunity for the development of a deep friendship. Many women discover that they can now take the opportunity to deepen a friendship that they always knew was on the brink of becoming important, but because of circumstances, never had a chance to develop.

Be careful to maintain these new and rich relationships with women even when you become involved in another romantic relationship. It is so easy to slip back into the old pattern of "couple" friends and let your single friends drift away. If you permit this to happen you are causing yourself a serious and unnecessary loss. Your new man need not like—or even know—all your other friends. It is all right, and very healthy, for you to maintain separate as well as shared friendship circles. Your circle can even include both men and women. Fortunately it is becoming more socially acceptable to have close friends of the opposite sex with whom there is no sexual expression of the relationship. Your own circle of friends adds a freshness to your romantic relationship, and provides escape valves for both of you. It also lessens the pressure to fill each other's every need.

It can be especially helpful to have among your friends a woman who has already experienced a separation and divorce and is far enough away from it that she can be objective about her own adjustment as well as yours. Simply by existing, she proves that you can survive, and that the pain will pass.

> *"Some people wanted to remain friends to both of us, but I didn't want that. I was so busy trying to establish a separate identity from his that I didn't want to share my friends with him anymore. I didn't want people telling me how he was, either; it just made it harder to think of myself as separate. I could cope with these friends later on, but not at first."*

> *"There was such a loneliness, even before the marriage actually ended, being with someone with whom I no longer had anything in common. But people don't always know from the outside, and it was so important to try to reach out to the one or two friends that I needed so badly."*

> *"People said afterward that they were reluctant to approach me honestly, because they sensed that I was still denying that there was any problem. So I had to reach out to them first, and let them know that I needed them, and that reaching out was so hard to do because I hated myself and naturally assumed that everyone else did, too."*

> *"I really needed women friends; I didn't feel I could trust another man with my feelings. And anyway, I didn't think that a man could understand what I was going through."*

> *"I owe my friends so much for just letting me talk my way through it all. Eventually, I began to hear my own words, and my arguments and rationalizations simply didn't hold water anymore. It was be-*

cause they let me rave on that I ran down, and began to reassess my own perspective and to develop a new one."

COUNSELLORS

There are many women who, for one reason or another, are unable to rely on friends for support, but who still need someone to talk to. They also need to know that other women have reacted much as they are doing, and that their feelings are a natural reaction to the stressful situation. Again, such women may approach one of the several counselling agencies within their own community. An objective counsellor can help without the complications and obligations of friendship. There are various community agencies, mother's-day-out organizations, and women's centres. There are also women's bureaus in most provincial capitals. A phone-call to any of these will put you on the track of a good counsellor.

BOOKS

The ultimate no-strings help comes from books, of which there are now many on the market, in your local library, or in a friend's bookcase. Referring to books as a resource is appropriate to much of the discussion in this book. Whether you are seeking self-help psychology, relaxation or exercise techniques, or a do-it-yourself divorce manual, the library or bookstore can help you. Read critically, selecting the advice appropriate to your situation—remember, there are different solutions for different people.

In any separation or divorce case, getting information on your own is much cheaper than paying an hourly rate while your lawyer explains things to you. You will save money and make much better use of your lawyer if you have done your homework. Take notes as you read, and make a list of questions for the next phone-call or office appointment with your lawyer. Whether you prefer novels, biography, academic studies, documentary information, or do-it-yourself advice books on divorce, they exist in abundance. Some are listed at the end of the chapters in this book. As well as the obvious lack of obligation and the objective reassurance that a book may supply, it can be read at your own convenience at home or at odd moments during the day, and can be consulted again and again. Many women have felt that the advice or reassurance that they can offer to other women is worth writing down. This is certainly an act of friendship, and such friendship is readily available.

Some cities have bookstores which stock books of interest to women and children, and may also operate as a sort of drop-in centre, where you can find some assistance both through the books, and perhaps through a new acquaintance, over a cup of coffee. Check the Yellow Pages under "bookstores," or call your local women's centre. Such no-strings help may be more difficult to seek, but often proves extremely beneficial.

ACCEPTANCE

The grieving process is concluded by acceptance; acceptance of yourself as a single person, and of the challenge that this implies. Acceptance is signalled by the end of the depression, renewed energy, and the beginning of a sense of enthusiasm and adventure for your new life pattern.

Learning to live alone, to be emotionally and practically self-reliant, is one of the most unexpected and satisfying results of separation and divorce. This sense of self-sufficiency doesn't come easily, especially to women who went directly from the protection of their parental home to establish a home with a husband. Still, learning to live alone is a very worthwhile and rewarding adventure, and equips you to enjoy more mature relationships in the future.

The phrase "learning to live alone" simply means learning to live without the companionship, shared decisions, and mutual dependency which are part and parcel of a marriage. Even if you have children, you must learn to live alone in the sense that you become fully responsible for the management of your own household and for the management of your own life. Decisions are yours alone, as is the responsibility. This can be alternately invigorating and terrifying.

Many women have achieved a reasonable level of self-confidence and self-reliance before or during their marriage from outside experiences such as a job or community work. Still, the sense of competence that they have in the office doesn't always come home at night, and many capable professional women are extremely dependent upon their mates for home-related decisions. Even with a job and a fairly good sense of your own capabilities, learning to live alone can be a major adjustment. This adjustment is often further complicated by a sudden drop in self-confidence that accompanies the process of separation and divorce.

Redeveloping—or starting to develop—a workable level of self-confidence and independence can only come with practice. You can read all the books and do all the thinking, but only evidence from everyday living can provide the reinforcement that you can indeed manage well on your own. This is certainly a pure application of the 4-H Club motto: "Learn to do by doing"!

Once you have passed through a month in which you have paid all the bills, or at least selected the ones that you can pay, planned the payment of the others in the future, and kept your budget and your own mood more or less in balance most of the time, a good feeling will begin to grow. This feeling of self-assurance feeds on itself and inspires you to go on sorting out new and better ways to get through each month, until one day you realize that you are no longer simply existing and enduring, but that you have control of your life in a new and exciting way.

Only when you have developed some confidence in yourself as a single person can you really begin to put the confusion of the end of the marriage behind you. Although this adjustment requires an enormous effort on your part, the passage of time in itself achieves a great deal. As painful events sink further and further into the past, the scars will heal over, unless you continue to aggravate them. It is during the early days on your own that your mind can play tricks on you. The marriage which ended in such unhappiness can take on a rosy glow in retrospect. You may find yourself remembering only the good parts and overemphasizing them, especially since these are the things that you miss. Or, you may find that you only remember the bad times and that you are overemphasizing those. In time you should achieve a balance of memories with which you can comfortably live, but this will happen only when remembering the marriage is no longer painful.

CHANGING LIVING PATTERNS

In order to achieve this state, you must inject enough new experiences into your life. Your separate identity as an individual will become clearer to you and others as you begin to express it by selecting new experiences, new places, new friends, and new patterns of living. As well as these new experiences, you must settle your accounts with the old patterns that you chose to leave behind, and even with the ones that you choose to retain. In other words, you must take this opportunity to take stock, to identify the patterns of living and the patterns of behaviour which are part of you, but which you would like to change. Then get busy and change them. You should do this as early as possible, before you get into a rut of self-pity or inactivity, such as the woman who, although divorced for many years, continues to live in the same house and take part in the same activities and friendship circles as when she was married, but without her husband. Her major conversational topic remains her marriage, her husband, her divorce. Whether she is bitter, or sad, she has not adjusted to her altered status and has no sense of her own identity outside the marriage. Of course, it is never too late to climb out of such a rut, but the longer you wait, the harder it becomes.

The changes and the new experiences which you seek out need not be earth-shaking. You may join a new club, or get a new job, or start a new hobby, or buy a series of theatre tickets, or you may move to a new house or apartment, or a different city. Although such decisions as the last should not be made impetuously, different women require different degrees of change in order to really begin to believe that they are separate individuals.

Determining your own need for change in where and how you live is a very personal matter. Some women need a sense of the familiar for awhile before they can make the break with the past. Others can't wait to be away from the marriage home and neighbourhood, and see a move as the first step in defining their new life. Just be sure that you are not staying in the old place in order to prolong your stage of denial. If you are still secretly dreaming that he will come back to you there, you should get out. Or, if he is back there all the time, interfering with your life and the children's on a daily basis because he still thinks of it as his home, again, you will need to do something—limit his access if you can, or move to somewhere where he doesn't feel as if he has a proprietary interest.

For some women, making such changes in their living habits takes a great deal of courage, particularly if they have spent many years bound by children and household and have been dependent almost entirely upon a husband for social contacts. Going to a movie, concert, museum, or art gallery alone is not only frightening, but fear makes such an idea totally unappealing. Still, the first steps must be taken, and the reward is a pleasant sense that you really can stand alone—and you will even begin to enjoy it, after awhile, if not at first. For other women, making the obvious changes in patterns, such as finding new friends and activities, is the easy part. For them, doing things alone is always pleasant, not terrifying. They are outgoing women anyway, and finding new activities and a few new friends doesn't present a big problem. For both types of women, however, the deeper changes still remain the most important, and are the most difficult to achieve.

YOUR PARENTS

Divorce is a shock to most parents, even if they have seen it coming ever since their son or daughter began dating the person that is now being divorced. The job of our parents was to bring us up to fit into the general fabric of society, creating stable marriages and secure homes in which to raise our own children. A divorce in the family flies in the face of the social values our parents have taught us.

Our parents often do not have much experience with divorced families, and so have only hazy concepts of "what comes next." They can't imagine life as a single person for their child, especially if it is a daughter, and if she has children. They may, at best, anticipate financial and social difficulties for their child, and at worst, see her as a social disgrace, forcing her children to grow up in a "fatherless" home, seriously disadvantaged.

From now on the traditional patterns of family relations will be different. Family dinners, celebrations and birthdays, Christmas, and so on, will never be the same. These occasions are often especially important to parents, who may not see much of their children in between such events. For them as parents and grandparents, there is only loss. They also face the possibility of losing the friendship of the son- or daughter-in-law, and perhaps even less access to their grandchildren. Whether or not these things actually come to pass, the circumstances for visiting these people will be quite different from now on. Some parents choose to remain friends with their son- or daughter-in-law, while others cut him or her off completely in their anger and defence of their own child. Although some of this sort of loyalty is reassuring, this extreme reaction only increases the pain of an already painful situation, for everyone.

Some parents come too strongly to the defence of their child by rejecting the spouse completely. This behaviour has a couple of results; it forces their child to defend the spouse she is divorcing to her parents, and it also causes her to have to work even harder to prevent herself from adopting the same attitude, believing that everything was "his" fault, as her loyal parents say, and ignoring her own responsibilities in the marital problems.

Some of the feelings that your parents may be experiencing may also be a veiled threat to their own marriage. If they have been unhappy for much of their marriage, one or both of them may see your courageous act of getting out of a bad marriage as something they should have done years ago. This can incite many emotions which they dare not confront directly, and which may be expressed indirectly as anger—or even rejection—of you.

The announcement of the impending divorce of a child causes a mixture of reactions in most parents. There is, of course, surprise, and usually sadness for the pain that their child and grandchildren will have to experience during the process of divorce. They may feel as if it is in some way their fault. Most of these negative reactions are fleeting. Some parents, however, are not able to put aside their own feelings in order to support their child through the divorce. These parents may continue to see only their own sense of anger or embarrassment.

It is almost impossible for the divorcing child to help such parents. Each attempt may lead only to recriminations and guilt from the parent, such as statements like, "How could you do this to me?", and "What will I tell my friends at the bridge club?" This attitude is a serious problem, but not something that the divorcing child can help the parent to confront.

For some parents, "what the neighbours will think" is a very real concern. They are deeply embarrassed by the idea of a divorce in the family. They may even deny its existence to friends and relatives in order to avoid coming to terms with the changed situation themselves. In a sense, coming to terms with a child's divorce may mean that the parents must experience many of the elements of the grieving process in order to reach a stage of acceptance where they can be of assistance to children and grandchildren. Here time may be the best healer, and you may have to take some time away from your parents to lessen your own pain.

You certainly have a responsibility to explain your divorce to your parents. You need not give them all the details; it is all right to preserve your own privacy, and reviewing the details may be very painful for you. Furthermore, you may decide that your parents will be more helpful to you and the children if they do not feel they have to take sides. You can achieve this, perhaps, by explaining simply and clearly that you and your spouse have decided to stop living together, and that it is no one's fault in particular that the marriage broke down. Telling your parents of some of the steps you have taken to try to preserve the marriage will be reassuring, but again, detail is not necessary. Divorce is a private affair, and you are offering an explanation to your parents with the hope that they will accept and understand your adult decision, and react accordingly.

THE OLD AND THE NEW—IN-LAWS

It would be so much easier to adjust to a new pattern of living if it weren't that many of the same old things keep right on happening. You may still live in the same house, and be visited by the same people. You may still see your husband or his relatives, and such situations are a constant reminder of the past. Further, they are often stressful meetings after a separation, full of emotional tension until everyone manages to adjust to the new arrangement. It is so easy to fall back into the patterns and roles of the past relationship. There may even be subtle (or not so subtle) pressure exerted upon you to discourage any change. Relatives may feel that there has been enough change, and it is a very normal reaction for people under stress to resist change. All of these things are likely just undercurrents, but if you recognize that they are happening, you are in a better position to cope with them.

Just as you need the freedom to grow and change, you, too, must permit and encourage those around you to do the same. It is extremely difficult for parents of the couple to accept divorce without taking sides, especially when the law is set up to blame one or the other partner. Even without the law, tradition has it that someone must be at fault. When faced with a divorce, whether or not there has indeed been a wrong-doer, they are likely to be loyal to their own child. And there is nothing wrong with this, in many cases. It is natural for a parent to want to support a child, and parental support at this time is very important to each of the couple. The more mature the two sets of parents are, the more objective they can be, but it is necessary for the couple to recognize the impact that the idea of divorce may have upon the parents. They may see it as a reflection upon themselves, and they may well be tempted to apply their own values and judgements upon the situation, values and judgements which arise from a different generation and a different perspective.

It is important that you give in-laws time and room to adjust. If you yourself take time to consider how they feel and can accept it, you are less likely to increase your own misery by feeling rejected by them as well. Further, it is up to you, at least in part, to help your in-laws to adjust to the separation, and in time, if you continue the relationship, to adjust to you in your new role. If you are trying your wings as a more independent, adult person, you will have to give them time to learn to see you this way, and you must realize that any changes you make in your own life pattern, or in the lives of your children, may be interpreted as a further rejection of their own child, your husband. This may require a great deal of patience, but to save the relationship, it must be changed so that your life can continue to grow all in one piece. Although you play different roles with the various people in your life, one of your major goals now is to integrate these roles as much as possible, making them all fall into line with the sort of person you are and want to become.

It is difficult to permit your in-laws the freedom to react and adjust in their own way, especially when you most need their support. They may feel that the changes you are making are a direct rejection of them and their values. They may withdraw, or they may be angry with you. Yet, your acceptance of their behaviour must once again be tempered with common sense. Permit them to react, but try to protect yourself and your children if their reaction is too strong, too prolonged, too immature, or inappropriate.

There are several things you can do. One is to take time to listen to them and to talk to them. Perhaps they would really like to accept the new situation, but don't quite know how to cope with it. They may be afraid of losing a relationship with you or with your children that is very precious to them. They may be unable to cope with the conflict in their own value system that your separation creates. In any case, they may welcome an opportunity to air these feelings with you and welcome the reassurance that you are trying to understand their point of view and wish them to accept yours. Once they realize that their relationship with you will continue and that their feelings of doubt, confusion, and concern are accepted, they may be able to be much more helpful. Remember, though, that each person's emotions are complex and that emotions don't always run along with intellectual decisions. Your parents-in-law may offer you their support, but it may not always be consistent; when they believe that their son is suffering, they may shift back temporarily to side with him, and this you must simply understand.

The ability of parents to support a couple of the next generation through a divorce is growing. There is more literature, more discussion, more television situation serials, all of which raise the consciousness, familiarity, and acceptance of a changing pattern of behaviour in society. Still, however, people react from the base of their own experience, and lucky is the couple that has the support and understanding of both sets of parents during the pain and confusion of divorce.

If a discussion doesn't achieve the minimum level of understanding that you need in order to continue with a relationship with your in-laws, you may have to declare a moratorium; explain to them that you need time to sort things out, and that you'd prefer not to see them for awhile, but that you will contact them when everyone's feelings have had a chance to settle down. This may not be a popular decision, but it does reduce the tension, and even if your decision breeds resentment, by the time you re-establish contact, you'll be stronger and in a better position to cope with it.

As with many of the aspects of the process of divorce, there is a side benefit to the in-law relationship. Society has clearly defined the roles of a daughter-in-law, father-in-law, and mother-in-law. Although none of us really fits into the stereotype, we are all measured from time to time against it. The act of separation gives you and your in-laws the freedom to hop out of these roles, to become friends, as honest adults, without the obligations of the defined in-law relationship. The encouragement that you wish to continue to see them, but that the relationship must change, may be all the assurance they need. It may even be a relief to drop the roles and expectations of being in-laws and become friends. Such a change may take time and effort on the part of everyone, but it is usually worth it.

From the point of view of the parents of the couple, they are victims in the divorce, because they are profoundly affected, but have absolutely no control over what happens. Some of the unpleasantness that occurs may arise from these feelings of powerlessness. Often the act of taking sides arises from the need to do something to relieve their own emotional pressure.

> *"It was unfair of me to feel that I was the only person growing and changing, but it was so intense for me that I ignored what was happening to our parents."*

> *"Parents do change. It's so hard for us as kids to believe that; we think of our parents as static, and our kids think of us as static."*

"Once my in-laws and I acknowledged the tension and brought it out in the open, everyone was relieved, and we could go on from there."

"My parents couldn't accept the divorce and cut me off totally for over a year, just when I needed them most."

"My Mom's reaction, when I talked about the possibility of divorce, was, 'I would be ashamed of you if you didn't divorce; I will not be ashamed of you as a divorcee. The marriage is over, and if you haven't got the guts to admit to the world that it is over, I will indeed be ashamed of you. If you do it, I will be proud of you'."

RELATING TO YOUR EX

Establishing a new relationship with your husband after the separation is often much more difficult than coping with new relationships with your parents and in-laws. The habits are strong, and if the marriage lasted for a long time, the patterns of behaviour which you had developed with each other will be very hard to break. Any changes you try to make may be greeted with animosity, since they may be interpreted as a rejection of him. This is only one possibility. Another is that he will not see the changes at all, because he is so involved in his own adjustment that he can only look inward for awhile. He may not be consciously blocking your development toward independence; he simply may not be interested any longer in what you do, or he may be unable to change his perception of you as you were within the marriage relationship.

Any of these negative reactions are tolerable to you as long as you have realized that you do not need your ex-husband's approval. If, however, you are still hoping, deep down, that he will notice you, that he will change his mind about you, that he will like you better as the new you, or even that you will prove something to him, the fault lies within you: your primary motivation to change and grow must come from within yourself, and the approval you should be seeking is your own. You are quite capable of supplying your own support, but you must learn to trust yourself. Seeking the approval of your mate, when you have chosen to separate, is simply a continuation of old patterns and may create a block for both of you. Until you learn to accept each other in your new roles, there will be an unnecessary degree of tension inherent in every phone-call and visit.

If you continue to rely on your mate for approval after the separation, you are also opening yourself up to further rejection. You may well delay the whole process of adjustment for each other, as well as prolong the legal aspects of separation and divorce unnecessarily. By seeking his approval, you permit him to disapprove of you; you give him the power to reject you again and again, which can only weaken your ability to create a new life pattern. You can prevent this by taking control of your part of the relationship. You can control the number of times you must meet, and you can control much of your own behaviour. If the relationship is too full of anger and resentment, put it on ice for awhile. Deal only through intermediaries (lawyers, not kids) until things cool down a bit. Or don't do anything at all until you feel ready for the next step. The power is yours, and you need not be a victim unless you choose to be.

Women who remain under the control of their mates long after the separation do indeed have a choice, but they may need a bit of help to realize that they have a responsibility to themselves as well to end the dependency. Old behaviour patterns die hard. Continued dependency is usually as much the woman's fault as the man's, in that they are both perpetuating a long-established pattern of behaviour.

The husband is often deeply resented for his "intrusion" into the precariously established independence of his wife. But she does not establish any new guidelines for their relationship, and until this is done, the old patterns must serve. If you do not want him dropping in without notice, say so and establish a specific time each week for visiting. If you do not want him coming to your residence, select a neutral place to which you can deliver the children—a park, museum, or McDonald's. If his frequent phone-calls are upsetting to you, ask him to call at a specific time, so you can prepare yourself. If none of this works, examine your own feelings to see if you are really being fair, and if you are and the situation remains untenable, see your lawyer about defining the terms of access more clearly.

> *"Every time I start to get a little self-confidence, he drops in to see the children and destroys me. It takes me days to recover."*

> *"I had to resolve to keep him right out of my life until I was really sure that I had become comfortable with this growing sense of me. It just couldn't take place while he was entering in and out of my life every day or two."*

> *"I have come to terms with the knowledge that he will never see me as I really am, let alone as I am becoming; and that is part of why the marriage ended, anyway. Why should things be different now?"*

If there are children, you must sooner or later work out a relationship that permits the visiting sessions to come and go without a major upset each time. If there is a lot of animosity, all one can do is minimize the encounters, and then make them short, polite, if possible, and very much to the point. Do not linger unless you are very sure that you can retain control of your emotions. If he can't, it is not your responsibility, but you can do him the favour of ending the meeting. The sooner you take responsibility for your behaviour in these inevitable encounters, the sooner it will become tolerable for you and for your children, friends, and relatives. In time, even a bitter relationship may alter, and with growing mutual respect, become defused. Sometimes, though, bitter relationships may remain bitter forever and after a reasonable effort, should be accepted as such. In time, most couples achieve a tolerable relationship following separation and divorce. Some develop firm friendships based on the new honesty that independence helps them to develop; some even choose to remarry each other (like Elizabeth Taylor and the characters of the television program "Dallas"); and some never see each other again after the divorce.

SELF-ASSESSMENT

The soul-searching that leads to an assessment and an acceptance of self presents a great challenge. Where does one begin? Can it be done alone, or should a counsellor be employed to guide you through it? Remember, you can change your mind. If you find that you reach a stage where you would like someone objective to talk to, find that someone. Or perhaps you would like someone with professional experience to start off, and then you will continue on your own. Or perhaps you will work your way through the entire process by yourself. In any case, you will have to do most of the work.

For those who have never looked at themselves other than superficially or through the reflection of society, it is a little more difficult at first. You are seeking to see yourself as you really are, the central elements of your personality. Not as you appear to your husband, or your mother, or your children; not in comparison to the magazine women or the stars of your favourite TV show, but as you really are. One way to do this is to get out your pencil and paper, and write down what you would like to be like. Describe the person that you would realistically like to be. This is your goal. Be fair, and do try to restrict yourself to the possible. Then a day or two later, write down what you think you are like right now. And then that evening, when you are alone and have a cup of tea or a glass of wine beside you in your favourite chair in your living room, or at the kitchen table—wherever your special place is— compare the two. Ask a few questions. What things do you have to change in order to bring the two closer together? Write these down, and then set to work on them, one at a time. Would you like to be better organized? Less critical? More patient with the kids?

Let's take the example of teaching yourself to do a better job of budgeting your time and energy. Start by preparing a things-to-do list each morning, or at night just before you go to sleep. Try not to be overenthusiastic; it may take you a few days to learn how to set achievable goals for yourself. You cannot control all the interruptions—kids, phone-calls, etc.—so set just a couple of important tasks for yourself each day. If you don't try to move mountains, you may find that you can get everything done that you meant to, and still have a bit of time left over. Use that for yourself—don't start another task. Reward yourself. Read a book you like, or go for a walk, or just sit and think. Or have a nap. Setting unrealistic goals for yourself leads to inevitable frustration and disappointment. Instead, make your plans so that you can get everything done, and give yourself that nice feeling of satisfaction, the feeling of being finished. So often when there is too much to do we start everything all at once, and end up with nothing done, and a dreadful feeling of frustration. The most obvious example is spring cleaning. You start working on each room in the house at the same time, and by the end of the day you are exhausted and the place looks worse than before you started. If you had started instead with a clearer goal such as cleaning all the kitchen cupboards, you would still be dead tired, but you would have finished, and you might have the incentive to get on with another task tomorrow.

It is the same with your personal reassessment. Maybe this week you will work on your relationship with your children. Think of something special that you can do for or with each child each day. You can develop a habit of being kind and pleasant most of the time, just as you can develop the habit of being a carping fish-wife. Since you can't be both, start consciously working on being nice at a particular time, say, in the mornings. At least at those particular times you won't be yelling. No one will notice the difference in your behaviour for awhile, but you will know that you are changing. Perhaps your children will never consciously acknowledge an improvement—they will just enjoy it. And it will become easier as you practice. This is how you change behaviour patterns—set realistic objectives and do just a little at a time. Remember to reward yourself for success—nobody else will!

Changes in attitude do not show immediately to other people; not even to people who know you well. They are set with their image of you, and it will take time and repetition before they really understand the changes in you. This works to your disadvantage, because once you have managed to change something as important as an attitude or behaviour habit, you want your achievement to be recognized. We are brought up in our society to work for praise and recognition. However, the person you must rely on for this recognition and even a bit of back-patting is yourself. Others may well benefit from these changes in the future, in that they will enjoy or respect you more in time; but you are really making these changes for yourself, so that you will like and respect yourself better.

A point to be remembered is that you are many different people. Each of your friends and relatives sees you slightly differently, and over time, you change and mature, so that someone who knew you when you were twenty may not recognize you at forty. The continuity lies within yourself alone. We commonly mistake our public self, our superficial self, with what we really are. This kind of mistake leads to constant discontent with ourselves, since we can never successfully reconcile ourselves with someone else's image, or with our own wishes of what we should be. There is a pay-off, though, for becoming acquainted with your real self and then accepting yourself; you are then able to recognize the perceptions that others have of you, and enjoy them, or reject them. This is much healthier than trying to live by the goals and expectations that others set for you.

Once you are aware that there are several versions of you wandering around, that you behave quite differently with different people and in different places, it becomes easier to distinguish some of your own motivations: are you behaving in a particular way to please someone else, or is your behaviour a sincere expression of yourself? This is not to say that you shouldn't try to please others, but only that you should not let yourself be entirely governed by their standards.

The ability to distinguish between the various images of yourself is especially important in reaching a sense of peace with yourself. It becomes less important that you fail to reach someone else's objectives for you, and more important that you reach the objective that you have set for yourself. We usually achieve this stage in our relationship with our parents during late adolescence, but we often simply substitute their values with another set, also external. It may be the values of a husband, or of a profession. To really grow up we must become capable of selecting our own goals, even though they may indeed be derived from other people's examples. These are no longer blindly accepted and followed, like a new fad, but have been carefully sifted and examined, with the final selection representing your own self.

One of the more brilliant portrayals of this process of coming to terms with oneself and putting the various images that others may have in perspective occurs in Margaret Laurence's book *The Stone Angel*. Hagar is an old woman who reviews the various episodes in her life: first, exclusively from her own point of view, but later balanced by the counterpoint of her increasing recognition of the perceptions of others. She has a great deal of difficulty reconciling the overt selfishness of her behaviour to her husband and her son and her daughter-in-law with her own idealistic perception of herself. She finally comes to realize the vast difference between what she says and how it is perceived by others; between what she meant to say and what she really said; between what she wishes she were and what she has become. For Hagar, since she has let the patterns develop for so long, she can only reconcile them, not change them. She is astonished at the insidious nature of her own personality development. She didn't become old and fat and miserable all at once. It happened slowly over the years. But she never really looked at herself, never listened to the kindly advice of her husband, and instead, finally drove him away with her pretentions. Hagar is a woman who cannot like what she has become, nor can she change it. She is about to die, and for her, it is important now only to recognize and to reconcile what she really is. In Hagar, Margaret Laurence draws a very clear and instructive picture of the difference between our internal and external selves. Such recognition is an essential step in the achievement of self-knowledge and the ultimate goal of self-acceptance.

Once you have begun the process of self-exploration and have discovered some of the things that you value, you will learn to protect them and nourish them. You may compromise on many things, but not on these. Perhaps you did deny these parts of yourself during your marriage, but now you must not, since to do so is a denial of your very nature.

What are these things, these core values? They don't have specific names, but they are the thoughts and actions which comprise your personal strength, your sense of rightness and fairness, your sense of honesty, your principles. They are most easily recognized when they are threatened or denied. They are signalled by the twinge you feel when you acquiesce on a point which is against your better judgement. You have a vague feeling that what you have said, or done, or are about to do is wrong, but you do it anyway. Other times it is what you don't do. For example, you don't stand up for yourself or defend your point of view to your husband or your boss or your friend. Such small denials of self, if they become habitual, breed frustration and resentment. They are a denial of the essence of you. Some people think of this as intuition or conscience. In any case, this is the precious part of you, the part which you will learn to identify and start to nourish.

Beginning to defend that self, to stand up for your own personal values, to trust your own instincts, helps you to learn to like and respect yourself. A side benefit of this self-knowledge is that it permits you to really listen to other people; you are no longer in competition with the people with whom you talk. You don't have to compare yourself with others, to convince them and yourself that you are equally bright or equally experienced. So many conversations are really contests, people attempting to impress each other and themselves. Yours need no longer be so; instead, you can really listen to what the other person is saying as something other than a challenge to you. This kind of non-competitive listening frees you to have deep and enduring friendships based upon mutual acceptance and respect. It also provides the firm base from which another loving relationship may develop, should you choose to consider it. Sometimes this process of achieving self-knowledge does indeed take place within a marriage and permits this kind of honest acceptance of self and each other which characterizes a rich relationship. Sometimes it only happens after the failure of a central relationship forces the process of self-examination and assessment.

Since the 1960s, scholars have taken a serious interest in the process of self-acceptance. Much research has been done, and many books written. This bodes well for the future, since couples are marrying later, and have much more information at their disposal. They will form more realistic marriages, with fewer fairy-tale expectations and much more realistic acceptance of each other. The dramatic increase in divorce of the last thirty years may indeed lead us to a much more secure concept of marriage.

References

Kübler-Ross, Elizabeth, *On Death and Dying*. New York: Macmillan, 1969.
The most widely known study of the grieving process.

Laurence, Margaret, *The Stone Angel*. Toronto: McClelland and Stewart, New Canadian Library, 1964.
A novel which examines the thoughts and feelings of an old—and somewhat unpleasant—woman as she prepares to die. She reviews her relationships with family members and learns to take responsibility for her part in them.

CHAPTER THREE

Kids and Divorce

It's time now to confront the subject of children. Readers who don't have children can skip this section if they wish.

TELLING THE CHILDREN

Wherever possible, children should be helped to prepare for the separation and divorce of their parents. Because it is so painful, parents often avoid discussing the impending end of the marriage with their children and unwittingly deny them the necessary time to adjust. For their part, children can be apparently oblivious to the tension and unpleasantness of even the worst marriages and may be completely surprised when their parents separate. This may be because children, like many adults, unconsciously deny unpleasant things, or it may also be that since this is the only marriage they know, they assume that their parents' relationship is normal and are, therefore, astonished when they find that it is about to end in divorce.

Divorce forces a tremendous emotional adjustment on a child of any age other than infancy. Once a child has come to know and rely upon both parents, any change in this pattern is upsetting. Regardless of the circumstances of the separation, the child stands to lose the day-to-day access to one or the other parent. Even if the relationship with the departing parent wasn't particularly good, the change in the status quo requires adjustment. The older a child is, the stronger the emotional involvement may be.

Any child deserves an adequate explanation of the separation, and the reassurance that he or she is loved by both parents. Often the parents are so wrapped up in their own emotional turmoil that they forget to go beyond the factual explanation to provide the reassurance that the child needs so desperately. It is very common for children to take the blame upon themselves, rather than accept that no one is really to blame. Kids are taught that if things go wrong, it is someone's fault, and in a child's world, the person who is wrong is often the child. It is therefore so easy for the child to assume that this is his or her fault, too. This burden is too much for a child of any age to bear. Each child needs to know that the trouble rests with the relationship between the parents, and is in no way the fault of the child.

The initial explanation should be given as objectively as possible. There is no need to recount the details of the breakdown of the relationship, but an honest explanation of the reason for the separation must be provided which is equal to the child's ability to understand. A reassuring fact for the parent is that kids only hear as much as they can cope with. Usually, even if you tell them much more than you should, they keep what they need and throw the rest away. It may take awhile for the initial explanation to sink in, and the parents should be prepared to repeat it as many times as necessary. Further, they should provide many opportunities for the child to ask questions and talk it over with each parent separately, and if possible, also with both parents together. Such discussion should always be accompanied by the reassurance of the love of both parents for the child.

The first question that usually pops into a child's mind is, what will happen to me? Children deserve to know immediately what will happen to them, to be reassured time and time again that their interests are being taken into account in your plans. Like the parents of the separating couple, the children are profoundly affected by the separation and divorce, and have absolutely no power over events.

A mistake that parents often make in the first rush of emotions following the decision to separate is to offer the child the choice of which parent he or she will live with. This is often terribly unfair, since the child is usually blissfully unaware of the complications of adult life and is not able to judge which parent or which situation or which combination of circumstances will be most suitable. Before such decisions are made, all alternatives should be carefully weighed. Outside advice from friends, relatives, and possibly a counsellor should be sought so that the final decision regarding the care of the children is made with their best interests truly considered and not made in the heat of the moment by a distraught parent. Many children are completely confounded by the horror of having to choose between their parents, and would much prefer to have the decision made by a grown-up. The children may or may not participate in the making of this decision, depending upon age, maturity, and circumstances.

The following questions, prepared by an eleven-year-old girl, reflect some of the thoughts she had about her parents' divorce.

You wonder if your Mum gets custody of you if that will hurt your Dad an awful lot, or vice versa.

If you have brothers or sisters, you worry if you might get split up.

You feel that whatever you decide to do, you will hurt someone by doing it.

You feel guilty about everything that is happening.

You worry that you are the cause of your parents' divorce.

You get jealous of other kids who have two parents.

You get teased at school and you feel embarrassed.

You feel you have to take sides, but you don't want to.

Sometimes you think about killing yourself.

You ask yourself, "Why is this happening to me, and not to someone else?"

Tell your children what they need to know to make good judgements and decisions, listen carefully to their questions from their point of view, as best you can. And listen even more carefully for the questions that they do *not* ask, for the comments they do *not* make. Give them the opportunity to say what they think and feel, and then let them know that you expect them to accept and cope with what has happened, just as you will. Do not offer too little information for the child to adequately consider the situation privately later. Too little information also implies that you do not trust the child to do his or her own thinking. Treat the child's intelligence with respect. A child of any age often responds well to expectations that he or she can behave in a grown-up fashion and cope with grown-up issues. Most children will adjust quickly to any new situation. Kids are remarkably resilient. Watch for signs, however, that a child is not adjusting, such as withdrawal, unusual mood changes, frequent and inappropriate crying, or an increased need for attention. Reassure such a child and try to provide the extra attention for awhile. If this goes on for too long, or is too strong a reaction, you may want to get counselling for the child and yourself.

CUSTODY

There are many different possibilities for the solution of the question of custody of children—the couple may agree between themselves that one of them will have custody, they may decide on joint custody, or there may be a full-blown custody battle in court.

JOINT CUSTODY

Joint custody is a fairly new idea. It may be undertaken with the best of intentions, or as a way out of an awkward and unpleasant decision. It is important that the child be made to feel that he or she belongs in each parent's home and is not just a visitor in both places. It is possible that the child will lose the essential security that comes from a sense of place. Joint custody puts a strong pressure on the parents to communicate regarding the needs of the children. This may be especially difficult after a marriage in which communication may have been a central problem.

When joint custody does work, the children usually think of one home as their main base, with one parent with whom they have a more regular and dependable relationship. North American society is set up to reinforce the concept of one home and a single-family dwelling. Often kids themselves lean towards one or the other parent and neighbourhood and build their social lives in relation to that home more than the other. The concept of joint custody is recent, and there are many gradations and interpretations of it. It requires a high level of maturity, sensitivity, and objectivity on the part of both parents.

Joint custody is a concept that moves away from the adversarial system of the courts. A joint custody agreement—or court order—is based on the assumption that both members of the couple are adequate parents. This contradicts present divorce law in Canada, which is still based upon the assumption that one party is guilty of a marital crime, and is therefore unlikely to act as a responsible parent. This essential difference between the rationale of divorce and joint custody can raise conflicting emotions in cases where the divorce and/or the custody settlement was disputed. It is difficult to adjust from an adversarial divorce battle to the accommodation necessary for practising joint custody. As the law changes to permit "no-fault" divorce, the philosophy of joint custody will be more consistent with divorce practice.

Divorce is an act of rejection. It is a negative experience regardless of how amicably it is settled. The decision to end the marriage is usually based on serious differences in value systems, or sometimes differences in attitude regarding the upbringing of children. Courts still tend to award joint custody only if it is agreed upon by the two parents. It is rarely imposed in a judgement against the wishes of the parents.

There are many arguments both for and against joint custody, or shared parenting. Little research has been done because it such a new concept. The effect on children of shared parenting after divorce as opposed to the exclusive parenting of the mother or father is still unknown: early studies in California indicate that there are fewer returns to court on custody issues when joint custody is ordered. Most studies to date, however, reflect the perspective of the parents and not the children. Many experts are very reluctant to argue in favour of joint custody because of the lack of security provided for the child. Two separate environments merely complicate the child's world, which has already been confused by the divorce. Guarding the parents' rights to equal participation in raising their child may preclude the child's right to a secure home environment with a consistent and reliable relationship with a parent. If a child is going to live regularly in two homes, make sure that each home is supplied with familiar items, toys, pictures, clothing, to provide continuity and lessen the adjustment period of each relocation.

Long, drawn-out custody battles may indeed convince the children that both parents want them, but the price is very high, both emotionally and economically, for everyone. Once the judge has made a decision, it should be accepted and the parent who loses custody must graciously acknowledge defeat, still reassuring the children of his/her continued love and concern. The fact that the decision was taken out of the hands of the parents and was made by the court can be comforting. The children and the parents are left without the responsibility of the decision; the judge decided. A custody battle creates a terrible strain for the children, and they should be given the security of the decision whichever way it goes and a chance to adjust to a new sense of permanence and safety.

CHILD CARE

The traditional view is that only a mother can properly raise her children. Although many women continue to hold this view, separation and divorce often force a woman to work outside the home. Alternatively, a woman may choose to continue her career, and to share her child-care responsibilities with others. Finally, to further cloud the traditional picture, many fathers are now arguing that they should have the right to play the principal role in child care, both within and outside marriages. Separation and divorce create a situation where such choices must be confronted directly.

The facets of the problem vary, depending upon the age of the children, but you are left with the question of who will be supervising the kids when you cannot be with them. There are many answers to this question. A convenient solution is to have a relative or neighbour care for your pre-school children, along with her own. Many women continue to work in their own homes by caring for other people's children. Because your child knows the person already, the adjustment is less than it would be with a stranger.

Many of us, however, live far from our relatives and must seek less personal places for our children if we are to work outside the home.

DAY CARE

Day care is a common solution for smaller children, although it can sometimes be quite expensive. Many day-care centres are now subsidized by provincial and municipal government grants, so it is wise to ask your local government Social Services departments what choices you may have before selecting one.

Before you decide on a particular day-care centre, visit with the teachers, and try to get a sense of what their objectives are. Ask about the child/supervisor ratio. Find out if there is a planned program or if it is basically a babysitting outfit. Take a tour of the physical location, checking the adequacy of the facility and the cleanliness of the kitchen and bathroom. Find out if nutritious snacks are served regularly, and if the kids have an organized rest time or quiet time. Make sure there is a reliable connection between the day-care centre and a doctor, nurse, and hospital nearby.

Once you are satisfied that these requirements will meet your standards and needs, ask around among your friends and neighbours, or get the phone number of a couple of parents who use the centre. Find out how their children adjusted to the centre. Also, phone the municipal day-care registry and check on their rating for the centre you are thinking of selecting. Then, take your child or children to the centre for a morning, if you can, when you can stay with them for a few hours, and see that they are happy and contented with this new situation. (Of course, this is not always possible if you have to be at work, but perhaps a friend or relative could go. Or perhaps it is better for the children to make the adjustment on their own.) The more involved you are with the day-care centre, the better service you are likely to get. Attend the parent sessions if you can, and bake for the bake sales (or buy some nice goodies at the local bakery). If you are known and respected as a concerned parent, your children are likely to receive more individualized attention.

NANNY/HOUSEKEEPER

The next alternative is the housekeeper/babysitter. This can be very expensive, but some people feel that it is worth paying as much as half of their salary for this service. There are many variations on the housekeeper/babysitter role. Some people are nannies only, and will just cook for the children. Others will care for the kids and do light housework. Find out what "light housework" means and schedule it to suit your needs. Some parents prefer to separate the two tasks completely and have a babysitter and a housecleaner (if they can afford it) or do the housework themselves on weekends. If you can afford to have an occasional house cleaner, try to arrange that it is done just before your days off so that you can really enjoy it.

A housekeeper must be carefully selected. Some of us are lucky: the ideal grandmotherly type appears in answer to our ad, and moves in to love the kids and bake brownies. Alternatively, you may end up caring for a neurotic or an alcoholic on top of all your other problems. It is extremely important to screen a housekeeper carefully. Treat the person as an employee. Conduct a reasonable interview in your home. Ask about previous experience in detail. Try to discover what the person's philosophy about children is. Find out if the person is ill very often, and discuss a procedure that will protect your own job...a neighbour or friend or relative who will cover for a day or two, or a day-care centre that will take the kids with no advance notice for a couple of days in the event of the sitter's illness. Get several references, and make sure you check them by phoning the people. After you have discussed the housekeeper's ability with a former employer, always remember to ask, "Would you rehire this person?"

Although you should retain a certain distance from the housekeeper, it is important that you develop a friendly and trusting relationship. This is based on honesty and straightforwardness. Discuss salary, and make sure that there is clear agreement between you on what the terms are going to be. Don't forget to discuss cost-of-living increases and vacations, because if these are not agreed upon, they will return to haunt you. What about time off over Christmas? Will you need help on some weekends or evenings? Try to anticipate your needs as carefully as you can.

You must clearly outline the job itself. What are the hours, and exactly what housework is the person responsible for? Help the housekeeper to prepare a schedule. This sounds a bit like overdoing it, but it is important. Once you both know that on Monday the kitchen floor gets washed and that on Friday the living room and dining room get vacuumed, and so on, you feel that you're getting your money's worth, and the employee is able to derive a sense of satisfaction which comes from completing a job. Make sure you distinguish between routine housekeeping tasks which should be kept up regularly, and the bigger maintenance tasks which only get done once a month, or less often, like window-washing, and scraping the wax off the kitchen floor. There should be two separate schedules for these very different kinds of tasks. You can also give yourself a real boost by scheduling the daily housework so that the house is pleasant for you for the weekend, when you are home. Be sure that your nanny/housekeeper understands that the children's needs come first and that the housework schedule is flexible enough to accommodate this.

It will take some time before you can really assess whether you and your new housekeeper see eye to eye about methods of child-raising. The initial interview can cover such things as diet restrictions and preferences that you may have for your kids, methods of punishment, off-limit places in the neighbourhood, and so on. As with any job, you should set an initial trial period, after which both you and the housekeeper/nanny can reassess the situation.

The first few weeks will be a period of adjustment, with the kids either being dreadful to her, testing her on every point, or being little angels, trying to win her over to their side in the continuing war between kids and grown-ups. Eventually everyone will settle down somewhere in the middle, and a working relationship will emerge.

There will be lots of times when the children "tattle" on the housekeeper, and when the housekeeper reports incidents where the children have been bad, or where she is having trouble disciplining them. Despite your natural instinct to side with your kids, it is important that you remain objective in these situations, and help the housekeeper and the kids to work out solutions to the problem. If you step in and side with the kids, or give the kids an opportunity to believe that they can influence your attitude toward the housekeeper, life becomes extremely difficult for the housekeeper. Both the children and the housekeeper should see you as a person who will listen, and perhaps suggest a reasonable alternative for everyone to try. During the hours that the housekeeper is in your home and on duty, you are not only mother, but employer. These roles can conflict sometimes. Your children must come to realize that you trust the housekeeper to care for them in your absence. The housekeeper must feel sure about this, too.

The relationship between you and your babysitter or housekeeper should be friendly, but remain at a sufficiently professional level that you will not be taken advantage of by your employee. Although this person may end up being one of your closest friends, make sure that you do not unwittingly make the working relationship more difficult by confiding your personal worries to such an extent that your own loneliness and confusion put you in the inferior position. Once this happens, it can't be undone. When you find yourself begging your employee to do a job, or apologizing too often for the inconvenience your requests may cause, then it is time to assess the relationship. Make sure that you get what you are paying for; reliable assurance that your job description will be carried out, without undue worry on your part.

This problem can be even more difficult if you have a live-in babysitter. There are terrific advantages, because, depending upon your agreement with the sitter, you may be free to go out in the evening and on weekends. However, a live-in sitter can also limit your privacy unless you are able to provide a separate room that also serves as a sitting room for him or her. You may, alternatively, enjoy the company of another adult during the evenings, and prefer to include the sitter as a new member of the family. Much of this depends upon your personalities, and the stage that you are at in redeveloping your self-confidence and new life patterns. You may need lots of privacy, and prefer to hop into bed with a book early each evening, as soon as the kids are in bed, and turn the living room and the television set over to your sitter.

Be sure to explicitly set regular mutual evaluation sessions where alterations in routine may be discussed and where either of you can decide to terminate the relationship. Of course, you can fire your employee with whatever notice you have stated at the time of hiring.

Evaluations are useful for more reasons than just the decision of whether or not to continue the relationship. These sessions should be used to discuss each child and compare impressions of the child's needs and interests. Routines need to be varied as children grow. Routines even vary with the season; for example, bedtimes and study times will change from school days to summer vacation days. Children's needs for supervision change as do their recreational interests. Household routine should also be reviewed at evaluation sessions so be sure that you both allow enough time for discussion of all these issues. Be sure to lead the discussion carefully, leaning towards a businesslike attitude and avoiding the danger of an emotional set-to over your inevitable differences of perspective and priorities in the household.

Nannies and housekeepers are undoubtedly one of the most abused groups of employees in North America. Often they come from other countries and must deal with a radical change of culture as well as with the often unreasonable expectations of their new employers. If you do employ such a person, help her to make friends in your city. See that she gets out often and that she discovers where the places are that she will enjoy. It is in your own best interest to help the person to adjust, and it is simply human kindness. There are so many horror stories about girls who come to a new job only to find that they are on duty twenty-four hours a day, seven days a week, and that they are expected to do everything from child care to cooking to housework to being butler and maid for company. All this, and they are usually appallingly underpaid. In fact, there are now several places in various cities which serve as rescue centres for nannies who simply cannot tolerate the conditions of their employment, but have no recourse since they know no one in the new country and lack the funds to return home. Often the agencies that brought them into the country no longer care about them, either, having collected their placement percentage.

Make sure that you pay at least minimum wage, and that your hours are fair and not excessive. Make sure that your employee has adequate time off, and that she or he has the opportunity to spend it in a truly recreative way. If you are not sure what you should pay, call the labour relations branch of your local government. If you aren't sure where to find some friends for your employee, call your local social service agency or the immigration office or take him or her to a local youth drop-in centre. You can arrange outings with other young people in your neighbourhood until an independent network is established. And finally, if you are aware of a nanny who is being badly used, report the situation to your local labour relations branch of the government, anonymously if you wish.

CO-OPERATIVES

Yet another possibility for day care and also for housework is a neighbourhood co-operative. By sharing the responsibilities, several families can save child care expenses, and often feel that they achieve a better quality of child care. Babysitting co-operatives vary from those which serve evening and weekend social needs to those in which parents with different work schedules care for each others' children. Alternatively a parent who does not work outside the home cares for all the children in the group in return for cash payment or other services from the group members.

The barter system and sharing of expenses or tasks are both techniques for exchanging services of value. As well as the obvious advantage of avoiding or reducing the need for cash, a very personal element is introduced to the transaction. And the obligation between friends or acquaintances is often of a higher quality than that of strangers.

The possibilities and combinations of exchanges for babysitting co-ops are only limited by your imagination. A work-sharing co-op may arise from a babysitting co-op, or it may be started on its own when several families agree that it would be fun and quicker to do some of the bigger tasks together.

Caring for each others' children, sharing heavier tasks like spring cleaning and window washing, putting in the garden, and building a new garage or basement room make the tasks more fun and provide some pleasant friendships as well.

If you choose to try to start a co-operative group to serve your own needs you will need to locate other parents whose needs are compatible with your own. Put an ad on the bulletin board of the local supermarket or in the local newspaper. Call the local social services organization to see if they can put you in touch with other working parents who might like to work out a system of sharing.

AFTER-SCHOOL CARE

If your children are all school-aged, you need someone to be there at lunch-time and after school, and sometimes you even need supervision for the morning. In some communities you can find an after-school program run by the community, by a social service agency, or by a group of parents. These programs vary widely. Some take the children in the morning until school-time, then feed them a hot lunch and care for them after school until the parents are finished work. Others do only some of these things. If you have such a program near you, you are fortunate. If not, it may be in your interest to start one.

Alternatively, you can sometimes hire a local teenager, who will be glad of the extra money, to come in the morning until school-time and then be there after school when the kids come home. They usually can't manage lunch-time, too, because of their own school obligations. If you are particularly lucky, you will find a teenager who will also prepare dinner so that it is ready to eat when you dash through the door exhausted at the end of the day. Even if this can only happen once in awhile, it is worth it!

EMERGENCY PLANNING

Whatever system you use, or even if you feel your children are old enough and responsible enough to manage on their own, make sure that they are very well prepared to cope with any emergency. This, of course, applies also to anyone you hire. The big dangers are fire and injury.

Most fire departments will be delighted to send a representative out to your home to discuss emergency procedures with your entire family. This is well worth doing, both for the obvious increase in safety and for the peace of mind it gives you. Rehearse with each child the best way for them to get out of their bedroom in the event of a fire, and see that the whole procedure is written down somewhere for regular review. Select a place outside the house where everyone is to meet once they have escaped from the house through the various specified routes. Determine which neighbours they approach to call the fire department, and make sure the neighbour is aware of this possibility. If possible, get the children to memorize the telephone number, although it is usually enough to call an emergency number like 999 in most cities. Once you have learned the procedure for fire, rehearse it every four months or so, so that it stays fresh in everyone's mind. If there have been changes, make sure that each child is trained for the circumstances of the new room. The best advice to give is that if there is any sort of a fire, get out of the house and call the fire department. Most damage can be repaired, and it isn't worth the risk for a child to try to deal with a fire alone, regardless of how it started.

Police departments are equally willing to visit your home and offer suggestions on making it more burglar-proof. They will also help you train your children about what to do if they are alone and hear a prowler. The police usually also instruct members of the community on ambulance procedures, too. Again, make sure that the information is written down, and that it is reviewed regularly. If there is a Block Parent program in your neighbourhood, it is to your advantage to join, and to instruct your children in the program. If there isn't one, maybe you can help to start one.

The most worrisome and unpredictable situation is injury. A carefully prepared first-aid kit and a carefully prepared emergency telephone list are essential. Your first-aid kit doesn't need to be terribly sophisticated, but it should have everything necessary to treat minor cuts and burns, including a pair of scissors, adhesive tape, some rolls of gauze, Band-Aids, cleansing solution such as mercurochrome, peroxide or Dettol, burn ointment and possibly a homemade sling and an elastocrepe bandage. Every child should know where the first-aid kit is kept, what is in it, and how to use it. In addition, you should have a comprehensive list of telephone numbers by the phone in plain sight for the use of the children or a babysitter in an emergency. We've provided a sample; take the time to prepare such a list, cover it with plastic, and put it on the wall by the phone. And make sure that it is always up to date. If you are covered by medical insurance make sure that a photocopy of your card or policy number is attached to the emergency phone list. Make sure that your children and babysitter know where the list is kept.

EMERGENCY PHONE LIST

General Emergency Number
Police—neighbourhood station
Fire Department
Ambulance
Poison Control Centre
Hospital Emergency

Mother—office
Father—office
Father—residence
Neighbour #1
        address

Neighbour #2
    address
Nearest relative
    name
    address

Family doctor—Dr. Smith
    address of office
Dentist—Dr. Jones
    address of office
Orthodontist—Dr. Best
    address of office

Power company
Gas company

Children's schools
    Elementary
    Junior High
    Senior High

Health insurance numbers
    Family code
    Patty
    Jody
    Jim

Many communities have started babysitting courses for teenagers, and such sitters are well-prepared to deal with most emergencies, but they still need to be supplied with information about where you are, whom to call, where to find your doctor, and so on. Everyone becomes excited during an emergency. With carefully set out instructions and information, most emergencies are quickly dealt with by whomever happens to be present.

These mechanical concerns, like fire, theft, and injury, are the very things that haunt the working parent. As we've seen, precautions can be taken to ensure that an emergency will be coped with adequately.

Kids usually cope very well, surprisingly well, with most emergencies. It is necessary to accept that you, as a parent, cannot be with your children all the time to protect them, whether you are working outside the home, or not. It is very important, therefore, to assure the children that you have confidence in their ability to cope and that you know they will be able to manage with unexpected situations. And when they do, tell them so.

MOM, THE RESCUER

With children, with in-laws, parents and friends, even with your spouse, one of the biggest things you may have to contend with is your own impulse or need to protect them, to save them from the pain of separation and divorce. This impulse to protect comes from our social conditioning that we must, as women, put our own needs last and protect and comfort everyone else first. Such behaviour is considered to be the sign of a good mother and wife, in terms of the mythology of the recent past. Of course, you should provide comfort and reassurance to these people whenever you can, but not to the extent that such behaviour denies the reality of your own situation, nor to the extent that it denies your own feelings and postpones your dealing with them for too long. The image of the woman as "rescuer" may influence many of the people that surround you at the time of a divorce. They may still, consciously or unconsciously, be expecting you to behave according to the traditional stereotype by continuing to put your husband's, children's, and other relatives' needs before your own. Admission of your own pain may be seen by yourself and others as weakness; inability to provide constant protection for your children, and even reassurance for your husband, may be considered selfishness or inadequacy. The social pressure towards supporting others before yourself is very strong.

If you sense that you are succumbing to this pressure, step back from yourself for a minute and assess what you are doing. Once you recognize your own impulse and motivation, it is easier to curb your unhealthy need to run around supporting everyone else.

What you are really doing is denying the others a chance to seriously consider the new situation and adjust to it. Further, you may be creating or perpetuating a pattern from the marriage which implies that you are responsible for "making everything okay." You should watch for signs of this behaviour and avoid it. Even if this pattern existed in the marriage, now is a good time to throw it off. This is a time for everyone to behave responsibly, recognizing their own feelings and coping with them openly with love and consideration for others' feelings, too. It is not a time to perpetuate unhealthy dependency patterns. Trying to protect children from the worry and grieving is wrong and will delay their adjustment. Children, like their parents, are suffering a serious loss and should be permitted to experience the grieving process too. Children's emotions tend to be more open and readable than adults'. You will be able to tell as your child passes through the stages of denial, anger, bargaining, depression, and acceptance. If the child does not show signs of grieving, make sure that he or she knows that it is all right to cry, and that you will accept the sadness and the anger, and will provide love and comfort.

Although you can still reassure everyone including yourself that everything will indeed be okay, you must each at the same time recognize that it will take time and effort on everyone's part to achieve that state of "okayness." The alternative, permitting children and relatives to avoid facing the consequences of changing perceptions and relationships which arise from divorce, cheats everyone in the long run. By permitting the expectation that Mummy will make everything okay to persist, you are also taking on a very unrealistic burden for yourself at a time when your emotional strength is already taxed. Even if you went through your marriage taking responsibility for everyone else's feelings, making sure that hurts were smoothed over, that fights were settled, that Daddy wasn't bothered when he was tired after work, that the kids bought birthday presents and Father's Day presents and Mother's Day presents for in-laws, and so on, now is the time to let this pattern lapse.

Just stop all the "have-to's" for awhile; the really truly important ones will float to the top of your mind eventually, and you will do them again—because you want to, not because of an obligation. Many women stop sending Christmas cards altogether and wait a few years. Certainly this is a time for reassessing personal obligations, whether with friends or relatives. It is a time, actually, to make things easy for yourself. Cut out as many pressures as you can. Avoid the impulse to prove that you can be Super Mom, even through a divorce, and instead be a realistic mom, dealing as honestly as you can with your own and everyone else's feelings. This doesn't mean that you lie around and worry and cry all the time. There is a real benefit to keeping busy, but not so busy that you cannot take time to think. As with everything else, you can err in either direction. Withdrawal and inactivity are just as dangerous as too much "busy work."

The rescuer pattern often comes out when visits with the absent parent, still usually Dad, take place. This is a time for Dad and the kids to be free to develop whatever their new relationship is going to be. Resist the impulse to organize it for them. Permit Dad to make mistakes, to cope with awkwardness and sadness, both his own and the children's. Give them time alone together, preferably in the apartment or home that the father has established away from the family home, so that the kids will have a chance to see that Daddy is all right and that he has a nice place to live.

Fathers report that it is extremely painful for them to return to the family home to visit the children. The home is now the symbol of the failed marriage. Almost any arrangement is superior to having Father visit the children only in the family home or in the home of the mother, since the children then are unable to get a sense of the father's new life pattern. They must know that Dad is adjusting, in order to carry out their own adjustment. The same rule holds for the reverse situation when Mother is the absent parent.

It is essential for the children to understand that life is moving on for both parents, that the separation may be a temporary slowdown in the pace of living, but that things are starting to move along again in a new pattern that very quickly becomes normal.

What children need most of all is an element of predictability. We owe them something more concrete than the assurance that "everything is going to be okay." They need to know exactly how things will be, what to expect, and how the changes in their parents' lives will affect them. Some of these things cannot be predicted at first, but parents tend to give blanket assurances to children accompanied by very few concrete facts upon which the children can base their own thinking. Facts provided as objectively as possible are equally as reassuring as hugs and should be supplied as often as possible without overloading the child. It is best to make the child's position plain as early as possible. Make it clear that the children are participants, but will not be directly involved in any decisions relating to the divorce; or, if they will be involved in some decisions, tell them which ones and clearly describe the circumstances and limits to their participation. Explain that they will be kept informed and that their interests will be safe-guarded as much as possible. They need this assurance, and are greatly relieved to know that they are not expected to be a confidante, advisor, or counsellor.

KIDS AS PAWNS

Children are always, to some extent, pawns in separation and divorce. Each parent will try to some degree, consciously or subconsciously, to seek the emotional support and loyalty of the children, unless they are tiny babies, though perhaps even then. Parents who are aware of this potential for manipulation and confusion can try to guard against it. Since it will happen anyway, in most cases, it should be recognized for what it is and then controlled or avoided where possible.

Try not to let your own insecurity at this time cause you to be unnecessarily dependent upon your children, since it will slow your own adjustment and theirs. It is very tempting for a separated parent to become exclusively dependent upon an older child for companionship and even advice. Although this may be healthy, and even encourage maturity in some cases, in others it creates an artificial adult façade for the child's personality. It may prevent resolution of the separation and divorce from the child's point of view, since it is subsumed in the much stronger perspective of the parent. Finally, too much sharing of one parent's pain can lead to a permanent bias against the other parent on the part of the child-confidante.

Such dependency and vying for loyalty can increase the already heavy emotional load that the child is carrying. This is not to say that you should hide your feelings from children. It is all right for them to see you crying, to know that you are sad, too, to cry with you. However, few children are able to carry their own emotional load, plus that of a grieving parent. It is not healthy to expect the child to be your main and regular source of comfort, or to listen to you as you try to sort out your feelings. Your perspective on the marriage relationship is that of a partner, a lover, a friend; the child cannot possibly see that point of view because of inexperience, and because of the very nature of the child-parent relationship, which is usually a life-long pattern. A child only comes to terms with the perception of parents as adult people when he or she reaches adulthood. Certainly it is unfair to ask a child of any age to achieve that difficult transition while adjusting to the divorce of the parents.

In complicated cases where divorce is contested or custody is an issue, or simply where one or both of the parents is immature, manipulation of children's feelings and loyalty can be carried to an extreme. There is a time when one or the other parent may have to step in and try to stop such manipulation. If you feel that this is true in your case, examine your own motivation as carefully and objectively as possible. Try to be sure that your interfering does not stem from your own need for loyalty, from your own loneliness, from your old patterns of competing for the children, or to get even with your spouse. Don't fall into the trap of trying to become a better manipulator.

If your husband is manipulating the children's emotions and loyalties during his visits, there is little you can do. You can spare the children some anxiety by not questioning them upon their return from their visits with their father. At least this saves them from some of your anger and pain. It is quite true in this case that "what you don't know won't hurt you." You really don't need to know every word that was exchanged during the visit with Dad, or who he is seeing now, or what his apartment is like.

Most kids recognize manipulation for what it is, and make allowances for it in their own assessment of both parents. If, however, you think that the manipulative behaviour of their father presents a serious danger to the adjustment of the children rather than just an annoyance, speak to your family doctor and your lawyer. They will advise you about options for corrective action such as counselling for the kids and the father (if he is receptive to this), or restricting and supervising the visits.

If you feel that your spouse should not see the children, or should see them less frequently, or should only see them under supervision, approach him directly first. Try not to create a confrontation, but attempt to examine the effect of his behaviour on the children as objectively as possible. Alternatively, you could quietly arrange that a mutual friend or trusted relative always be present during visiting times.

If the other parent is unable to discuss this problem with you because of anger, or tension, or other unresolvable conflicts, see your lawyer. You can only interfere with the right of your ex-spouse to visit the children if there is real danger to the children. In such cases a court may order him to stay away. (See discussion of Restraining Orders in Chapter Four.) Normally, however, the courts are governed by the principle of maximum access to both parents, insofar as this is in the best interest of the child. If your lawyer decides that visits should be supervised, make sure that it is not by you, since this simply leads to a higher level of confusion.

A final point is to make sure that the children are aware of what you are doing. Do not interfere unless the behaviour is causing them some problems, so that your interference in their relationship with the absent parent will seem justified to them. Then inform them honestly and briefly, without an emotion-laden diatribe on the faults of the other parent. Do not ask them; tell them how it is going to be. Speak with assurance and finality, so that they do not feel that they are involved in this decision, since this is another example where objectivity is all but impossible for a child.

A warning is necessary here, because there is a danger that you will set yourself up to be the "bad" parent by interfering. Again, remember that children are remarkably resilient and pragmatic people, and that they are often not being hurt as much as you think. We, as individuals, find it almost impossible to really see a situation through someone else's eyes, even those of our own children. We tend to base our actions and reactions on how we would feel if the same thing were happening to us, and this can be quite inaccurate. Kids do not have the emotional experience that many more years of living have given us. Thus, they usually just take what they can cope with from any situation, and ignore the rest. If your children do not perceive themselves as being manipulated in a harmful way by the other parent, maybe they aren't. Maybe it is simply your perception, based upon much more knowledge and many more experiences, and further complicated by your own resentment and unhappiness.

THE FANTASY OF THE ABSENT PARENT

Sometimes, the parent who leaves goes some distance away to another city. In such cases some things become easier, and some more difficult. For example, the question of frequent visits is solved, but those visits that are planned will cost more in energy and money to arrange. Retaining a realistic relationship with the absent parent becomes more difficult for a child, since he or she becomes at least partially dependent on both parents to make the arrangements. It is in everyone's best interest to make contact frequent and reliable, if possible, so that the child is assured of the other parent's well-being, and has a realistic idea of what life is like for the distant parent.

Whether the departing parent is nearby or distant, if communication is curtailed very much and contact is inconvenient or simply dwindles over time, you may confront a new phenomenon: the fantasy of the absent parent. This is a very common occurrence and is a manifestation of the child's attempt to deal with a difficult situation, the loss of a parent. It is very easy for the parent who lives with the child to resent the fantasy of the absent parent, but try to avoid this. This is a situation which will sorely tax your sense of humour, but nevertheless the fantasy should be tolerated. If you try to fight it, you will lose, since you are not the star of your child's fantasy. The other parent is. In fact, you don't even have a walk-on role. If you interfere, you will put yourself in a bad light, since you can't possibly compete successfully with an imaginary hero. Pointing out the faults of the other parent which are inconsistent with the dream is a pointless exercise, because it may indeed be these very faults which caused the fantasy in the first place.

A fantasy is something that we create to make up for deficiencies in reality. They are not harmful, usually, and are also much less troublesome, in most cases, than the actual person would be. So, even though it is hard to stomach the image that your child seems to have of Dad as the rich, important, interesting businessman, while you in contrast wash dishes and clean toilets, grin and bear it. Often the image of the rich, busy dad is invented to make up for the fact that Dad seems too busy to phone or visit. It is important to remind yourself that kids with two parents at home often create fantasy parents, too.

It is so easy to lump your own feelings about your ex-spouse with the children's feelings, to forget that they do have a separate relationship with him, which should be allowed to continue. It is tempting to believe that since he left you, he left them, too, and he doesn't have any right to see them. This is unfair to everyone. If they are little, you must help the children to stay in touch with their absent dad or mum, although you should refrain from stage-managing, or even being present at most of the visits. They must develop a continuing, growing relationship which withstands the strain of separation and divorce and which accommodates these changes, as well as the changes that occur in the growing-up stages of children and of the parents themselves. Life is full of momentous changes; a divorce is one of quite a few milestones that the children will encounter and pass through.

"I didn't realize that the children's father could still love them when he didn't love me anymore. Yet the kids really needed to know that."

In the last few paragraphs we have been assuming the worst. It's time to spend a few minutes looking at some of the alternatives, such as a set of parents who agree to divorce, but who work hard to maintain the relationships with the children, without falling into the trap of denial, of pretending that nothing has really changed. There are lots of ways to do this, and it depends on the age of the kids, and the circumstances of the parents. If they are still living in the same town, the absent parent may continue to attend parent-teacher meetings, or may choose to take turns attending so that both parents stay in touch with the child's progress. The absent parent may babysit for occasional weekends to give the resident parent a break, as well as to have a more extended visit with the children. Many of the same activities that were shared before the end of the marriage can be continued despite the changed circumstances, given a set of mature and loving parents who can surmount their own feelings and provide for their children's emotional needs separately.

This last sentence sounds as if anything less than such an arrangement is a failure. This is not true. For many couples, such adjustments are desirable and possible; for others, there is too much animosity; and for still others, there is an adjustment in between, after the tension has died down.

Much of the trouble that arises regarding children in a divorce comes from the common misconception that love is a limited commodity. Subconsciously we may believe that if the kids continue to love the other parent, the love they have for us will be in some way diminished. Despite the overwhelming presence of negatives which flow over you during the time of separation and divorce, they do not necessarily flow over everyone else in your family, since their perspective and emotional make-up are totally different from yours. Your feelings of rejection, failure, being unloved, and angry may not be shared by your children. In fact, it would be surprising if they were.

MANIPULATION OF AND BY CHILDREN

There are three things to remember about children in a divorce situation: first, they are involved in the divorce; second, they are pawns, regardless of how careful you think you are; and, third, they are unbelievably resilient. If you can accept the first two premises, you have come a long way in learning to be honest; and if you learn to believe the third premise, you will worry less and feel less guilty.

Regardless of the age of the child or children, they are involved and will be affected by separation and divorce. Even if they are babies, the pattern of their lives is still altered. Kids react differently at different ages, and according to their own personalities and social background. Their adjustment is further affected by their relationship with each parent and the existence of an outside support system of friends or relatives or a counsellor. Even though it is easy to see from an objective perspective that children are certainly involved in a separation, they are the forgotten people in so many cases. Parents are so overwrought at the time of a separation that they often provide little or no preparation for their children. When they do, it is often laden with bias against the other parent or with guilt from parental feelings of failure. Even though you are experiencing an emotional turmoil, you must somewhere find the strength and wisdom to help your children to cope with their feelings and adjust to the new situation.

The best way to do this is to confront the truth together. The truth is simply that the marriage has ended. Regardless of why or under what circumstances, this truth must be faced openly by everyone—parents and children alike—in order for a healthy adjustment to take place. The longer parents try to fool themselves or their children, or even outsiders, the longer it will take to accept and adjust to the new reality. And yet, it is so tempting to continue the old behaviour patterns, to extend the period of denial by telling the children that nothing has really changed. Daddy will still come over often, and Mummy and Daddy are still good friends, and so on. The truth is that you have decided never to live together again. It is such a simple statement, but it takes some women years before they can acknowledge that this is the irrevocable truth, permitting themselves and the rest of the world to adjust.

Although parents often believe that they are protecting their children by not telling them the marriage is over or by "breaking it to them gently," they may actually be unwittingly cheating their children. Parents consistently underestimate the abilities of their children. We simply don't recognize their intellectual ability to accommodate a change as big as divorce. Further, it is a natural reaction for parents to try to shield their children from any hurt, whether physical or emotional. Similarly, it is a natural reaction for children to blame themselves for the divorce if they are not given a clear explanation.

Parents who have experienced divorce are continually astonished at how well their children accepted and adjusted to the new situation.

The pragmatism and resilience of children simply cannot be underestimated. In fact, contrary to the old myth that mixed-up kids come from broken homes, we now know that just as many mixed-up kids come from homes that are apparently happy, and lots of healthy kids come from homes which have experienced divorce. Many mixed-up kids come from homes which have been preserved despite an unhappy relationship between the parents. Tension and stress are bad for parents and for children. Prolonged, such tension can only lead to emotional and often physical problems.

Even after the custody issue has been long since decided, children will tend to imagine that they can choose between the parents. This is a classic opportunity for manipulation, and is common to many divorce situations. (We should remember here that manipulation of parents by kids is not limited to post-divorce families. Nevertheless, divorced parents often feel more vulnerable to such manipulation.) It is normal for kids to compare one parent with the other, one home with the other, and especially when things are unpleasant, to imagine that life in the other home would be better than where they are. Many children will play one parent against the other, and this seems to happen when tensions are high, and you may not be able to communicate well with the other parent. You are left resenting the child and resenting the other parent, although he or she may not be responsible. Children often sense when you are vulnerable. If early on they discover that they can successfully make you feel guilty and then get their own way, you are in trouble. You must learn early on to keep from flinching and giving in to a child who says, "Daddy would let me do that. I wish I were living with him. You're mean.", or "Daddy is nicer to me and always gives me extra money," or "I can always stay up late when I visit Daddy," and other such remarks. Once children learn that the technique doesn't work, they will usually move on to something else. But if you let them believe that you feel guilty and that you can be made to do what they want if they play on this guilt, your power and credibility as a parent, leader, and decision-maker will be severely curtailed.

The best strategy is to ignore such behaviour, but if it persists, you may choose to tell the child that you do not like this behaviour and that it must stop. If you have a working relationship with the other parent, you may wish to co-ordinate some of the rules in the two homes to minimize the differences. The real problem, however, is not derived from such differences, but from the insecurity and tension that arise from the changed circumstances to which the child is adjusting.

A final comment on the issue of custody; as more and more women enter the work force, the rationale for the traditional belief that the children are better off with their mother is wearing thin. Mother may not stay home to look after the kids in the traditional pattern. She may choose or be forced by circumstances to work outside her home and so, whether the kids are awarded to Mum or Dad, they will likely be in day care. This is a major factor in the transition to fathers becoming serious contenders for custody.

GRANDPARENTS

Kids and grandparents have the right to continue their relationships through the divorce procedure and on into the future. This subject was touched on earlier in the book, but here it is stressed from the point of view of the children and the grandparents themselves. It is so easy to have your perception of in-laws coloured by your resentment or anger or hurt related to their child, your ex-mate. Regardless of your feelings, the relationship between children and grandparents should continue. You may even have to help a bit if the children are young, so that they don't have to suffer the loss of their grandparents as well as the major shift in their home life. They and the grandparents should be assured by you at the time that they are told of separation that their relationship with the kids will continue unhampered. In fact, you may very well enlist their support to help the kids through the first adjustment with extra visits. If the grandparents have a good relationship with the children and if they are not too biased about the divorce, they may very well serve as a great source of comfort, wisdom, and understanding, as well as a slightly removed set of listeners for the children. Further, grandparents on either side may be willing to help you by babysitting and giving you a break from time to time. Asking them to babysit now and again may give them the opening that they need to realize that they will indeed be a continuing part of your life, as well as giving them an opportunity to help you. This, of course, can be abused if you end up using them only as babysitters and don't see them otherwise. Even if you feel you must sever your connection with your in-laws temporarily or permanently, you should see that this does not affect the children's relationship with them for too long. Your feelings and your choices should not impose decisions on the children or the grandparents to which they are not a party.

DEALING WITH OUTSIDERS

Conversations with friends who really care about you and mean well can be very painful during the first months. One of the reasons for the pain is that you may not have sorted through what has happened yourself as yet, and it is awkward to try to explain it to someone else. Another reason is simply the reminder that such conversations present. There are many tactful ways to change the subject, and you should practise some of these. You can always say something like, "I find it difficult to talk about that right now. Do you mind if we talk of something else?," to get you through most situations. If you feel that the person really deserves an explanation, create for yourself a brief and polite explanation only a couple of sentences long, and if possible, an explanation which does not blame either of you. Something like: "We just weren't getting along well, and it was time to end it." Or: "We simply can't communicate anymore."

Neither you nor your children should feel obliged to respond to questions like: "Whose fault was it?" "How much alimony are you getting?" "Why did you leave him?" "Why did he leave you?" and so on. Do not let yourself start on a verbal diatribe defending your position. Respond briefly, or change the subject. Finally, there is the multi-purpose answer to almost any question: "I'm not sure; I guess I need to think about that."

Kids may need to be prepared to deal with the questions of well-meaning or not so well-meaning friends, neighbours, and acquaintances. Curious and perhaps well-meaning people try to get information from children. If you have children, you should help them to develop a repertoire of polite, unemotional, and uninformative answers for people with whom they would rather not have a long discussion. You might even want to prepare them for the sort of questions they may encounter, so that they can avoid embarrassment. A few of the answers that you have prepared for yourself, such as, "I'd rather not talk about that right now," or "Thanks for your interest, but I really don't know what plans my parents are making," or "Let's talk about something else, because this makes me feel uncomfortable," will help. Or they can simply say, "You'd better ask my parents about that."

At the same time, you should encourage them to talk to other people about what has happened, freely and without guilt. It helps kids to meet other kids whose parents are also separated or divorced. They are reassured to know that they aren't so different. They can talk to someone else who has had similar experiences, and both receive and give support. Kids are very good at reassuring one another. This becomes extremely important if the kids are over ten or so, and have begun to try to figure things out for themselves. Once they begin to rely on outsiders for many of their ideas, they should have the opportunity to meet children their own age who have been through a parental divorce. Some communities offer a discussion group for kids who are experiencing divorce. This is a fairly new idea, but it offers kids a chance to talk about what they see happening to them with both other kids and a qualified adult. Since the group is quite removed from the home situation, many of the feelings and reactions are somewhat defused when they are discussed with objective outsiders who understand.

KIDS AS INTERMEDIARIES

If the relationship has seriously deteriorated between the couple so that intermediaries are needed for communication, don't use the kids to give messages to the other parent. This is very unfair, because they are not equipped to carry emotion-packed communications from one parent to the other. Kids should never be put into the position of hurting one parent on behalf of the other. Lots of parents consciously or unintentionally send hate messages through their kids, and this causes deep confusion in the children's minds, as well as unnecessarily complicating and possibly damaging the children's relationship with the other parent. Further, it puts the children in the middle, and gives them reason to believe that if they weren't responsible in the beginning for the separation, they certainly are now, because of the messages they have been forced to carry. Using children as intermediaries can also reinforce manipulative behaviour. They see that by saying certain things about one parent to the other they achieve a certain power to influence events. Very soon this becomes a habit, and the messages are often exaggerated or completely fabricated in order to perpetuate the children's power.

Children must be as free as possible of parents' reactions to each other, free to carry on separate relationships with each parent without interference. If an intermediary is required, get someone else, someone who is removed from the family situation and who will not be unduly influenced by the messages and the reactions of the couple.

ADVANTAGES OF DIVORCE FOR KIDS

Kids who grew up in families with only one parent, or with more than one mom or dad often say that they feel that they were lucky. Instead of only one role model for adulthood, they had several. There were housekeepers, various friends of the single parent who take an interest in the children, and other adults such as counsellors or friends or neighbours who might not have been close if the divorce had not occurred. These children feel that they were better prepared for adulthood and marriage than many other people from two-parent homes who still had an idealistic and unrealistic conception of marriage. Children from divorced families can be very selective when it comes time for them to choose their own mates, and much more discerning and realistic than their parents were. They have had to think about what goes into a marriage relationship, at least as far as their parents were concerned, and they know that "happily ever after" is a myth. They have come to recognize the difference between a good relationship and a bad one.

KEEPING IN TOUCH WITH YOUR CHILDREN

FAMILY MEETINGS

Children of all ages like to feel that they are worth listening to and that their feelings are valid. In fact, their insights are often very wise because they have not had their reasoning covered over by many layers of conditioning. Lots of kids grow up without having many opportunities to try out their new ideas with their parents. Parents who do not provide opportunities for long chats with their kids are often surprised by the things that they do outside the home. They find themselves dealing with situations after the fact, rather than preparing themselves and their kids for some of the events of growing up in advance.

Left to chance, such things as heart-to-heart talks or serious discussions with children may never take place. There are lots of ways to build such opportunities into the family life pattern. One of the ways is to hold regular family meetings to which attendance is compulsory for all members of the family. The following suggestions can be modified to meet your own situation. These meetings should be set up in advance, so as not to conflict with other plans. Plenty of time should be allotted, at least an hour at first, although some will take more time and some less. Hold the meeting in a comfortable room where everyone can sit in a circle in chairs or on the floor. Appoint someone chairperson and someone recording secretary—this is a great opportunity to teach kids a bit of parliamentary procedure. The positions should rotate from meeting to meeting unless the kids are very young. At the beginning of the meeting, go around the circle asking each person what he or she would like to discuss, and have the secretary write these things down as an agenda, along with the name of the person who suggested the topic. Then, either follow the order in which the subjects arose, or create a more logical order, and begin. Each person gets to speak first on the issue(s) he or she put on the agenda. After discussion of potential solutions a vote is taken. Remember, this is a time to respect the ideas of each person. Everyone should feel safe to present their thoughts, without fear of criticism or derision. The recording secretary will only write down any action that is undertaken, such as Dad will fix Peter's bike on Saturday morning, or Carolyn and Diana will do the dishes for the next week, and so on.

At first, the meetings may become complaint sessions, because everyone finally has an open forum for their chief beefs. This should be tolerated but controlled so that the discussion remains fairly objective and the meetings do not deteriorate into arguments. Properly conducted, such meetings can often clear the air between family members by creating an opportunity for each to really look at and understand the point of view of the other. If the meeting must be a complaint session, make sure that it ends with a happy topic, like planning a family outing or a special dinner, or something of that nature, so that everyone has a chance to relax again before the meeting ends.

Although it is very likely that the first few meetings will be complaint sessions as well as question periods where kids ask Mom or Dad for more information about the separation or future plans, this passes quickly into a time where the kids feel free to raise other questions, such as what about drugs in high school, how do kids get pregnant, what should I be when I grow up, and so on. Family meetings are not relaxing for parents, but they are extremely enlightening, and provide a unique opportunity for a parent to understand more about what the children are thinking. Later, as the children get older, some meetings may be held without the parent, with specific problems to be solved by the children, and the consequent solutions to be brought to the parent for final approval. Even if these solutions are not exactly what you had in mind, you are well-advised to let the children learn from their own mistakes. Only interfere if you really think their solution is dangerous. Their commitment to their own ideas is usually much stronger than to parentally imposed solutions, and the family can benefit from many intangible elements of the children's independence and co-operation.

AGENDA FOR FAMILY MEETING

Review curfews—school is out for the summer: Molly
Plans for grandpa's birthday: Dad
Revise dog-walking schedule: Mum
Review housework duty list: Carolyn
Change suppertime to accommodate baseball practices and games: Steve

---

Another benefit of a program of family meetings is the spin-off, the research committees of children. When the meeting is asked for a raise in allowances, a child or children can be appointed to research the issue, to get the feelings of each member of the family and perhaps some friends, and bring a proposal to the next meeting. The same procedure can be followed for family vacation plans and many other aspects of family life. Although this looks like a parental evasion of responsibility, in fact it creates a fine sense of responsibility in the kids. Rather than taking a radical stance, they are forced to listen to the opinions of other members of the family and represent them fairly at the next meeting.

The above suggestions and the sample agenda are merely ideas to start your own thinking along. If this concept of family meetings sounds too formal to you, modify it, but remember that children have a tremendous sense of order, and seek to organize nearly everything.

They love the formality of a chairperson and a recording secretary. Even if you haven't held such meetings before, when a big change in the family pattern such as separation and divorce has taken place, it is as good a time as any to start.

OTHER STRATEGIES

Another way to keep in touch with your children is to make a point of spending time alone with each child each day. This doesn't have to be a long time, but it should be time when you can give the child your full attention so that he or she can feel that telling you what happened today is important to you. This may take a little effort on your part, because you are often tired and rushed at the end of the day, and your nerves may be a little frayed from the evening rush-hour traffic. Perhaps this is a good time to sit and have a restful cup of tea while you listen to a child. Or maybe you will have a cup of coffee with another after dinner. Perhaps your special time with each one is at bedtime, when you sit on the edge of the bed and share confidences.

As well as spending some time alone with each child each day, you should arrange to have a periodic outing alone with each one, something that is out of the ordinary, a treat. Perhaps it is dinner out, or it can be a visit to a museum or an art gallery. You can include the child in an adult activity, such as taking the child with you to work while you catch up some evening or weekend. The child can sometimes help by running the photocopier or answering the phone or playing with the typewriter. You may even choose to take a child along with you to a committee meeting, or a community meeting where your child can discover another role that the parent plays. This can be a political meeting, a church meeting, a social club, or whatever you happen to be interested in.

Some special things cost money, and some are absolutely free. Many cities have endless activities which are very interesting and cost nothing. Maybe you can start exploring the attractions and history of your own city or town. Visit the library, the archives, the city or town hall, or provincial legislature. Or visit the tourist office in town and get a map and then visit every single park, over a period of time, for a picnic. Find all the museums and art galleries, and request that you be put on the mailing list for notice of coming exhibitions. See if there is a Nature Centre. Have a winter picnic in a park on a bright sparkly blue and white winter day. Get up very early and go to the local market, if there is one. Find a pretty place to sit and watch the sun rise, with a Thermos of hot chocolate. Ask at the tourist office about tours of various local industries; most of these are free. Sometimes you can just phone up a cookie factory or candy outfit or bottling plant and arrange to visit with your child. Once you begin to explore where you live, and even the surrounding area, your own life is enriched, as well as that of the child.

Discover the various ethnic communities in your town or city and spend some time wandering in the grocery stores in each neighbourhood. The Italian pastas, Ukrainian sausages, Chinese vegetables, Vietnamese delicacies, and so on will perhaps inspire you to experiment with special national dishes at home. Children and adults love celebrations and parties. If your child is studying Mexico, have a special meal one evening with Mexican food. It needn't be elaborate—Spanish rice, tacos, and so on, but add a candle, serve the milk in wine glasses, and have a child decorate the napkins with crayons. Suddenly you have a fiesta. Or have Chinese food, but sit on the floor (which you may want to cover with newspaper) and eat with chopsticks at a low coffee table. You can declare "Children's Day" and buy a birthday cake on the way home that says "Happy Children's Day." Suddenly there is a special dinner. These are simply suggestions—you will soon develop your own special times.

If your time is very limited, you may choose to combine time with a child with something that you want to do anyway. Take tennis lessons together; join a gym and exercise; run; take a cooking class; learn to knit; start a collection (match folders, stamps, comic books, butterflies—whatever you happen to like). Sharing your own interests with children helps them learn to be alone and to entertain themselves, too, with a special interest. Your enthusiasm will be contagious.

A final thought on special times. One of the stages that parents and kids find most difficult to deal with is the on-set of puberty. This, too, can be a cause for celebration, as indeed it is in many other societies. When a boy's voice begins to change, when a girl gets her first period, these may be times for a special dinner out with a parent. Such a welcome to adulthood will be anticipated impatiently by parent and child and will provide an opportunity for a discussion of the confusing things that are happening to the child's body and emotions. These changes are often glossed over by parents, because of a vague sense of discomfort, but kids need the reassurance that the drastic mood changes and the strange sensations and the rapid physical growth are all normal phenomena. There are lots of books on the market now to help kids and parents alike with explanations, but one of the best sets are *What's Happening to Me?* and *Where Did I Come From?*.

Although a child's privacy and shyness should be respected, the topic of physical maturation should be open for discussion now and then, and whenever the child needs to approach a parent, the channels of communication should be open, and the opportunities apparent.

Thoughtfulness and consideration and love can be shown in so many ways. Yet another is to give unexpected gifts to a child; not big expensive things, but things that remind the child of your love and understanding. A diary with a lock and key for private thoughts; a new hair ribbon or barrette; a magazine; a can of favourite food; a book; a flower; a magnet. Such presents can be given any time just to say "I love you" or "Thank you for being so good lately" or "I am sorry that you were sad yesterday" or "Congratulations on the great mark you got on your test," or whatever seems appropriate.

Divorce and separation are times when major life patterns are changing, whether you like it or not. It is wise to balance some of the more difficult changes with some more pleasant ones. Although such changes may at first require an effort from the parent at a time when energy reserves are low, they pay off as you see the deepening of your own relationship with your child and you both become confident that the life ahead will have some very nice times, too. Such activities, if they can be counted on by the child, help the child to begin to trust the single parent again, and to trust in a secure future, despite the changes.

References

Gardner, Richard A., *The Boys and Girls Book About Divorce*. Toronto: Bantam, 1970.

_____, *The Parents Book About Divorce*. Toronto: Bantam, 1977.

FOR SMALLER CHILDREN

Mayle, Peter, *Divorce Can Happen to the Nicest People*. Toronto: Macmillan, 1980.

_____, *Where Did I Come From?* Toronto: General Publishing, 1973.

_____, *What's Happening to Me?* Toronto: General Publishing, 1975.

Thomas, Marlo, *Free to Be You and Me*. Toronto: McGraw-Hill Ryerson, 1974. (Companion cassette tape.)

FOR PRE-TEENS

Berger, Terry, *How Does it Feel When Your Parents Get Divorced?* New York: Julian Messner, 1977.

FOR TEENAGERS

Robson, Bonnie, *My Parents Are Divorced, Too*. Toronto: Dorset, 1979.

CHAPTER FOUR

The Law

Once you have recognized the beginning of the end, the fact that the marriage is not working and that separation and divorce are possible, if not inevitable, it is time to assess your situation and the resources available to you.

This chapter is based on the assumption that you will sooner or later legally end your marriage. There are two steps: legal separation, and divorce. The first step is often skipped. This chapter explains how to find and use a lawyer. It also describes the legal implications of some of the various options for separation and divorce in Canadian law, including the new Divorce Act. Remember, though, that family and divorce law are changing constantly these days, and that your case will be strongly influenced by the recent decisions made by the judges in the courts of your province. Make sure by reading current periodicals and talking with friends and with your lawyer that you are up to date on the trends in property settlement and custody.

IDENTIFYING THE ALTERNATIVES

The first thing you should do is to sort out the various alternatives from which you can choose your future. There are books on the market which describe the procedures for ending a marriage. Remember, although divorce law is under federal jurisdiction, each province interprets it slightly differently, so the advice of a good friend in another province may or may not be applicable to your situation. The general principles are the same, but there are variations in property and maintenance laws. Some useful books are listed at the end of this chapter. You might also phone a good-sized bookstore to request a book reviewing family law in your province, or you could visit your local community or university library.

If you can't afford a lawyer, but you need advice on the impending break-up of your marriage, there are free or subsidized legal counselling services in most cities. There are a wide variety of agencies serving the needs of women in most cities now, but these do change in focus, and because of irregular funding, they come and go. Various women's centres may maintain a list of feminist lawyers in your city or province. To find out which agencies exist near you, phone your local YWCA, or the provincial government department that deals with the status of women. Both of these resources are fairly permanent and keep track of the other related non-profit agencies. Another possibility is your provincial government social services department, which often provides funding to such agencies. Many of these agencies maintain libraries on issues affecting women, and there are often support groups which meet periodically to help each other through stressful times such as separation and divorce. Some other possible sources of free legal advice are the student legal services at most universities, and the shelters for battered women. For general information, several provinces have initiated a telephone service, Dial-A-Law, which is listed in the yellow pages of the phone book under "lawyers," and which will play pre-recorded tapes relating to your area of concern. The service is toll-free, and covers laws specific to your particular province. This service is currently available in Alberta, British Columbia, and Ontario. Have paper and pencil ready, as this information will help you to be prepared to direct more specific questions to your lawyer. Further, many women's centres also have lawyers associated with them, which will offer free advice.

As well as the legal factors, you will have to assess the more personal ones. You will be weighing the impact of your possible choices on your children, if you have any, and of course upon yourself and your spouse. You will also want to prepare a realistic assessment of your financial status, both present and future (see Chapter Five). It is very wise to make an appointment with a lawyer at this time. This will not necessarily mean that you are beginning divorce action, nor that if you do, you will hire this lawyer.

It isn't always possible to be as methodical as this in planning a separation, but if you are deserted by your spouse, or forced to leave your home precipitously, see a lawyer at once.

INFORMAL SEPARATION

There are two main kinds of separation—informal and formal. Informal separation exists without having gone through the contractual or legal procedures which characterize formal separations. You can choose to simply live apart and never legally break your marriage tie, but this will limit your freedom in many ways. Under the Matrimonial Property Act your spouse will continue to have a claim on anything acquired while the marriage remains in existence. Your bank may refuse to lend you money without your husband's approval, because you may still be liable for each other's debts. Unless you post public notice announcing that you are no longer responsible for his debts, this, too can remain a potential threat. To remove this danger, it is important that you close out joint bank accounts and charge accounts. You remain responsible for any debts incurred on such accounts, even after separation. A disclaimer does not protect you from this.

Until you are divorced you cannot, of course, marry anyone else—which may be the farthest thing from your mind, anyway. But finally, your ability to adjust emotionally and psychologically to life on your own may be severely hampered if the legal bond remains.

FORMAL SEPARATION

There are two kinds of formal separation agreements, both of which are considered valid by the courts. The first is a contractual agreement which can be written by yourself and your spouse, with or without the aid of a lawyer. For various reasons, religious and otherwise, some people want only a separation. It is possible and considerably cheaper to do some of the paper-work involved in ending a marriage yourself. A separation agreement can be drawn up by you and your spouse, agreeing as to property and maintenance. Such a document legally establishes the separation and can carry a lot of weight in divorce court later on should you choose to divorce as well. You should make at least four signed and witnessed copies, one for each of you, one for the income tax department, and one for any other eventuality. If such a contractual settlement has worked well, a judge will seldom see any reason to change it, and it will likely become the basis of the divorce settlement.

This source of contractual agreement works for many couples as either an interim or permanent settlement. If, however, the custody and visiting arrangements or maintenance payments to which you agree are challenged later on by either spouse, you will have to go to court and start again from scratch. Your contract, although not necessarily binding any longer, will still carry a lot of weight because of the fact that you both did agree to it. It is treated like any other contract in the eyes of the law.

It is also valid to the income-tax people. In fact, maintenance agreements can now be back-dated as far as a year, as long as the agreement is made the year following the year in which the maintenance agreement was made. The person paying the maintenance deducts the full amount from his taxable income; the person receiving the maintenance must pay income tax on the amount received.

If your separation agreement covers the property division, remember that each province has different laws regarding what constitutes matrimonial property—for example, pensions—and how it should be divided. Agreements regarding matrimonial property are not valid unless each party has had independent legal advice. If your separation agreement is meant to be an interim device, you may choose to have it cover only maintenance and custody, and leave the property division until you are preparing for divorce court. Alternatively, you can each get legal advice and proceed to draw up your own agreement.

The second kind of formal separation is called a "legal separation" as opposed to the less formal separation agreement. This is a separation which has gone through the court process and been announced by a judge. These are quite rare because by the time you have gone to all the trouble and expense of a legal separation, you could have had a divorce—the process for a legal separation is as complicated and as expensive.

If you find that the process of drawing up a separation agreement is getting out of proportion to its value, you may choose to switch horses, and put your energy and money into getting a divorce.

Divorce can similarly be arranged without hiring a lawyer, but only if it is straightforward and uncontested. If there is any question of custody or maintenance conflict, a lawyer for each party is essential.

CHOOSING A LAWYER

For some people, making that first appointment with a lawyer—and keeping it—is extremely difficult. It is a public acknowledgement that the marriage didn't work. It is part of the process which will end the partnership and cancel the vows of "'til death us do part." Lawyers are aware of this reluctance and are usually very understanding. They expect people to be upset at such a time. They are not surprised by tears or even by total confusion. They realize that people often have little factual information about divorce, despite what they have heard from their many friends who have preceded them through divorce court. Men are often worried and defensive because they have heard that they can be "taken to the cleaners," and women are frightened because they do not understand their rights regarding money, the home, and the kids. In both cases, confidence is usually very low, and emotions run high. Lawyers are prepared and experienced. It is their job to protect your interest in an impartial way and to see that you get a fair and adequate settlement without trying to "get" your partner, and they should also see that you learn quite a bit along the way.

The first decision you must make before selecting a lawyer is to decide whether you want a male or a female lawyer. Some people prefer a lawyer of their own sex, and some men seek a female lawyer in order to make sure that they are fair to their wives. Some women continue to be more comfortable with male lawyers, despite the possibility of sexual bias. Remember, however, that female lawyers may also be sexually biased—many women still feel that women should stay home with the kids; these are the sorts of things that you must determine.

Before you make an appointment with a lawyer, check with your local law society to ensure that your potential lawyer is a member in good standing. You may also wish to check with some friends who may be acquainted with him or her for personal impressions. Alternatively you can ask the Law Society to give you the names of several experienced lawyers specializing in the field of Family and Divorce Law. It is important to realize that there are many subspecialty areas in law. Some provinces permit lawyers to advertise now, so you may select a lawyer from an ad in the paper. Since professional advertising is fairly new, and there are many professional constraints, many lawyers still prefer not to advertise. Even if you select a law firm from an ad, do check its reputation with other sources as well.

THE INITIAL INTERVIEW

After a few hours on the phone you may end up with a short list of possible lawyers. Try to meet two or three of them before you make your final selection. Some lawyers will not charge for an initial appointment, or will charge only a minimal fee, as long as the session is short. Your objectives in this interview are: (1) to gather information about the various alternatives of separation, divorce, custody, and access, their likely cost, duration of the process, and the steps involved; and (2) to decide whether or not the lawyer can adequately represent your perspective.

It is important for you to remember at your first interview with any lawyer that he or she is bound by the law to ask you quite seriously if you have considered marriage counselling and if there is any possibility of reconciliation, before divorce proceedings can be started. If you are unaware of this, the question can come as a bit of a surprise.

The next thing you need to find out, of course, is cost. How much will the lawyer charge, how much is the divorce likely to cost, where will the money come from, who will be paying it, and when? This is straightforward information which you receive in response to direct questions, either on the phone before or during the first interview. Bear in mind that there is a wide range of prices for divorce, depending upon the lawyer and the degree of complication of your particular divorce. Nevertheless, your lawyer can give you some ballpark numbers to help you with your financial planning.

Your first appointment with a lawyer is merely to gain information and to get a general impression of the particular lawyer. This may be the lawyer who will assist you through your divorce, or you may decide to look further. Based upon the information that you have gathered from your reading, you should by now have prepared a list of questions that you need a lawyer to answer. Included here is a suggested list of questions that you might ask at the first appointment, both to discover the attitude of the lawyer and to get some of the information that you need before you can get your financial life in order.

---

1. What is my legal status now?
2. How long does it take these days to get an uncontested divorce in this province? A contested divorce?
3. How much is my divorce likely to cost? Who will pay this and when?
4. What steps would you suggest I take?

During your first appointment, try to decide whether or not the lawyer is receptive and supportive of the rights of women in divorce. You can get a sense of attitude by asking about the current status of divorce legislation directly affecting women. If the response is a blanket assurance not to worry, beware. What you really want is a reasonable explanation by someone who will treat you as an intelligent and competent adult, and whose general personal philosophy is compatible with your own. It is not so much what is said, but how it is said that will help you to assess the lawyer's attitude toward women in general and your divorce in particular. Find out how long appointments with your lawyer last. Are you allotted fifteen minutes, half an hour, an hour? This is not always terribly important, since the lawyer will let you know when the time is up, but it is nice for you to be aware that you have a specific amount of time to get your point of view across and to try to govern yourself so that you are not half-way through your story and still snivelling when it is time to face the secretary and the waiting room.

Often the male partner in the marriage is acquainted with a lawyer from business contacts, and it may seem logical for both partners to go to this lawyer to obtain the separation or divorce. First of all, this lawyer may not even be a divorce lawyer. You should, however, realize that it is impossible for a lawyer to adequately represent the points of view of two people without bias. Differences of opinion are inevitable. Contentious items are usually items that have been held or owned in common. Even if it is comforting at first for a woman who may have had no previous dealings with a lawyer to go to one known to her husband, she may soon begin to feel resentment at the camaraderie between the two who have known each other longer. Although it may seem difficult at first, you should find your own lawyer. Lawyers usually refuse to act for both parties, anyway.

Hiring a lawyer should give you a sense of relief in that you need only provide the right information, and the process will run along its own course, with just a bit of prompting on your part. Once you have selected a lawyer, you must carefully discuss the various alternatives for action and decide whether you want to start with a legal separation, to proceed right to a divorce, to get custody of the children, and so on. Your relationship with your lawyer should permit a healthy balance of times when you take advice or pause to reflect on a new alternative, and times when you must disagree with the advice offered in order to stay in tune with your own conscience. Your lawyer should see that you are fair to yourself and your children, and that your petition for divorce reflects this fairness.

If you are emotionally overwrought, you may find some of the best advice difficult to take at first. For example, if you are full of anger and don't want a penny from your spouse, you must still try not to let your emotions interfere with the rights of the children, who are entitled to be maintained with a continuing standard of living much like what they are used to. In fact, you do not have the legal right to refuse money for your children even if you want to.

You can change your mind about divorce right up to the time of the court day, and you can even remarry after that if you have a mind to. So make the best decisions you can, with the best advice you can get, making sure that the final outcome will be something that you can live with without either guilt or resentment. This is not always possible, but it is certainly a worthy goal. You can take as long as you like to get a divorce, but arrange that first lawyer appointment as soon as you know that the marriage is ending. You should try not to prolong the process, since you risk having your life become a no-man's-land of indecision, where you aren't really married and you aren't really free, and you remain dependent upon your spouse with unsettled financial arrangements; planning and getting on with your own life are impossible. Yet many women cling to this limbo through fear of the unknown alternatives. This state is hard on everyone, and if extended, it prevents adjustment to the fact that the marriage has indeed ended. Be reasonably sure before you return to the lawyer with instructions to proceed for a divorce, but don't wait for a new star in the sky, or a special sign to underscore your certainty—just make the best decisions you can at any time, considering all the possibilities and all the people. But make those decisions and get on to the next stage in your life.

If, further down the road, you lose your trust in your lawyer, pay the bill, ask for your file, and find another. Although both doctors and lawyers have a mystique about them which gives them a great deal of power, remember that you are the employer, and your lawyer is providing a service. Shopping for a doctor or a lawyer and changing to a more satisfactory one, if necessary, are perfectly acceptable things to do. If, however, you are on your third lawyer, either there is a flaw in your selection process, or the fault lies with you.

THE LEGAL PROCESS OF DIVORCE

There are two more things you should do in preparing yourself for the legal process of divorce. One is to attend divorce court, and the other is to study the Divorce Act.

Divorce court is public. Anyone can sit in on divorces unless the judge expressly orders that the case be held privately. In fact sitting in on court is considered a good recreational pastime by some people. Uncontested divorces are usually run through the court on a specific day each week. Each case can take as little as five minutes. Spending half a day observing these cases helps you to achieve a sense of proportion about your own divorce. It also provides a rehearsal of the procedure and the behaviour of the lawyers, the judge, and the petitioner. You will be much more confident if you have an idea of what to expect when you are on the stand. Just being in a courtroom for someone else's trial helps demystify the process and the formality, and allay your own fears.

The second thing you should do is to become familiar with "legalese," the language of the courtroom. The language of the law is quite different from everyday English. The phrasing of the Act is standard, and has been designed to serve in most cases. Being asked by your lawyer in court if your spouse "so behaved as to render further cohabitation intolerable" can be upsetting, however, if you haven't heard it expressed like that before. In fact, much of the wording of the Act is very general and non-specific, as the above phrase, and usually saves you the trouble of having to "wash your dirty linen" in the courtroom. Some sections of the Divorce Act are printed later in this chapter in the section on "grounds." Read them carefully and get used to the sound of the terminology.

YOUR DIVORCE TRIAL

Your own divorce trial will likely be an anti-climax. All the work is done before, and even most of the grieving may be over. You have established a budget, and are well on the way to life on your own. A few days before the court appearance your lawyer will likely run you through a rehearsal. The procedure will be reviewed, along with the questions likely to be asked by both your own and your spouse's lawyer. The idea is to reduce the element of surprise, and to make you feel as relaxed and confident as possible under the circumstances.

You may not even have to appear in court. Usually only the "petitioner," the person who initiated the divorce action, is required to be present in uncontested cases. The "respondent," the person being sued for divorce, is represented by his or her lawyer. If any aspect of the divorce is being contested, both parties will be present along with their lawyers. Under the new Divorce Act, in some circumstances *no one* has to go to court.

ALIMONY AND MAINTENANCE

INTERIM MAINTENANCE

This is an amount ordered by the court to cover the time until the proper application for maintenance can be made. It is often required immediately after an unexpected break-up, when the woman is left with no money, and may not have a job. She may also not have had the time to prepare a budget. Interim maintenance is granted on the basis of need and not on the basis of your standard of living before the divorce. It is meant to prevent the need for welfare. Therefore, you have to be able to show the court clearly how much money you need and for what. This often takes place at a time of maximum pain and disruption. Nevertheless it is worthwhile to take time alone or with a friend to figure out what you really need, rather than just adding up the bills that are shouting to be paid. Go to court to request interim maintenance prepared with a list of expenses, as well as figures for how much you have and how much you need.

ALIMONY AND CHILD SUPPORT

Alimony is money paid on a regular basis to a spouse after legal separation or divorce. Child support is money paid to a spouse for the support of a child of whom one does not have custody. Both are ordered by a court. Maintenance is a combination of the two. Alimony has bad connotations because of the connection with Hollywood and rich and glamorous stars divorcing each other quite often, with the women demanding and often being awarded fabulous allowances for alimony. Most of us will never be in that league, but nevertheless, that is how the idea of alimony has become associated with the concept of "taking him to the cleaners."

Alimony is the physical manifestation of your original promise to care for each other for the rest of your lives. Usually, the husband is the one in the paying position. Older women may accept alimony with alacrity and not with guilt. Although divorce was not likely even a possibility in their minds at the time of their marriage, it is still a reality of the present, to which they must adjust. Women over fifty may still choose to re-enter the work force, especially if they have had earlier careers upon which they can build. Many, however, will be supported by alimony and eventually by the old-age pension system. Younger women may receive alimony until they have completed courses, or re-training, or until they have become re-established in a job. Women with small children may choose to receive alimony until the youngest child is in school full-time, and then go through training, or take a job for which they are already qualified. (There will be a much more detailed discussion of re-entering the work force in a later chapter.) It is still, and will be for the foreseeable future, quite legitimate to be receiving alimony. It is only unfair if you really are taking him to the cleaners, if his earning capacity has decreased, or if you could indeed be out working but are lazy or just scared. Alimony ends upon your remarriage. Some divorce agreements also include clauses whereby alimony ends if the recipient enters into a steady relationship with another person for a long period of time, for example, six months.

Alimony is not simply a financial obligation; it is a recognition of the continuing existence of personal obligation in a marriage, even if it has ended. The marriage ceremony is a serious commitment. The promise to care for each other throughout life cannot be easily cast aside if our society is to continue to provide security for its members. Although we still talk as if men are the payers and women the recipients of maintenance payments, and we assume that mothers will get custody of children, the reverse situation is becoming increasingly more common. Now, a woman may be earning a higher salary than the man, and custody may be awarded to the father, two fairly new precedents. A woman may be asked to contribute to the maintenance of her spouse, especially if he is keeping the children.

Society still meets these situations with a high level of prejudice. It is still strongly believed by many people that the children belong with the mother, regardless of her mental, physical, or economic ability to provide for them, and often without regard for her preference. A woman who decides simply that her children will be happier with their father is severely condemned by society and may even be ostracized by her friends and family. It takes a great deal of courage to make such a decision. Even strong feminists may reveal a streak of prejudice when confronted with this concept. This is because they have fought so long and hard to achieve recognition of the value of the woman's work in the home as child-raiser and homemaker that it is almost inconceivable that women would now choose not to retain custody.

The idea that mothers should keep their children is deeply ingrained in our society. It is this idea which can create a trap for the single mother, and can prevent a willing and able father from raising his own children. If a couple agrees in advance that custody goes to the father, such will indeed be the case. If, however, the case of custody is contested, there is still a far greater likelihood that children will live with their mother. Judges and lawyers often harbour this bias, too. This attitude of society will change with time, and with the example of many more women agreeing to paternal custody and many more fathers doing a good job of raising their children. Such liberating ideas contribute much to the equality of both men and women; men should have an equal right to choose to raise their own children, and women should have an equal right to choose to focus on a working career.

We are witnessing a gradual change in this attitude which should be recognized by men and women alike. We are in a period of transition, and we are still fighting for equal rights for women, the right to pursue a career, to permit the father of her children to raise them and to pay support to a husband and/or children if the situation warrants. Some of these "rights" may not sound terribly desirable, but equality implies equal responsibility, and responsibility often has negative as well as positive connotations.

As it stands, we live in a society where most of the recipients of maintenance payments are and will continue for awhile to be women. The whole question of alimony is loaded with layers of emotion. With the emphasis on financial independence for women which arises from the women's movement, the concept of alimony is now tinged with embarrassment. Some women feel that receiving alimony is an admission of their own inadequacy. This feeling is further complicated if there is animosity towards the ex-husband and the woman wishes she were not beholden to him. But the question of alimony is much deeper and more complicated than this. A woman who has stayed at home during her marriage has made a valuable contribution to the family and has the right to continued maintenance until she is able to provide for herself, or if she is unable to enter the work force for some reason, until she dies. Women must not be taken to task for following the patterns of the society in which they grew up. There are, of course, cases of abuse. The women who choose to sit back and collect alimony when they are perfectly capable of partial or total self-support are referred to in legal circles as "alimony drones."

ALIMONY AS EQUALIZER?

Alimony has a bad name. It conjures up illusions of lazy women being kept in luxury at the expense of their hard-working ex-husbands. Alimony was meant to be a form of equalization payment, and may indeed form at least part of the solution to the continuing search for a fair and reasonable way to end a marriage (after having exhausted the search for a fair and reasonable way to continue the marriage). Otherwise, although the house is split, one spouse must share one-half of the proceeds with one or more children; again, hardly equitable.

Lillian Kozak, chair of NOW's Domestic Relations Law Task Force in New York state, puts forward the analogy of "dividing up a business partnership by giving half the capital and inventory to each partner—but letting one of them keep the entire income-producing business." It would seem that some sort of equalization payments would be in order in the business setting. We need to institute them in the divorce setting. Alimony, based on allowance for completing educational or employment upgrading, if appropriate, or as compensation for a large income disparity between spouses, seems fair in this context. The new Divorce Act does have room for something of this nature, in that one of the explicit directives for judges making maintenance orders is that such orders should alleviate economic hardship which is a result of the marriage breakdown. This could be limiting, however, depending upon how it is interpreted—whether or not early decisions to stay home with the children constitute hardship resulting from the breakdown of the marriage, in terms of lost income.

Assuming that a formula can be developed to fill this need, there is still the question of collecting payment, which will be discussed elsewhere. There is also the problem of the second family. Should a man be tied to his first wife and children economically forever? The answer seems to be yes, insofar as the dual obligation as parents and as investors in the business of being a divorced family is concerned. We are not there yet, but we need legislation which reflects a society in which decisions to marry and to have children are taken seriously for life, even if the circumstances are altered. Although you may not love, honour, and obey till death you do part, there is an obligation to ensure that the years that you spent together do not exact an unfair price on the life of either spouse.

MAINTENANCE

Refusing to accept alimony because of resentment or bitterness is your own business. Refusing to accept child support, however, is another matter. You do not have the right to make that sort of decision, either for your spouse or for your children, despite your strong feelings to the contrary. Child support is a tangible connection for the departing parent to his or her children. It is a right as well as an obligation. It has nothing to do with your ability as the parent who retains custody to support the children. If the other parent is willing and able, support payments should be made until the kids are grown up. Even if the other parent isn't willing, courts will go to great lengths to enforce such payments.

The children also have a right to feel that the other parent is contributing to their support and well-being, even though the marriage is over. Although it may be tempting to prove that you can support the family yourself, you should permit the other parent to pay a fair share, because of the importance that such support has for their relationship. Further, children should not suffer a major decrease in their standard of living unless this is unavoidable. There are, of course, many cases in which it is indeed unavoidable, such as when the other parent is unable or unwilling to pay.

Unfortunately, the issue of alimony is complicated by the emotions and attitudes of the couple. If the alimony or maintenance payment, for that matter, is treated like an undeserved gift, given out of the goodness of the man's heart to his undeserving and grasping wife, if the monthly payment carries with it obligations and guilt and unnecessary accountability, then the procedure should be altered. The best way to avoid at least the personal encounters that seem to bring out such behaviour patterns is to arrange for a monthly automatic bank transfer from his account to yours. This moves the transaction to the business level and helps to defuse some of the feelings.

Maintenance payments and visiting rights cannot legally be used as clubs. Maintenance orders are made regardless of the conduct of either spouse, and visiting rights can only be changed by a court order. In other words, the father cannot withhold payments to punish the mother for what he considers bad behaviour; nor can the mother withhold the children on visiting day because he hasn't sent the cheque. Of course, both of these things do happen, but the courts will attempt to enforce maintenance and access orders. The law, if followed, protects the children from becoming pawns in the money game. If you feel you are being treated unfairly by your ex, tell your lawyer. Don't try to make the children your allies against their father—this can only hurt them.

Even though housework and child care are still not valued economically in our society, you must learn to value your job yourself. Your self-respect, which gives you the confidence to accept the alimony or maintenance payment for what it is, is derived from the firm belief that what you do is important and valuable and certainly deserving of the support you receive. Whether or not your ex-spouse values what you do, it is essential that you learn to; if necessary, you must be able to retain that certainty in the face of disdain from the source of your support. In fact, these attitudes, which can be described as the "beneficent giver" and the "grateful receiver" are usually simply perpetuations of old patterns which were unhealthy during the marriage. They should be recognized as such and ended.

ENFORCEMENT

Once payments for maintenance or alimony are ordered by the court, the problem becomes collecting. Less than 35 per cent of such orders are paid regularly. The Alberta Institute of Law Research found in a recent study that a third of husbands pay none of the court-ordered support at all. Until recently little could be done about this, because the courts did not punish these men, nor did they assist the wives in collecting. An already struggling woman had to pay the legal fees to try to collect, usually without results. Manitoba has started a serious program for enforcing maintenance orders, and payment has increased to 85 per cent. There is a new law which can enforce payment of alimony and maintenance orders. Several other provinces are following suit; for example, the Alberta Maintenance Enforcement Act was passed in June 1985. Non-paying spouses can actually be put in jail in some provinces. The courts hope that this will cause a number of errant spouses to get back into line.

Provision can now be made for money to be transferred from the non-paying spouse from a variety of sources, including income-tax returns. Under the new legislation data banks related to unemployment insurance, Canada Pension Plans, and health care are now available to the courts. Wider access to personal information banks permits errant husbands to be traced through their charge account records and certain other sources.

The final word on this is that parents are responsible for their children until they are grown up and independent. This responsibility frequently supersedes subsequent marriages and children.

THE NEW DIVORCE ACT, 1985

Since my work began on this book, a new law has been passed governing divorce in Canada. It is called *The Divorce Act, 1985*, and will have been proclaimed law by the time this book is published. This law reflects the mounting pressure for reform in divorce legislation in Canada. The central achievement of the new law is that divorce can be achieved more quickly. There is an option whereby a couple can divorce if they have not lived together for one year— avoiding some of the pain of accusations and counter-accusations inherent in the old system. It is now possible to obtain a divorce without either spouse or lawyers appearing in court. This should substantially reduce the cost of many divorces. (See Appendix II for the form "Request for Divorce [Without Oral Hearing]".)

This section will examine the new Act in the light of the old, and discuss its advantages and disadvantages, and the mechanics of its use. Since it is new to Canada, I have relied on the kit prepared for lawyers by the Legal Education Society of Alberta, and on some of the American literature regarding the fall-out from similar legislation in the United States. A list of references is included at the end of the chapter.

This law will go a long way towards dispelling the adversarial attitudes that currently accompany divorce. It may still be necessary for one person to initiate the divorce action, however. This would be unfortunate because "who divorced whom" will continue to be an issue. Only when the courts will receive an application from two people to dissolve their marriage on the basis of voluntary separation will we really have "no-fault" divorce. This may be a possibility under the new Act; only time and case precedents in courtrooms will tell.

GROUNDS

There are three types of marriage breakdown recognized by the new law: one year of separation; adultery; or mental or physical cruelty. Thus, the popular term for the new Act, "no-fault divorce," is only true in some cases. Divorce is now granted exclusively on the basis of "marriage breakdown," eliminating the need for one spouse to blame the other for a marital offence (although this remains an option under the new law). In a sense the change is somewhat semantic, as can be seen in the accompanying chart. Although marriage breakdown is now the only ground for divorce, this category includes subheadings similar to those encompassed by the matrimonial offence clause in the old Act.

GROUNDS FOR DIVORCE

1968	1985
Marriage breakdown	Marriage breakdown
—3 years separation	—1 year separation
—5 years desertion	—adultery
	—physical or mental cruelty
matrimonial offence	
—adultery	
—sodomy	
—bestiality	
—rape	
—bigamy	

Divorce is only granted in cases with adequate, provable grounds as specified by the Divorce Act, and if an offence is being used as the grounds it must have been committed by the spouse who is *not* initiating the petition for divorce. In other words, you cannot both commit the offence and apply for a divorce; if you committed the offence (for example, adultery), your spouse must initiate divorce action. Canadian divorce law is predominantly adversarial; its language and historical interpretations tend to create a polarization of "guilty" and "not guilty," which is often inappropriate to the circumstances of marriage breakdown. The times are indeed a-changing, and although grounds are necessary in court, no one really cares afterwards what they were, or who was the "guilty" party, except in extreme cases. It used to be a common belief that divorces were almost always caused by philandering husbands, and sympathy always went to the poor wife. Nowadays it is not polite to ask about the specific grounds in a divorce of a friend or acquaintance; society has come to accept that the grounds may or may not represent what really went wrong. For example, the fact that the marital offence cited was adultery on the part of one spouse on a particular day does not exclude the possibility that both spouses had been having affairs as the marriage deteriorated. It is a commonplace now that infidelity is merely the sign of a marriage already in trouble; although this generalization sounds trite, there is some truth in it.

The courts will operate under two central principles: (1) to promote the economic self-sufficiency of each spouse within a reasonable period of time [Section 15:7d]; and (2) to ensure that the children have the maximum contact with both parents that is consistent with the best interests of the children [Section 16:10] within a reasonable period of time. The first of these principles has led to the tendency of the courts to split the assets of a marriage down the middle upon divorce, and the second principle has led to a dramatic increase in joint custody awards. The implications of these principles in practice are not clear, but various aspects will be considered throughout this book.

The Canadian new divorce act is quite clear and specific, and the passages describing acceptable grounds for divorce are printed below as they appear in section eight of Bill C-47, the Divorce Act 1985.

Divorce

8 (1) A court of competent jurisdiction may, on application by either or both spouses, grant a divorce to the spouse or spouses on the grounds that there has been a breakdown of their marriage.

(2) Breakdown of a marriage is established only if
(a) the spouses have lived separate and apart for at least one year immediately preceding the determination of the divorce proceeding and were living separate and apart at the commencement of the proceeding; or
(b) the spouse against whom the divorce proceeding is brought has, since celebration of marriage,
    (i) committed adultery, or

(ii) treated the other spouse with physical or mental cruelty of such a kind as to render intolerable the continued cohabitation of the spouses.

(3) For the purposes of paragraph 2(a),
(a) spouses shall be deemed to have lived separate and apart for any period for which they have lived apart and either of them had the intention to live separate and apart from the other; and
(b) a period during which spouses have lived separate and apart shall not be considered to have been interrupted or terminated
(i) by reason only that either spouse has become incapable of forming or having an intention to continue to live separate and apart or of continuing to live separate and apart of the spouse's own volition, if it appears to the court that the separation would probably have continued if the spouse had not become so incapable, or
(ii) by reason only that the spouses have resumed cohabitation during a period of, or periods totalling, not more than ninety days with reconciliation as its primary purpose.

A note regarding the establishment of the ground of separation: Many couples cannot afford to maintain two residences, although the marriage has broken down irreparably. It is quite acceptable to establish separate living patterns in the same house, each occupying a different part of the house, and not serving each other in terms of sexual access or shared responsibility for laundry, cooking, etc. After one year of such separation, you are both eligible to sue for divorce.

The terminology of divorce can be confusing. In the old Divorce Act there was a distinction between a Decree Nisi and a Decree Absolute. Since some divorces will continue to be granted under the old Act for awhile because of overlap, some of the terminology should be reviewed. Usually the judge ordered a Decree Nisi at the divorce hearing. This was followed by a waiting period of three months to permit time for an appeal. Divorce orders, like other court orders, can be appealed to a higher court. If an appeal were to reverse the divorce order after a remarriage, bigamy is the embarrassing result. Thus, the time for an appeal is built into the divorce procedure. (It still is in the new Act but it is one month rather than three.) During this time you can still call the whole thing off and stay married. At the end of this period, the divorce automatically is final, and you can apply for a Certificate of Divorce. Once you have this document, file it safely with your important papers. You will need it from time to time, to prove to the income-tax people that you are indeed divorced, or that you do indeed have custody of your children, and other similar things. You must show your Decree Absolute (old Act) or Certificate of Divorce (new Act) to obtain a passport or to remarry.

Under the old Act, occasionally a Decree Nisi and a Decree Absolute were granted simultaneously at the time of the court hearing; this was only done if it was in the best interest "of the Canadian public." In other words, there are special situations involving children or common-law relationships, where the delay of the divorce may cause harm to others.

In the new Divorce Act a divorce is granted by the court and automatically takes effect in thirty-one days, unless the court, recognizing special circumstances, orders it to take effect sooner, or if an appeal has been launched.

RECEPTION OF THE NEW DIVORCE ACT

Because of unforeseen effects of such changes, this new Act has been received with mixed reviews. Even before it has been officially proclaimed, there are lawyers, other professionals, and women's groups all expressing serious misgivings. (See references at the end of this chapter.) A similar divorce law has been followed in California and various other states for several years, and we can learn from their experience. The major problem is that although the new Act permits quicker, cleaner divorces, because material possessions (money, house, furniture) are generally divided as evenly as possible by the courts, less tangible possessions and assets (pensions, education, job experience) cannot be split.

ADVANTAGES OF THE NEW DIVORCE ACT

The obvious advantage is that divorce need only take one year instead of three. This means that you can file for a divorce on the day that you stop living together, and a year later, having done all the paper work, go to court; or, if you have already lived separately for one year, you may proceed immediately. The old Act required a waiting period of ninety days to allow for an appeal, and the formality of a Decree Absolute; the new Act has a waiting period of thirty-one days, and no Decree Absolute.

Another advantage is that both you and your spouse can file for the divorce, agreeing that the marriage has broken down, without having to accuse one or the other (or both) of various offences in order to establish grounds. This is certainly an improvement from the point of view of any children, who will benefit from reduced animosity. This provision also permits you to retain a more reasonable attitude in deciding who gets what, since, at least in theory, no one needs to be at fault. The other forms of marriage breakdown are still available, because many divorces will still be contested, and there will indeed be those which can only be tried on the basis of matrimonial offence, and the related legislation governing property and maintenance.

Because the ideal no-fault divorce implies agreement between the spouses to end the marriage, it would appear logical to share a lawyer. This is still a bad idea. Despite the no-fault principle, amicable divorces are rarer than hen's teeth. It is sometimes easier for a couple with no children to reach an agreement, but property is still a contentious issue to some degree in most cases. It is always worth having your own lawyer advising you on your best interests, even in uncomplicated cases.

DISADVANTAGES OF THE NEW DIVORCE ACT

Some religious bodies and other groups in society are arguing that the reduction from three years to one year does not provide enough time for due consideration and attempts at reconciliation. There is certainly more time for doubt and changing your mind in a three-year period. But the new Act still permits up to ninety days' reconciliation (not necessarily continuous) within the one-year separation requirement. As with the old Divorce Act, a lawyer must ask each client during the first appointment in a divorce action whether or not reconciliation and counselling have been seriously considered. The potential for reconciliation seems to have been allowed for.

The more serious disadvantage has to do with financial settlements. The principle that maintenance awards will be made with a view to the early establishment of self-sufficiency for both spouses, combined with the trend toward splitting the assets of the marriage down the middle, have led to some unpredicted hardships for many women. Material assets are fairly straightforward to identify and to assess; but there are other intangible assets within a marriage for which we have as yet no formula for assessing, and thus they cannot be split. These are things like education, professional and business goodwill, pensions, and insurance. These assets are most frequently accumulated by the male spouse in our society for many reasons. Women tend to take on a greater share of the child-care responsibilities, and consequently have less time and energy for career development. Insurance and pensions are usually attached to the person with the higher earning power, and dependants still frequently lose most or all of that protection upon divorce. And finally, men tend to be paid higher salaries because they have more education and well-established careers and business contacts, some or all of which was achieved during the marriage, and also because, even with equal qualifications, women are paid less for the same work.

All of these points relate directly to the fact that even with the material assets of the marriage split down the middle, women, especially those with children, do not get a share of the less tangible assets, to which they made a direct contribution, although home labour and child care are not valued monetarily. The fact is that women tend to be forced to a considerably lower standard of living following divorce. Lenore Weitzman's study in the United States revealed that the standard of living of the average divorced woman and her dependent children is reduced by 73 per cent, while her ex-husband's is increased by 42 per cent. Hardly an equitable settlement. This is largely because of the lack of provision for evaluating and dividing the less tangible matrimonial assets, but the situation is aggravated by another fact, that 60 to 80 per cent of maintenance orders are ignored by those ordered to pay. Weitzman discovered that this amounts to over $4 billion annually in the United States.

Although the new Act does seem on the surface to provide for a more immediate and equitable resolution of financial arrangements, in fact it is, at least in the following sense, a step backwards. The old Act, with its adversarial stance, had the court and society judging one spouse to be at fault, and thus demanding that he or (less often) she pay. Thus, women who had spent their lives being homemakers and mothers were awarded lifetime alimony payments, and the family home. Now the family home is likely to be sold, and each spouse will receive half the equity. This is not enough to buy another house, and constitutes a serious risk to the security of the spouse who has a low earning capacity, because of child responsibilities, low educational achievement, or inadequate job experience—or all three. Furthermore, the new Act explicitly states that any support should be given with a view to early self-sufficiency.

With some reflection, it appears that neither is right, but that women were at least in this sense better protected under the old Act.

This is not to say that women should either have the right to be entirely dependent for life upon an ex-husband's income, nor that women should avoid providing for their own support. What seems to be missing is a formula for a division of the intangibles, the factors that ensure that the man's economic transition to single life will be considerably less painful—and shorter in duration—than a woman's.

SOLUTIONS

For a couple without children, with roughly equivalent incomes, the new Act should be an advance in the evolution of divorce legislation. For a couple with children, where the wife has been the chief child-raiser and the husband has provided the bulk of the economic support, the interpretation of the new Act to achieve maximum protection for the woman will take a skilled and imaginative lawyer. Certainly the new Act is superior to the old in many respects. The current maintenance legislation is important in enforcing collection of alimony and maintenance. Pensions are now being split by some courts at the time of divorce. Insurance policies are less clear, but there are recommendations that equal provision for insurance be part of the divorce settlement. Yet another possibility is the deferment of selling and dividing the proceeds of the family home, so that the custodial parent and the children can continue to live there until they no longer need it because they have achieved a reasonable financial level, or because the kids have moved out.

PROPERTY

Property law is often a source of surprise and disappointment at the time of a divorce settlement. Until the late nineteenth century a woman and all her possessions became possessions of her husband upon marriage. She ceased to be a person in the eyes of the law. In the subsequent years much has changed, and there are certain guidelines for the division of property at the time of divorce.

Current law sometimes takes into consideration the woman's contribution to the home in terms of time and labour, although there is as yet no established formula for this. Even now, the most valid contribution to the home in the eyes of the court is a documented financial one: records of purchase payments, insurance, receipts for furniture and housewares are what count. In many cases these financial responsibilities were undertaken by the male spouse, and the female has actually bought little or nothing that wasn't paid for from her husband's earnings. This situation is a problem at the time of divorce, one which could have been at least partially prevented with competent legal counselling regarding property ownership before the wedding.

By the time you are drawing up a divorce agreement, that is all water under the bridge. Generally, any gifts you received prior to the marriage remain yours (money, furniture, jewellery). Gifts you received during the marriage are usually yours, too. Property acquired jointly during a marriage is more complicated. There is as yet no general rule that the non-working spouse gets half of the matrimonial assets; much is left to the discretion of the judge. The safest position is to have joint ownership of the house and property legally documented during marriage.

Once you believe that the end of your marriage is near, don't do anything until you are sure of your legal and financial position. Find out who really owns the house before you redecorate it; find out if you own the car before you sell it. These and many other spur-of-the-moment acts may cause you embarrassment later on, and even if you have joint ownership of some major items, this does not necessarily imply equal distribution at the time of divorce. If there is something you really want, remove it to a safe place (mother or equivalent), remembering the fine old adage, "possession is nine-tenths of the law." Don't forget the safety deposit box!

You can save yourself and your lawyer a lot of trouble if you can make copies of your spouse's income tax returns, brokers' statements, the serial numbers of his Canada Savings Bonds, any insurance documents, and anything else that looks important. Otherwise these will have to be collected by your lawyer, for a fee.

This seems an appropriate place to insert a word of caution about desertion. Although desertion is almost never used as grounds for divorce anymore, you should check with a lawyer on the implications of this action in your province. Do this before you leave the matrimonial home if you can; if not, as soon after as possible. In the eyes of the law you can leave without being guilty of "desertion" if circumstances of physical or mental cruelty make it impossible for you to stay. The best way to establish this is to go directly to a shelter for battered women, or into psychiatric care. These are extreme cases.

Leaving is now being considered the same thing as "separation" in most cases, rather than "desertion." Real desertion, as in truly vanishing, seldom happens. Usually there is some communication, even if it is just through lawyers.

There may be some other possible disadvantages to leaving in terms of custody and property settlement. Try to make sure you are protected *before* you act.

MARRIAGE CONTRACTS

Marriage contracts are optional in most provinces, with the exception of Quebec, where they remain a mandatory step in preparation for marriage. They are useful if, for some reason, you wish to over-ride the current legislation, and ensure a particular pattern of distribution of the assets of the marriage. A marriage contract gives you control over who gets what, regardless of the fifty-fifty principle practised in the divorce courts today. You can, for example, be sure that the items you purchased yourself remain yours, or that one spouse will receive more than the other, or list various other exceptions which you wish to safeguard. Some provinces require that the contract be prepared prior to the marriage, others permit contracts during the marriage. In any case, there are specific formats and requirements, and these vary from province to province. In any case it is wise to get the advice of a lawyer before signing.

In cases of divorce where there has been a marriage contract, it is usually upheld by the judge even if many years have gone by and conditions have changed considerably. Only in exceptional situations, for example, where one spouse might be forced onto social assistance if the contract were enforced, will a judge consider over-riding it.

It is advisable to consider preparation of a contract if you plan to live common law. Although this is not exactly the same as a marriage contract, its purpose is similarly to ensure a particular pattern of distribution of assets upon dissolution of the relationship. Although in some provinces common law spouses have property rights protected by law, in other provinces there is no protection.

For more detailed information on marriage and live-in contracts call your lawyer, check at the public library, and check both Lynn King's book and the Self-Counsel Press book, *If You Love Me, Put It in Writing*, listed at the end of this chapter.

COURTS AND THEIR LEVELS

In Canada divorce is governed by a federal statute, the Divorce Act, the current revision of which was prepared in 1985. Although divorce is covered by federal legislation, it is usually dealt with in the provincial Supreme Court of Queen's Bench or equivalent. The name of this court varies from province to province. (See examples in chart below.) Many of the issues which relate to divorce such as property and custody disputes are governed by other provincial agencies and courts at a lower level of the judicial system.

The courts at every level, however, have a common responsibility, which is twofold: first, to protect the rights of the individual, and second, to protect the best interest of society as a whole. The first responsibility is readily understood; the second must be seen as an insurance for the orderly continuation of our society. Since trends in law are partially developed on the basis of cases, the decision of each judge will be used as a guideline or precedent for future decisions in other cases by other judges. This characteristic of the law ensures continuity in its interpretation and exercise over time. Note, though, that trends in case law can vary from one province to another.

Another aspect of the best interest of society as a whole is the economic ramifications of a court decision. A judge must make the fairest decision for the individuals, while not increasing the economic burden upon society unless this is absolutely necessary. Sometimes the two aspects of judgement, individual and societal, appear to contradict each other. For example, a divorce may occasionally be denied if there is no apparent financial support available for the other spouse. Thus, maintenance orders are intended to prevent an individual or family from having to rely on social assistance.

THE COURT SYSTEM

SUPREME COURT OF CANADA (FEDERAL)

PROVINCIAL COURT SYSTEM

Alberta
Provincial Court of Appeal
Provincial Court of Queen's Bench
Provincial Family Court

Ontario
Provincial Court of Appeal
Supreme Court of Ontario
District Court
Unified Family Court

Each court in the above chart overrules the one below it. A divorce can only be granted by the Court of Queen's Bench level or higher, but many related issues are decided by Family Court. Also, you cannot go backwards down the system. If you start in Court of Queen's Bench, for example, you cannot then go to Family Court on the same issue. As you go up in court levels, it gets more expensive, too.

The provincial court procedures vary from one province to another. For example, in Alberta, you don't need a lawyer to make applications for custody and maintenance in Family Court. This court even provides legal counsellors to help you through the procedure. To find out how the Family Court in your province acts, consult your library or your lawyer. Although Family Court can rule on many issues, the actual divorce can only be ordered by the Court of Queen's Bench. All lawyers can act on behalf of their clients in all courts, but law is customarily divided into sub-specialties, such as Family Law, Criminal Law, Corporate Law, and so on. A lawyer specializing in family law is the first to admit a lack of experience and knowledge in criminal or corporate fields.

AFFIDAVITS, RESTRAINING ORDERS, EX PARTE ORDERS AND OTHER LEGAL DELICACIES

You may be asked by your lawyer to help to prepare many legal documents during the course of obtaining your divorce. In order to demystify the process, some of these are described briefly here, and samples appear in the appendices.

AFFIDAVIT

The most common legal document that you will be asked to help your lawyer prepare is an affidavit, which is simply a sworn statement of your situation. An affidavit is mandatory with divorce petitions in some provinces. In others it is not required. An affidavit sets out the facts which comprise the grounds for your divorce in a logical sequence, and describes your financial status. It is prepared by your lawyer on the basis of what you have said, and you are required to read it through and sign it. This can be a shocking experience: the frank statements about your spouse, once typewritten on a legal document, take on a new importance; equally shocking is the first time you read an affidavit prepared by your spouse. (It is hard to believe that there can be two such entirely different views of the same events, and yet each person has a right to his or her version of the story.)

An affidavit is used in court as a sworn statement of the truth as it is seen by the individual. An affidavit speeds the court procedure by forcing each person to think carefully through his or her position in advance of the court appearance. In some applications it even avoids the need for you to appear in court in person. When it is attached to a petition for divorce, it provides the judge with a clear statement of your reasons for applying for a divorce. It also provides your spouse and his lawyer with a clear statement to which they can reply.

EXAMINATION FOR DISCOVERY

Your lawyer may choose to schedule an Examination for Discovery in order to determine the financial position of your husband, and other details which will affect the case. This examination includes both you and your husband and both lawyers. It takes place in a small room in the court house, and a court reporter is in attendance, to record the proceedings. You are each placed under oath in turn, and then questioned by each other's lawyer. You may not interrupt while the other person is being questioned, and you are asked to reply only to the questions you are asked directly. Make sure you speak clearly and slowly for the benefit of the court typist. It is a good idea to take notes during the interview of your husband, so that you can tell your lawyer about any inconsistencies after the session. Save your remarks until you are alone with your lawyer.

Both you and your husband may be asked about your sources of income, your possessions in and outside of the home, and your intent regarding custody. Often you will be asked to produce documentation after the Examination for Discovery, papers which back up your claims, such as copies of past tax returns, pay stubs, cheques, bank statements, and so on. These are carefully listed by the reporter and your lawyer, and you are under oath when you agree to supply them.

Try to remain calm and detached, as if this were a business meeting. Nothing will be solved here; it is merely one more technique for establishing what the facts and the resources in the case are. This is not the place for an argument between you and your husband, or between you and his lawyer. Conduct yourself with dignity, and you will win the respect of your lawyer, possibly the other lawyer—and the court reporter, who, despite presumed objectivity and the presence of a tape recorder, has some power in deciding how the events get written down.

An Examination for Discovery has another purpose; it gives your lawyer a chance to assess the level of co-operation or animosity between you and your husband, and to assess your husband and the other lawyer as the opposition. Often the lawyers already know each other, but lawyers may behave differently with different clients. After the Examination for Discovery, you and your lawyer are in a better position to finalize your strategy.

RESTRAINING ORDER

In some cases where custody of children is contested there may be serious concern on the part of the custodial parent that the other parent will attempt to harm or abduct the children. In such cases the custodial parent can swear an affidavit stating these concerns and the previous actions of the other spouse which gave rise to them. The Court may then grant a Restraining Order, which orders that the spouse cannot approach the house or the children without prior consent or supervision, or other limitation. Restraining orders vary in the degree of restraint, and are usually time-limited. If you need such an order, make sure that you obtain several certified copies from the court, since the police may not act on the basis of an uncertified copy. Keep one copy with you always, file one with the principal of your child's school, day-care centre or babysitter, and one with the local police department, if there is any likelihood that you might need the police to enforce the Restraining Order.

EX PARTE ORDERS

This is a temporary court order made in the absence of the other spouse. A fairly common example of this occurs during custody disputes soon after separation, when both parents still have legal custody of the child or children, and the non-resident spouse is likely to make an attempt to abduct them. The Ex Parte Order gives temporary custody to the applying parent until the matter is heard in court with representation from both sides. Again, it is advisable to obtain several certified copies of this order. These are prepared at the court house or by your lawyer. These copies should be distributed the same way as suggested for a Restraining Order.

GARNISHEE

This is the final word in this section on speaking "legalese." If the court has ordered maintenance payments but the order is not being observed, i.e., the payments are not being made, the court can order that the salary of the non-paying spouse be garnisheed. This means that the employer of the offending spouse will be required to take the specified amount from earnings before issuing the next paycheque. The money thus garnisheed is forwarded to the court where it must be held for at least thirty-five days, and then sent to the other spouse. The disadvantage to the garnishment procedure is that by the time the required money is paid, more is needed. A recent alteration in some places to this process is that of the "continuing garnishment," where the court orders that the money be taken from the paying spouse's paycheque off the top every month, without the need to apply to the court each time.

OUT-OF-TOWN, INTERPROVINCIAL, AND INTERNATIONAL DIVORCES

Many other things can create legal problems during the process of a divorce. For example, your spouse may live in another province or country, in which case you will definitely need legal assistance to help you wade through the laws and precedents of two provincial legal systems. (Here again, you are referred to the end of this chapter and your bookstore or library. Both your local bookstore and library will order books for you about other provinces, if you can supply the title, author, and publisher.)

In Canada a woman's domicile is no longer legally that of her husband. Your domicile is Canada. The term "residence" refers to where you live—which province you live in. To be divorced in Canada you have to have a domicile in Canada, and you have to be a resident in a province for one year. Then you can file for divorce in that province. If you have been separated from your spouse and you live in different provinces, you may be divorced in the province where the spouse is resident and, if you both lived in your respective provinces for a year, either residence can be used for the purpose of divorce. Sometimes this is very important in that wherever the divorce is granted, any subsequent changes to be made in the divorce regarding custody or maintenance have to go back to the same court. Therefore it is very convenient to have divorce proceedings in the court closest to where you intend to live, to save the expenses of travelling for you and your lawyer and long-distance phone bills. In any case, distant divorces are usually more expensive than local ones, especially in contested cases.

According to the Divorce Act, divorces granted in other countries have been recognized in Canada since 1968 if performed by an authority duly recognized by the law of the other country.

It is also possible for a Canadian resident to divorce someone who lives in another country, although the process becomes long and drawn out. The big problem is serving the spouse out of the country, because you have to show that the person has been served with the petition. Usually this involves a special order of the court which will state that service on this person who, for example, is in the armed forces in Germany, or who has returned to India, can be done in a particular way. Then the court will specify how the petition will be served, such as by putting it in the newspaper in the Indian town, or by serving a close relative if you know that the spouse is in contact with that close relative. It is up to the petitioning party to convince the judge that the person in the foreign country has had notice, personal notice, that the divorce is happening. It also takes longer because they are given generous amounts of time to get to Canada or to hire a lawyer in Canada to defend the divorce if they want.

INFORMAL MARRIAGES, OR COMMON-LAW RELATIONSHIPS

Common law is a term originating in traditional British law which refers to the generally accepted customs which are respected by society, despite lack of formalization through proper statutory channels. In the past the term had a more general meaning, but now it is taken to mean marriage without formalization.

The break-up of a common-law relationship is as emotionally wrenching as the end of a marriage. Depending on where you live there may be much less protection for common-law wives, however, than for legally married wives in terms of rights both to maintenance at the dissolution of the relationship and to the estate in the event of the death of a spouse. If you are involved in or are contemplating a common-law relationship, it is wise for you and your spouse to prepare a contractual agreement, with the advice of a lawyer. You can compose this on your own, have your lawyer do it, or use one of the kits that are currently available; for example, the International Self-Counsel Press provides a kit called *If You Love Me, Put It in Writing*. Although a contract increases the security of both spouses, it can still be challenged in court by legally recognized relatives.

CURVES AND REDUNDANCIES YOU SHOULD KNOW ABOUT

Not all out-of-date laws have been changed yet, and there are a few which can cause problems, especially to women, if they are not anticipated and countered, or at least understood at the time of divorce. For example if the "dum casta" clause is included in a divorce agreement, alimony payments need not be paid if the recipient spouse has sexual intercourse with someone other than the ex-spouse. Similarly the "dum sole" clause permits the paying spouse to cease payment of alimony when the recipient remarries or establishes a common-law relationship. Both these clauses are based upon the outdated view of women as sexual and material possessions of men, and of marriage as a dependency situation for women. If such a clause is to be built into your divorce agreement, make sure that you fully understand its implications for your children and your own future relationships.

The law is always conservative. Its role in society is the preservation of the integrity of the society. Laws are generally changed only after social change has taken place. This delay ensures that laws are not arbitrary or trite and are less vulnerable to social trends and fashions. Laws are changed by a long and thorough process which protects society as much as possible from susceptibility to interference from political lobbying. There is, of course, a link between the political and judicial sectors of society through both formal and informal channels, but care is taken to limit their effect.

Laws may be drawn up by specially appointed committees as the need arises. The drafted laws are read in the federal parliament or provincial legislature three times, then once in the Senate, after which they receive Royal Assent from the Queen's representative. The last is, of course, a formality. Alternatively, old laws are modified after one or more court decisions signal the inadequacy of an existing law in the light of changing conditions in society. A well-known example of this occurred in the case of *Murdoch v. Murdoch* in Alberta; a farm wife was judged under the law to have no claim to a farm upon which she had laboured with her husband for many years. This decision and the public outcry which followed led to a revision of the property law, the Matrimonial Property Act of Alberta of 1979.

To sum up, the legal system provides a formal way of ending your marriage and dividing up the property. Whether you are able to agree on most of the arrangements informally with your husband, and need the legal process only minimally, or whether your lawyer will do most of the work in arranging your divorce, your understanding of the system will save you time and money. Take the time to select a lawyer you can trust, but trust your own instincts, too. You will have to live with the results of your divorce. Try to be as fair to yourself, your children, and your ex-spouse as you can. A divorce almost always means increased financial hardship—the income of one family is seldom enough to establish two new homes at a level comparable to the marriage home. This in itself is a serious adjustment, and must be faced realistically. The legal system puts some distance between angry couples, and because of the nature of the process, provides time for tempers to cool. However, the time required to settle a contested divorce causes a perpetuation of a limbo-like state for everyone.

You can make the system more efficient by ensuring that you are well-prepared for your appointments with your lawyer, that you have gathered the important information, and can present it efficiently. Your lawyer's fee is high enough—you can choose to pay for long, intimate chats about what a stinker your husband is, but it is cheaper to air your complaints to your friends. Learn to use your lawyer as a trusted business associate who is helping to negotiate your divorce in your best interest.

Social values and patterns are always a long way behind the latest ideological trends. It will be awhile before society will be able to accept the full range of possibilities implied by the concept of equal rights, from women in responsible jobs to men staying home to raise the kids; from women receiving total financial support to men receiving alimony payments. In a society as varied as ours, all these answers and many others are right for various people, but it will take time before acceptance of the full spectrum is reflected either in the general attitude of society or in all courtroom decisions.

References

FROM THE INTERNATIONAL SELF-COUNSEL PRESS

306 West 25th Street,
North Vancouver, B.C. V7N 2G1

Powell, Wayne, *Divorce Guide for British Columbia*, 1983.

Dickson, Robert Gary, *Divorce Guide for Alberta*, 1983.

James, Jack D., *Divorce Guide for Ontario*, 1982.

Fayers, Heather, *Divorce Guide for Manitoba*, 1979.

Kruzeniski, Ronald, *Divorce Guide for Saskatchewan*, 1983.

Packages of forms are available for the above provinces from the publisher.

ALSO FROM THE SELF-COUNSEL PRESS

Auxier, Jane, *Marriage and Family Law in British Columbia*, 1982.

Fayers, Heather, *If You Love Me, Put It in Writing: Marriage Contract Kit for Canadians*.

_____, *If You Leave Me, Put It in Writing: Separation Agreement Kit for British Columbia*.

McBean, Jean, *Marriage and Family Law in Alberta*, 1980.

Mungall, Constance, *Changing Your Name in Canada: How to Do It Legally*, 1977.

David, Rodica, *Marriage and Family Law in Ontario*, 1982.

OTHER REFERENCES

Alberta Rules of Court, 52nd Amendment. Edmonton: Alberta Attorney General, April 3, 1986.

The Canada Gazette, Part III, Vol. 9, No. 1. Ottawa: The Queen's Printer for Canada, April 7, 1986.

Freeland, Halyna and Sonia Maryn, "Where We're Going: Issues for the '80s," *The Newsmagazine for Alberta Women*, July 1985, pp. 24-28.

Galper, Miriam, *Joint Custody and Co-parenting: Sharing Your Child Equally: A Sourcebook for the Separated or Divorced Family*. Philadelphia: Running Press, 1980.
This book is strongly pro-joint custody.

Ishwaran, K. (ed.), *Marriage and Divorce in Canada*. Toronto: Methuen, 1983.
A statistical picture of changing marriage patterns in Canada.

King, Lynn, *What Every Woman Should Know About Separation and Divorce*. Toronto: James Lorimer & Co., 1980.
A detailed discussion of legal issues. Much of the information remains relevant under the new Act. Author is now a judge in Family Court in Ontario.

Legal Education Society of Alberta, *The New Divorce Act*, materials prepared for seminars in Calgary and Edmonton, Alberta, on the 5th and 6th of December, 1985, respectively.

Takas, Marianne, "Divorce: Who Gets the Blame in 'No Fault'?," *Ms.* XIV (8), p. 48, February 1986.

Weitzman, Lenore J., *The Divorce Revolution: The Unexpected Social and Economic Consequences for Women and Children in America*. New York: The Free Press, 1985.
A careful critique of the effects of current American divorce legislation on women and children. It supplies a detailed study of the effects of splitting property "down the middle" and other recent concepts. The book serves as a serious warning to divorced and divorcing men and women, lawyers, counsellors, and judges in Canada.

CHAPTER FIVE

Budgeting and Finances

When you first got married you often heard the cliché, "Two can live as cheaply as one." This is another myth, as you soon discovered for yourself. Maintaining a household for two, and later on for children as well, costs much more than your single apartment did. Similarly, after a separation, maintaining two households costs more than running the family home did. Well-meaning husbands often find that their new bachelor apartments, plus meals, visiting the children, and their own dating can cost a lot more than they thought. A salary which was just enough to cover one household may not be enough for two.

INTERIM PROTECTION

This is as good a place as any to tuck in a warning: separation and divorce can make nice people behave in nasty ways, especially with regard to money. It is always a shock when an estranged husband cuts off financial resources to his wife and children. It is seldom expected. Nevertheless, you are well-advised to be aware of this possibility and to guard against it for the protection of your children. There can be a long dry period between the initial break-up and the arrival of the first court-ordered maintenance payment.

One thing you can do is to empty the joint bank accounts and put them in your own name on the day you know you are separating. You have the right to anything that is in joint accounts. It is perfectly legal for you to take it all and put it in an account in your own name. Your spouse and others may object, but again the cliché, that "possession is nine-tenths of the law," is very relevant. At least you will have some money to feed your children for the first month or so, until the dust clears. Without that money you may end up having to go on welfare, unless you have a hefty paycheque or personal savings to rely on.

Because the courts are increasingly recognizing the rights of a wife to a share of the family business, entrepreneurial males are being especially careful about divorce. Even if the wife has never been directly employed by the company, her work in maintaining a household is considered by some judges to be a valid contribution to the family business. The assumption is that without the support and security of the home and the child care provided by the wife the husband would not have been free to pursue and develop the business. This possibility constitutes a serious threat to a man. In order to protect the business, a self-employed businessman can salt away his company profits during a long divorce process, and rewrite the company books to create an impression of near bankruptcy. This is done to protect the business assets from being divided as property of the marriage. Alternatively, he may blow the money on a fancy new car—the wife gets to keep the family station wagon, while he gets a new Mercedes. Be warned that this sort of thing happens often, and that much of your spouse's stalling might simply be a strategy to allow time for the business books to be rearranged. There isn't much you can do to counteract this, other than to have your lawyer proceed with haste, and monitor the company's financial statements.

As soon as you are convinced that your marriage is going to end or in the event that it already has, you had better get busy and find out how much it costs you to live. At first this may sound like a horrendous if not impossible task, but it isn't. In fact, it will become a source of satisfaction and pride once you have mastered the art of budgeting and financial planning. The following discussion is primarily for women who have not had the responsibility of managing the finances for the family before their separation, though others may pick up a few hints, too.

STEP ONE: ESTABLISHING HOW MUCH

The first thing that you must do is to acquire information. How much does it really cost you to live, to raise the kids, to run the house and the car? You won't know whether you are in a good position or a bad position until you come up with these numbers, regardless of how little or how much support you may receive. Your lawyer will need a basic budget in order to proceed to prepare your separation or divorce agreement.

STEP TWO: BUDGET AND RECORDS

In order to establish a basic budget it is necessary to keep records for a month or two. You will then have a good idea of how much money you need to live each month, how much maintenance/alimony you will require (if any), and how much money you will need to earn if you are returning to work. You will need to be quite meticulous for the first period of record-keeping, just to make sure that you don't overlook anything important and find yourself short, after the divorce, when it is much more difficult to make a change in the settlement. Once you have a reliable income each month, and have a clear idea of where your money goes, you can stop keeping track in such detail if you choose. However, once you start a careful budget process, you may also choose to maintain the sense of control you get from close monitoring of your finances.

This chapter explains in detail the various procedures for setting up your budget. It is one thing to decide how much you will need, but quite another to live on it later, unless you learn to budget spending and saving on a weekly, monthly, and yearly basis.

You can get budget booklets free from most banks. These booklets help you to identify and organize your expenses. Some of them are just record books; others offer suggestions for managing your money.

If you need additional assistance, there are many courses in budgeting available in most towns and cities. Community organizations such as the YWCA and community colleges offer such courses from time to time. Before you sign up, try to meet the instructor, or at least check the curriculum topics to see if the course will meet your needs. You may even choose to take older children along with you. Just make sure that the course is somewhere between being too simplistic and too close to a chartered accountancy course.

KEEPING THE RECORDS

There are many budgeting systems around. You can use envelopes, file folders, a looseleaf binder, or anything else that will help you to get organized. However you do it, though, the success of the system depends upon faithful record-keeping. Once any system is set up, it shouldn't take long to maintain. Once it falls behind, it is the devil's own job to straighten it out again. The most important thing is to choose an account book of adequate size in which to do the recording. A child's school exercise book will do, as long as it has lots of pages. It should be kept near the drawer or box where you are going to keep your receipts (in separate envelopes or folders) and where you will also keep bills and bank statements. It should be near a desk or table so that everything is handy, and doing the accounts doesn't require re-organizing the entire house.

In the account book label a page for each of your monthly expenses. At the top of each page put the amount you feel you can afford to spend on this item. The actual expenditures will be listed on this page as they occur. Leave several pages at the end because other things will occur to you and new expenses will crop up; make sure you have labelled one page "miscellaneous."

Then, each month under each heading write on the appropriate page the amount that was due on the bill, the amount that you paid, the number of your cheque (or the bank where you paid cash), and the date of the payment.

In allocating funds to operate your budget, you may wish to adopt the envelope system. Label an envelope for each of the monthly expenses, into which you put the allotted cash at the beginning of each month so that you won't be tempted to spend it on something else. You should have a matching envelope system for receipts. Each expenditure is recorded on the appropriate page, and the receipt is filed. Receipts for major purchases or repairs should be kept for two years, or until the warranty runs out. File these where they can be located quickly.

You can put all the basic unchanging monthly expenses on one page. If they are paid automatically, make sure you always remember to deduct them from your cheque book balance each month.

Do the same for quarterly items and annual expenses. Once they are all written in, you can figure out your basic costs for a month or a year, simply by adding up the monthly, quarterly, and annual expenses with your itemized monthly expense allocations, and dividing the total annual expenses by twelve. Don't forget to make some plans for long-term expenses, too. For example, it takes somewhere around $4000 a year to send a child to university.

The accompanying chart is a sample monthly budget checklist for a family with a take-home income of $1,865 per month, or, not counting the Family Allowance, $22,380 per year. For some women this budget will seem ridiculously high, for others painfully low. You will notice as you read it that there is a gap, a deficit of several hundred dollars. Adjustments will have to be made, and suggestions will be considered in the section to follow. Additional budgets are included in Appendix I.

Sample Monthly Budget

1 Adult, 2 Children

	Monthly	*Annual*
Rent/Mortgage	$ 600.00	$ 7,200.00
Food	425.00	5,100.00
Utilities	74.00	888.00
Heat	45.00	540.00
Phone	11.00	132.00
Transportation	175.00	2,100.00
Dog and Cat Food, Vet	30.00	360.00
Car Payment	190.00	2,280.00
Bus Passes	37.00	370.00
Clothes	135.00	1,620.00
Personal Care	60.00	720.00
Office Coffee Fund	18.00	216.00
Entertainment	125.00	1,500.00
Medical/Dental	35.00	420.00
Household Expenses	115.00	1,380.00
Gifts	45.00	540.00
Allowances	100.00	1,200.00
Savings	50.00	600.00
Savings (Christmas and vacation fund)	100.00	1,200.00
Emergency	50.00	600.00

Additional Annual Expenses:

Car Insurance	32.00	384.00
School Insurance	2.33	28.00
House Insurance	13.67	164.00
Property Taxes	70.83	850.00
Total	$2,538.83	$30,392.00

Budgeted money which goes directly to child care:

Food	300.00
Bus Passes	37.00
Clothing	100.00
Personal Care	40.00
Entertainment	40.00

Education	60.00	
Medical	25.00	
Allowances	100.00	
	702.00	/month

Monthly Income

Take-home salary	$1,434.16
(Note: this figure assumes that employer is deducting income tax at source)	
Car Allowance	131.00
Maintenance	300.00
($350 less $50 set aside for income tax)	
	$1,865.16
Family Allowance (goes directly into savings for children's education)	76.00

Shortfall/month:
$2,538.83 – $1,865.16 = $673.67

STEP THREE: ADJUSTING YOUR BUDGET TO FIT YOUR INCOME

The budget in the preceding section was prepared for a lawyer, in anticipation of a divorce trial. No one can live on a budget that is short by nearly $700. There may be tactical advantages to continuing your pre-divorce standard of living during the time before the court hearing, if you can. There is a danger that if you prove you can live on less, the court may award you less. In any case, after the decree, and possibly before it, you must get on to living on what you have, quite possibly paying off the debts that have accumulated during the divorce period.

Records are useless if you do not have enough money to buy the groceries, or pay the phone bill, or fix the car. Similarly, a list of expenses that exceeds the available money by several hundred or thousand dollars is a guaranteed cause of frustration, depression, ulcers, and sleepless nights.

A budget is a series of planned expenditures, and it must be all-inclusive, and yet match your income. If you don't follow the plan, you will not achieve what you want, and "crucial" things will be eliminated only because they occur at the end of the month, after the money has run out.

The best, simplest, and most controlled system is a cash system with a series of envelopes. The labels on the envelopes match the pages in your account book. At the start of each month, or immediately after your salary and/or maintenance payment has reached the bank, you put into each envelope the amount of cash budgeted for each item. Bills are paid, and items purchased from the cash in the envelope—when there is no money left, you stop. Try to avoid switching and cheating because this will destroy the system. If your first budget has the wrong allocations, adjust them next month. If you find you borrow from the envelopes, use a chequing account instead. A budget is not carved in stone. It is just a method to let you accomplish your aims within the reality of your available money.

Let's start from the top of the proposed budget above and consider ways to find that $673.67 per month. It isn't so hard, but because everyone has different priorities we'll still examine all the possibilities. One person's economy is another person's hardship; economize as it suits your family and your way of living. And discuss methods of cutting back with the children—they may have some good ideas, and it will sure help to have them understand and co-operate.

RENT/MORTGAGE

The payment of $600 per month is very reasonable, perhaps even too low. Nevertheless, you may choose to move to less expensive accommodation by getting a smaller apartment, or a house or condominium with a lower mortgage. Or you may select another place to live that costs the same, but is in a less expensive neighbourhood, and thus reduce the expected level of living, and the pressure on the kids to compete at an unrealistic level.

FOOD

There are many ways to reduce your food budget—unless you are already converted to healthy cooking and eating habits. In this category, unlike most others, economizing often means *improving* the quality of your family's diet. No more junk food—stop buying potato chips, taco chips, candy, and pop. Reduce the chemicals that you all eat, improve the kids' complexions, especially if they are teenagers, and solve the weight problems of chubby children (and possibly yourself). Substitute fruit juices—not flavour crystals, but unsweetened natural fruit juices. For snacks, serve fruits, nuts, celery and carrot sticks, and other cheaper things. Stop preparing desserts. If you must have something sweet at the end of the meal, serve fresh fruit. Buy only cereals which have no sugar and contain whole grains. Although these are more expensive, you get far more mileage out of them, nutritionally. And they are very filling. Reduce your meat meals to two or three a week, and buy cheaper, leaner cuts. This will mean that you have to reorganize your cooking schedule, especially if you work, because some of those meats will need longer cooking than a minute steak. Check into the possibility of a slow cooker—dinner cooks while you are at work. Or cook on the weekend for the coming week, or the night before for the following day.

You may need new recipe books if you are not used to cooking rice and beans and lentils and other more nutritious and more economical foods. Francis Moore Lappe's *Diet for a Small Planet* is a good beginning, because she explains the concept of maintaining a balanced diet while experimenting with these foods. You can also browse in your local health-food shop, and select the books that best suit the taste of your family. If this kind of diet seems like a drastic change for your family, introduce it slowly. It will start to pay off when you find that you are all feeling better with less sugar and additives, and you are also seeing the reduction in your grocery bill.

UTILITIES AND HEAT

You may need to have a "turn-off-the-lights" campaign, where everyone reminds everyone else to turn off lights in rooms that are not being used. This is just a matter of habit, but it really does make a difference. If you find that you often leave the outside lights on all night consider buying a timer and attaching it to the light switch. It can be set very easily to turn the lights on and off at certain times. Alternatively, buy a light fixture that is photo-sensitive, and comes on automatically as the daylight fades, and goes off at dawn.

Heat can be controlled by turning down the thermostat as everyone goes off to school and work in the morning, and at night when everyone goes to bed. You might also decide to get used to living at 18°C instead of 22°C. At first it means wearing sweaters in the house, but your body soon becomes acclimatized. An automatic timer is again a good idea—they can be bought in any hardware store, and are not difficult to install. Set it to lower the thermostat during the day and from midnight to 6 a.m. You can always over-ride the setting on the weekends if you wish with a flip of the switch.

PHONE

If you have extensions rented from the phone company, you can return all but one. Similarly, you may have a more expensive, stylish telephone—exchange it for the old standard. If you already have just the bare bones service, there isn't much you can do here, other than stop making long-distance calls. This budget already assumes that you have done that, at $11.00 per month.

TRANSPORTATION

It takes more than gas and parking-meter money to run a car. There is a continuing need for maintenance and a periodic need for replacement. The sample budget includes running and maintaining a car and car insurance. It does not include the cost of buying a replacement car. Use a realistic figure when you budget for car maintenance and repairs. Check with a reliable mechanic for a reasonable figure for your car, and together create an annual schedule for car maintenance. And don't forget to include what you spend on gas and oil. In fact, it is a good idea to have your car checked by a good mechanic twice a year, spring and fall, rather than waiting for it to fall apart on you. It will usually cost much less in the long run and increase the life of your car. Remember, you will have to buy new tires periodically, and you may need a set of snow tires, depending upon where you live. The bus is a lot cheaper! There are still a number of ways that you can economize if you need to continue to operate your car. If you are driving an expensive car you may consider getting one that is cheaper to run. It isn't wise to economize on insurance—keep your full coverage, especially if your teenagers drive your car. If you are running two cars, perhaps you should get rid of one, and the kids will take more buses or ride their bikes, and share with you when your car is free.

You can spread out your payments for expensive items like tires and insurance, or even a new/used car, either by using a charge card, or by making an arrangement for time payments with the supplying company. The only advantage to saving in advance towards cash payment for such items by making regular monthly deposits to a savings account, as budgeted, is that you get the benefit of the interest, and not the company from whom you are purchasing the item or service. You may not, however, be far enough ahead financially to do this for the first few years.

DOG AND CAT FOOD, AND VETERINARY FEES

This is really a personal issue—if Spot and Puff are really members of the family you can hardly find new homes for them. But if the kids are not really interested in the pets any more, think about it. And make a few phone calls before you take a pet to the vet—there are big price differences.

BUS PASSES

This figure represents two bus passes for ten months of the year, for each of the kids. If the school is within a mile or so, perhaps they could start walking or taking their bikes. Otherwise this is a fixed item—just make sure that they get the student price.

CLOTHES

Reducing your clothing budget can be fun, because you may enjoy the unique things you can find in second-hand shops (now called gently used, second look, and so on). Some of these will still be beyond your budget—there are used clothes and used clothes—but there are certainly bargains. Garage sales can also yield some terrific buys, especially for baby equipment and small children's clothing. Garage sales in the wealthier areas of town can supply you with some nice clothes, too. Watch for sales, and find out where the discount stores are. Some people argue that sewing still saves money, and it probably does if you enjoy doing it. Otherwise, careful shopping will provide the same sorts of things for much less effort. You really have to like knitting to justify the cost of wool these days, but if knitting and sewing are hobbies, keep them up if you can. Hobbies are healthy.

PERSONAL CARE

This includes things like make-up and hairdressers, and may include sanitary supplies if you don't include those in the grocery bill. A friend who has three teenage daughters finds it costs over $40 per month for sanitary supplies. Although some things can be cut from the budget, this isn't one of them. Hairdressers can be eliminated if you grow your hair long and avoid permanents. If you colour your hair, learn to do it yourself, or have a friend do it. And select inexpensive cosmetics from inexpensive shops. The door-to-door, private-sale cosmetics are more expensive than the drugstore variety, and the general effect is indistinguishable to the naked eye.

OFFICE COFFEE FUND

This item is here to remind you that if you work there are related expenses that should be included in your budget. You may choose to drop out of the coffee fund, but you may find that you wish to continue to contribute to the office gift and entertainment fund. You can probably take your lunch, so lunches are not included in this budget at all.

ENTERTAINMENT

This looks like an obvious item to cut, but think carefully before you do it. You can change your style of entertainment, from dinner out with your friends to a pot luck at your place or a picnic. You can take the kids to the free movie at the museum or the art gallery instead of the first-run films, or you can rent a video, if you own a machine. But you will want to do things, both with your friends and with your children, so make sure there is at least enough for dinner at McDonald's a couple of times a month, or whatever the equivalent is for your family. Maybe you can have a special dinner at home—Chinese food, or a pizza. But make sure that those special times still happen.

MEDICAL/DENTAL

It is false economy not to have your own teeth and the children's checked and cleaned twice a year. You are fortunate if your employment includes a dental plan. You can, however, put off having braces put on a child for a couple of years (or in many cases forever) with little or no permanent effect, or installment plans can be negotiated. Braces cost up to $5000 by the time the whole business is done. The most economical thing to do is to keep everyone's teeth as healthy as possible through regular check-ups and healthy diet.

Medical expenses should be covered by your provincial health-care plan. Avoid doctors who extra-bill. If your doctor does this, question the practice directly, and if there is no offer of compromise you can find another doctor, or utilize the community medicentres that are springing up in every neighbourhood. They keep much longer hours, don't extra-bill, and do not require appointments. You can see the same doctor each time if you wish, and thus have a much more accessible family medical service, in many cases.

A major expense in some families can be medications. Your employment may also have a medical plan which reimburses your family prescription drugs. Or your husband's job might include this. If so, discuss including this coverage as part of your maintenance settlement. When you are buying drugs, always request the generic form of the drug ordered. If your drugstore doesn't stock generic drugs, it will be worth quite a bit of money to find one that does.

HOUSEHOLD EXPENSES

This figure, $115, covers household repairs and replacement of broken or worn-out furniture and appliances. To economize you may choose not to replace some things, and to buy from bargain stores when you need to. Here again, the used market is worth considering. Although you don't get a warranty with used appliances, they are much cheaper. Just check them over carefully, and buy from reputable people, if you can. Small appliances can usually be replaced for a fraction of their original cost at garage sales and flea markets, or through bargain-finder's presses or the newspaper. Whatever you do, do not drop this item from your budget—there will be things to buy for the house each month, and some will take more than one month's quota.

GIFTS

These are birthday gifts for your family and friends, and gifts for the children's friends as they are invited to parties. It also includes gifts for grandparents, anniversaries, valentines, Easter eggs, wedding presents, and other assorted gifts that you and your family may wish to give. This item should be scaled down to suit your income. You can make some of the gifts, or you can give intangibles, like dinner at your house, or an overnight sleepover for a child. (See the section under New Traditions for more suggestions of this nature.)

ALLOWANCES

There are various ways to think about children's allowances. Smaller children need little or nothing, but as kids get older, an allowance is a good way for them to learn to manage money. You may even choose to give teenagers a clothing allowance. This is instructive for them, and a relief to you, as long as everyone sticks to it.

SAVINGS

This is the $50 which you deduct from your maintenance payment for income tax. Many women are surprised when they find that they have to pay income tax on alimony and maintenance. Make sure you budget enough, and resist the temptation to touch this money during the year because the tax collectors are not known to be sympathetic and understanding. It will collect a little interest for you if you select the right savings plan.

SAVINGS (CHRISTMAS AND VACATION MONEY)

Twelve hundred dollars isn't very much to pay for Christmas expenses and a summer vacation for three people, unless you like camping. If you don't, you might consider it as an inexpensive way to travel and have a holiday with your children. You can visit friends and relatives without imposing too much if you have your own tents and equipment. This is also where the money for summer camps for the kids comes from. If you feel that this is an item you must reduce in your budget, still plan some kind of holiday treat, even if it is a series of picnics at a nearby beach.

EMERGENCY

This is for the unexpected trip to see a sick relative, or for the window at the school that the kids accidentally broke. If this money isn't spent by the end of a year, you can reallocate it to Christmas, or whatever else you choose. But make sure that you maintain a slush fund there of several hundred dollars—enough for an emergency air fare to your most distant close relative.

MISCELLANEOUS CONCERNS

This budget does not have any provision for saving for the future or for holidays, retirement, or the children's education. Perhaps you should discuss with your lawyer the possibility of having a clause in your divorce agreement about an education fund for the children. Some divorce agreements stipulate that maintenance continues until the children are eighteen and self-supporting. If they choose to continue their education, the father may pay an equivalent amount to the fees and book costs at the local technical school or university.

As time goes by you will want to establish your own savings account. Do this as soon as you can.

This point-by-point discussion should leave you with a number of ideas on how to reduce your spending in order to live within your present income, or to free up some extra money for a small savings account. You will become proficient at budgeting as you go along, and you will make your system fit your needs.

Record-keeping and bill-paying of current expenses aren't the whole story. A budget is a realistic plan for your financial well-being. When you compose it, be fair to yourself, not overly generous and not overly stingy. Try to hit the middle range at first, and then, if there is some elasticity later on, you can reallocate, if you wish. Be sure that you do indeed build in a little allowance for entertainment, even if it is only enough to take the kids to McDonald's for dinner once a month and yourself to one movie. You must have a little fun, and many women forget this, insisting that they can do without. Of course they can, and much entertainment is free. But you and your kids should be able to do at least some of the things that you have done in the past.

There are, of course, many variations on budgeting priorities. The Family Allowance may be desperately needed to meet some immediate expenses. The appendix at the end of this book includes a couple of samples of affidavits of expenditures. Other items that might be added by someone else are:

Medical and/or dental insurance
Life insurance
RRSP
Car replacement fund
Major appliance replacement
Landscaping
Cable television charge
School supplies and books
Clubs and associations
Lessons for children (dancing, music, sports, driving)
Church and charity donations
Haircuts
Day-care and babysitting
Lawyer's fees
Counsellor's fees

It is wise to check a number of lists in order to compile your own, so that you don't miss important items.

STEP FOUR: BANKING

Before this all becomes too confusing, let's turn to the question of how one keeps track of these various funds. Once you have a figure for monthly expenses, and another for periodic and annual expenses, make a visit to your bank. The money for the monthly expenses should be in a current, or chequing, account. The money for periodic and annual expenses should be in a savings account to which you can have access as required, but which pays as high a rate of interest as possible. Find out about the various accounts before you make your decision. You may want several accounts, but make sure you are fully aware of the advantages and disadvantages and, more importantly, the hidden charges for each type of account. Is chequing a free service? What is the charge per cheque? Can you pay bills at the bank, and if so, which ones, and is there a charge?

CASH OR CHARGE?

How you pay your bills is a personal choice. Many people find that by paying by cheque, they have a record of their expenses. However, the information in the chequebook should still be transferred to your record book. This is compatible with the envelope system since you use cheques for rent, utilities, telephone, etc., and cash for food, entertainment, allowances, etc. Some envelopes have cheques in them instead of cash, but the amounts still correspond with your budget. You will still need another method as well, since you cannot pay absolutely everything by cheque, and you will need to keep track of the little bits that trickle out on other things.

Credit cards and charge accounts are risky at any time, but they can make a mess of a new budgeting system. You are well-advised to put them away in a safety deposit box for awhile. Do not cancel them; the problem for a divorced woman of re-establishing credit can be horrendous. The interest rates on credit cards are extremely high, and contrary to popular belief, you don't need them for identification purposes. A driver's licence and social insurance card or other card with your name are equally acceptable.

If you put yourself on a strictly cash basis you are much less tempted to spend money that you don't have. Some people argue that they can continue to use charge cards and keep track of their day-to-day financial status by writing every amount that they charge into their chequebook and deducting it from the balance. This technique doesn't protect you, however, from the awful end-of-the-month outlay to pay off all the charge accounts. However, you must pay it off completely every month if you are going to avoid paying unnecessary interest charges. Some banks have a new service whereby your charges are deducted from your bank account as the slips arrive at the bank, and the bank pays your bill. Breaking the charge-card habit is difficult, but very worthwhile. Instead of charging things, and delaying the miserable moment of ante-ing up, you can pay cash right on the spot.

PLANNING FOR THE FUTURE

SAVINGS

Soon you will be able to start a series of savings programs. When you have a little extra money, put it into a jar for your weekend away or some new clothes, or a new frying-pan. You will appreciate it much more if what you buy is really yours, free and clear, from the start. Furthermore, account day at the end of the month is a lot more fun if you actually have the money to pay everyone, and don't have to juggle and pay interest because of a weak moment and an unnecessary purchase.

INFLATION

When you are planning ahead, you must also remember about inflation. Not only should you build this into your own budget, but you should be sure that your alimony or child-support payments are indexed to the government cost-of-living rate. This becomes a major amount in years of double-digit inflation. Insist on this as a clause in your divorce settlement; many lawyers don't bother with it. Remember, your spouse's income will be tied to the state of the economy—yours should be too. Otherwise you may find yourself trapped as the cost of living rises and your income doesn't, even though your ex-spouse is paying the court-ordered amount faithfully. The cost of returning to court to increase maintenance payments may be high, and you may lose. Try to anticipate these things at the time of the divorce.

BILLS THAT WILL SURPRISE YOU!

Household maintenance is difficult to put a number on, but if you sit and think for awhile, you can remember many of the things that had to be repaired or replaced during the last year. Estimate what each one cost, and put an allocation into the budget.

Clothing expenses, if you have children, vary widely. Little kids don't need as much as school-aged children, and people in warm climates need less than people in cold climates. Take into account the fact that most of your spending may take place at special times of the year—for example, the big August–September back-to-school shop.

Remember, special occasions cost money. Don't forget Christmas and birthdays and Easter and Valentine's Day and Hallowe'en and your kids' friends' birthdays. With a little imagination you can scale these expenses down with home-made presents or other imaginative things like outings and special privileges. But you will still need money. Even Christmas, an annual expense, should be counted into the total budget and divided into monthly allotments, so that it doesn't come as a big surprise; much of the joy goes out of Christmas if you are in financial trouble or if you think that Christmas shopping will definitely put you there.

YOU'RE NOT IN IT ALONE

Budgeting can be a family affair, too. Kids are less likely to nag for extra spending money when they know exactly how much money there is and where it has to go. Not only does this knowledge generate understanding and support, but it is very good training for adulthood. There are various ways to include kids in budgeting. A child can help to address the envelopes the night you pay the bills, or run the calculator when you need to do the arithmetic; or sort and file the receipts. You can figure out with a child how much money you have to spend on supper, on an average, and have the child help plan and shop for a meal that is within the range permitted.

INSURANCE

Often your ex will have life insurance, either purchased, or more often as a part of his employment benefit package. However, he can change the beneficiaries of the policy with the stroke of a pen or a phone-call. To ensure that you and the children are protected in the event of his death, you should see if you can take out a life insurance policy on him.

Make sure that you include standard policies for household insurance for the house and its contents and insurance for your car(s) in your budget. Your jewellery should also have a separate policy if any pieces are too valuable to be covered by your household policy. This separate rider is usually available quite cheaply as an add-on to your household policy. If you are the sole support of your children, you must have an insurance policy to replace your salary in the case of your illness, incapacity, or death. Such arrangements should be balanced by those made by your ex-spouse in his will and insurance plans.

Another suggestion is that a life insurance policy in the amount of the husband's share of the equity of the family home be bought, with the wife as beneficiary. This could be relatively short-term also, in cases where the sale of the family home is deferred until the children have grown up.

RETIREMENT

You must start planning for your old age now, if you haven't already. Although some divorce settlements are now including a partial pension allocation for the wife from the husband's employment pension program, it is still necessary for you to make your own plans for retirement support. This may be a pension plan where you work; or it may be a series of registered retirement savings plans (RRSPs) through your bank or insurance agency; or it may involve gradually purchasing savings bonds; or investing in carefully selected and scrutinized ventures with a maximum of security.

Whatever method you select, do make some consistent arrangement as soon as you can, no matter how little you can afford to put away now. As time goes by your salary will increase and your children become more financially independent. You will be able to put more into your retirement savings. Every five years or so re-evaluate your retirement financial planning with a trusted adviser—a bank manager or other financial counsellor who is as unbiased as possible. Your insurance agent is not a likely adviser, because of the conflict of interest inherent in a salary based on premiums paid by clients. If you do decide to consult insurance sales personnel, see at least two in order to compare. They are selling a product from which they get a commission, so be aware of this reality.

ESTABLISHING A CREDIT RATING

You may not know whether or not you have a good credit rating, or worse, you may think you have one when you don't. If, during your marriage, the banking and other financial affairs were managed through either your husband's or a joint account, if the house and the car are in his name or under joint title, if charge accounts are in his name with you listed as a user, you may not have a credit rating at all, even if you were working and depositing a salary into the joint account. To find out your credit rating ask your bank manager or the loan officer.

It can be difficult for a single woman to establish a credit rating, but persevere, because you will need it. The first step is to approach your bank and get a charge card, either Visa or Mastercard; use it for a few months, but pay it off at the end of each billing period. Secondly, make sure that the title to the car and your house, or your lease, are in your name only, along with your utilities and phone. Finally, as soon as you can afford to, borrow some money from the bank, a thousand or two, and put it into a term deposit. Make your monthly payments regularly, no matter what. By the end of this process you will have established a good credit rating, so that if you ever need or want to borrow money, or if other institutions run a credit check on you, there isn't a problem.

INCOME TAX

One of the most important things to remember is that once you have a legal separation or divorce, you are responsible for paying the income tax on the money you receive, so be sure that you take that into account when you determine the final amount of maintenance or settlement money. (Or, if you are the one who will be paying maintenance, it is in your interest to get a legal separation or divorce, at least from a tax point of view, since you no longer have to pay tax on that portion of your income.) Your lawyers should tell you this, but many women still are absolutely astonished to discover that they have to pay tax on support money, and are often caught in the embarrassing position of not having planned or budgeted for this.

If you are receiving income of any sort from employment, investments, social assistance or maintenance payments, you must file an income-tax return each year. Check with your local income-tax office before you decide that you don't need to file. Many women have found that they owe large amounts in back taxes because they didn't understand the income-tax law, and didn't file because they thought their income was below the taxable minimum.

Another point concerning income tax: if you have never done your own tax return before, this may not be the time to begin. There are lots of companies in every town, such as H & R Block or Sears, which will do your tax return for a very small charge, and they are more likely to know how to do it correctly and to your best advantage than you could on your first try. Often friends offer to do it for you, but unless they are experienced in doing tax returns for people who are divorced, you are still better to go to a professional. When selecting a professional, you are usually wiser to choose one who charges a flat rate, rather than a percentage of your return. For a straightforward tax return, the charge should be below $20. Stay with reputable firms. Avoid discounters; they give you a cash advance on your potential tax refund and then you pay them the actual refund when you receive it, no matter how high it is. The government is trying to make them illegal—they prey on single mothers who need ready cash.

Make sure that you have a big brown envelope in a drawer near where you open your mail. Tuck any relevant slips of paper into this tax envelope as the months go by, so that a month or so before tax time you can grab your envelope and run to the nearest tax office and save yourself many headaches. You may choose to watch the professional prepare your tax return so that you will be able to do it on your own next time.

When you do decide to fill out your own tax return, there are many guide-books as well as the detailed information from the government which accompanies the form itself. (See the pamphlets listed at the end of this chapter.) Most cities operate a special telephone question line for the last month or so before the due date so that you can get help preparing your return while you sit at your desk at home puzzling. The earlier you do this the better, since the phone line is very busy as the deadline approaches. You can also drop in to the Revenue Canada office in your city for information regarding your tax return. Income tax need not be a major problem if you file your salary stubs and receipts for business expenses and if your income-tax payment is one of the annual expenses for which you have budgeted.

The amount of your tax payment can be fairly accurately predicted by either your lawyer or the government tax office. Once you have an idea of what it will be, tuck a monthly allocation into a savings account. It can collect interest for you, so choose the account plan at your bank which is most advantageous. Alternatively, in some cases the government demands installment payments of your tax in advance, in which case you must still plan in advance in order to have the money ready.

HOW MUCH IS IN THE POT?

Try not to worry about your spouse's income for the time being. It is more important to establish your own budget before you do any planning. If you don't know how much your spouse earns, it is easy for your lawyer to find out by requesting last year's income-tax return. Once you have established a realistic budget, your lawyer can put together a reasonable request for financial support. Even before the court settlement, you will have an idea of what you will be likely to receive, and then you can begin to plan your own future.

Will you have to work? Will you be working anyway, and if so, will the combined incomes be enough to meet your needs? If not, how will you achieve an up-grading on your job? Or should you seek another job? Should you consider going to a technical school, college, or university, incurring more debt in the short run but a better salary in the long run?

Must you scale down your standard of living, and if so, what is the most reasonable way to do this? Should you move to a less expensive house, apartment, neighbourhood, city? What other expenses can be reduced? Can you do without a car? Can you reduce your entertainment or clothing budget? Can you change your eating habits? More pastas and legumes and cheese, and no desserts!

Budgeting is a skill, and it is acquired with practice. If you do it successfully, you will have the satisfaction that you can indeed manage within your income, control your spending, and even save a bit, and you can do it on your own.

References

Lappe, Frances Moore, *Diet for a Small Planet*. New York: Ballantine Books, 1977.

Revenue Canada, *Separation and Divorce*, Income Tax Family Series Pamphlet.

_____, *Child Care Expenses*, Income Tax Family Series Pamphlet.

_____, *Child Tax Credit*, Income Tax Family Series Pamphlet.

CHAPTER SIX

Change and Serenity

As you pass out of the first months of sadness and grieving, of anger and invective, you should begin to look for the roles and habits you have accepted in a woman's stereotypical role, and reject those which no longer suit you, which constrain you and slow or prevent your own personal growth. This is the time when you must fully accept responsibility for yourself, for what you are and for what you will become, as well as for what has happened in the past. With this responsibility comes power; power to control your own life. With the power to govern your own life also comes the responsibility to control your own emotions and behaviour. With the power to live more freely comes the responsibility to develop independence. With the power to make decisions about your pattern of living comes the responsibility to develop self-confidence.

If you see yourself as a victim, whether of your husband's values, or of society's view of the stereotypical woman, you must realize that you are a victim only because you yourself permit it. You are permitting another person or society itself to make your choices and decisions for you. You lose by default because you don't exercise your own power. Your mate undoubtedly filled the gap with his own values unwittingly; it is part of the stereotypical role of a husband that he should make all the important decisions. Your pattern of dependence may simply have evolved during the marriage, or may be a carry-over from a strong father during childhood.

In any case, once you recognize that you did indeed relinquish your power for a time, you can begin to see this as a pattern of behaviour and take action to change it. Once you can say, "Oops, here I go again, asking someone else to make up my mind," you are well on the way to independence and a new maturity.

The image of the woman on a pedestal, unchanging, idealized, persists in our minds and in the collective mind of society. The stereotype of the perfect wife and mother is still very strong.

Even when you have managed to escape from the stereotype, many of the attributes of the unrealistic ideal remain evident in your patterns of thought and behaviour. It is almost impossible to drop them entirely after the conditioning of a lifetime. We know some of the attributes we should aspire to, such as selflessness, but we can't agree among ourselves as to how much of the quality is desirable. We don't know, for example, whether absolute selflessness is possible, and if so, is it even desirable? These notions are related to the Protestant tradition, and have been handed down from the centuries past.

Set beside the stereotype of the perfect wife and mother is the idea of the basic, unalterable imperfection of humanity, a product of medieval times. This ideology was used by the upper classes to convince the common folk that they were less worthy than the nobles and monks. The concept of permanent imperfection is contradictory to the concept of improving. Rather than accepting the futility of the human condition, we have come to believe that it is indeed possible to achieve happiness, goodness, and peace during a single lifetime. Late twentieth-century thought encourages independence, growth, and change towards individual freedom.

CHANGING SOCIAL VALUES

Change is an essential part of human nature. Life is really a continuum. Much as we long for a completely fresh start, it cannot be. Rather, we must come to terms with the past in order to exist fully in the present and to enjoy the future. We hang onto the ideals of the past long after they are really useful to society, because we aren't sure how to replace them. Replacement of ideals usually happens over time and after society has accepted the new value in practice anyway. Perhaps the ideals embodied in the myth of the woman on a pedestal are best seen as a monument to an older set of values from the Victorian Hangover and even before. These values have not altogether vanished, but are changing and evolving into the values of today and tomorrow.

Change is a slow process, not a step-by-step procedure. Because many of today's values appear at first to be exactly the same as those of a century ago, it is difficult to detect change. If one looks a little deeper, however, it is obvious that many changes have occurred; for example, although most women still inhabit the roles of wife and mother, nearly 50 per cent of them are now in the work-force. Although men still earn the higher wages than women, many are defending equality in the work-force for women; although most of the housework is still done by women, many men are beginning to see home maintenance as a task to be shared equally. In other words, the superficial stereotypes are still dominant, but there are changes in the making.

CHANGING PERSONAL VALUES

Personality is a complex notion, a set of ideas, stimuli, and behaviours which make us both behave as we do, and make the choices and decisions that we do. It is impossible to change all at once, and in fact, impossible to change some of the basic components of personality at all. But it is certainly possible to alter various reactions to common and frequently occurring situations. With such complexity, it is not surprising that old patterns persist into the present, even if they are no longer useful or relevant. When change is seen as a continuum, the annoying retention or flashbacks of old behaviour patterns becomes easier to accept and to cope with.

It is not surprising to find that you are still competing with a long-gone spouse to be best parent, even though he is now rarely a part of your daily life, and the stimulus for active competition ended long ago. Such hangover competitions are destructive in that they prevent the growth of honesty and self-confidence, and they prevent acceptance of the new situation. Continued competition quickly becomes obvious to the children, too, and prevents them from coming to terms with the two different parents as individuals who are living separate lives. Such competition, rather, encourages comparison of the parents by children, and leads to manipulative behaviour as they learn to play on your sensitivity about being a better parent than your past mate.

During the transitional stages, patterns of dominance and submission may also continue. It is not surprising, for example, that a woman who was submissive throughout her marriage behaves submissively to her boss at her first job, and finds it difficult at first to make decisions on her own. A woman may feel that because she receives alimony or child support payments, she is still obligated to the husband, that she must submit to his decisions and his values, and in extreme cases, to his sexual demands. Alternatively, the man may feel that because he is paying for the support of the wife and kids, he should continue to have the right to drop in whenever he feels like it, to work in the garage or the basement or the garden or otherwise continue to impose his presence and authority. As long as a former couple lets this sort of thing happen, they are perpetuating a stereotypical pattern and preventing their own and each other's growth. Further, they are preventing the children from adjusting to the reality of the separation.

Independence in this case means defining your own personal space, both mental and physical. What decisions are you going to make for yourself, and what decisions are you willing to delegate to someone else? (Note: There is a big difference between delegating and simply accepting the decisions of someone else.) By physical space, we mean that you should now control your own home, and you should decide when and under what circumstances others will enter it. You should not still be subject to unexpected visits to the children or yourself from a mate who lives elsewhere but retains the key and a homing instinct. What in fact happens is that you come to constantly expect such interruptions if the potential exists, and you are prevented from behaving normally or relaxing, because "he" might drop in at any time. Granted this seems extreme, but it is also common. Many women find that it is easier to perpetuate submissive behaviour than it is to take responsibility for their own lives when such action is so foreign to them. They are still very sensitive to the disapproval of an ex-spouse.

Make it clear that advance notice is mandatory. This is hard for many women who were submissive during their marriages, but it is essential to any sense of independence and freedom. You need to know that you are free to run your life and your home without the constant possibility of an unexpected interruption.

FLASHBACKS

Flashbacks are emotional reactions that arise from unresolved issues in the past. They are things that are important enough to your subconscious mind that they keep on recurring, long after the actual situation has ended. Just when you think that things are really going well, that you are making great strides toward becoming the real you, you will notice traces of the old, ingrained patterns that continue to hold you back. Some of these patterns of behaviour are harder to break than others, especially when they fill a deep need.

CARRY-OVER BEHAVIOUR

The worst of it is that even when you have become consciously aware of these bad habits, such as still playing Mom the Rescuer occasionally, there can still be an unconscious trigger somewhere inside you that goes off in unpredictable situations, and there you are, right in the middle again, stage-managing everyone else's life, or playing out other old behaviour patterns which are no longer appropriate to your life.

Habit—and society—decree that Mummy should make everything all right for everyone, sometimes even including the now-distant spouse. The "everything's okay" syndrome is even more dangerous if it is accompanied by the urge to manipulate the actions and behaviour of the others or the circumstances so that things will indeed be all right. The role of rescuer dies hard.

It may take a great deal of effort to let go, to let the children learn on their own, to make their own mistakes and discover their own feelings, their strengths and weaknesses. The point here is that you don't have the right to try to interfere with the behaviour of others, except insofar as you are responsible for teaching children a set of social values and ensuring physical safety. Even children must be encouraged to test these values by making as many of their own decisions as they can. They should be allowed to make mistakes, and to grow gradually but consistently toward independence—the ultimate goal of child-raising. Many parents do not permit their children to test and develop their decision-making abilities. Instead such parents manipulate, interfere, and otherwise influence their children to do "what is best for them."

The children, however, have been cheated of the opportunity of handling the situation independently. They need to realize early on that they are responsible for the consequences of their own actions. Only then will they stop relying on others to make their decisions for them and, worse, blaming others for their own mistakes.

The habit of indirectly controlling the behaviour of others is hard to break. Flashbacks like this will occur, especially in times of stress when you want to protect your children from worry and pain. All you can do, even for your children, is to give them the knowledge of how to behave well, and then you must stand back and let them learn.

OVERREACTION TO FLASHBACKS

There are other kinds of flashbacks, or reactions to a present situation on the basis of outdated behaviour patterns. One of the kids may say something that is unwittingly reminiscent of the critical comments your ex-spouse used to make to you, and suddenly you are over-reacting, based on emotions evoked from the past, and the child is wondering what went wrong. Flashbacks can be triggered by movies, television programs, books, or even conversations. They are usually unexpected, but if you recognize them for what they are, inappropriate reactions carried over from the past, you will find that they are more easily controlled, and they will start to fade.

TWO-O'CLOCK GOBBLIES

As well as unexpected reactions to present stimuli, flashbacks can take the form of the "2 a.m. gobblies" or the "if onlies." During the day you may be suddenly reminded of an uncomfortable event from the past, and you manage to put it out of your mind. When you are in bed alone in the quiet of the dark night these things take on exaggerated importance. Old memories take on strong significance and can cause intense emotional discomfort and of course, loss of sleep.

There are many ways to deal with these night-time disturbances. One is to keep a light but absorbing book by your bed, and when you wake with your mind churning through the past accept that you will be awake for awhile and read. Another way is to practise your relaxation exercises. The 2 a.m. gobblies are a fine incentive to learn some of these techniques, if you haven't already. Or you can get out of bed and write down what you are feeling and thinking, because dealing with such issues on paper often reduces them to manageable proportions. If the subject is recurrent, and the disturbance continually upsetting, you should discuss it with someone else in the light of day. It may be a friend, or a group of friends, or it may be a counsellor. Another suggestion is to get lots of physical exercise during the day so that you are really tired at night.

Issues from the past must be resolved somehow in order for you to move on intact, with your subconscious accompanying the rest of you. Many such issues can be explained away, or figured out and put to rest; some must simply be examined, and accepted as things which cannot be really resolved, but with which you can now live with some understanding and peace of mind.

PLAYBACKS

Learning to deal with such ghosts from the past is a valuable skill. The serenity prayer from Alcoholics Anonymous is especially apt:

"God grant me the serenity to change the things I can, to accept the things I cannot change, and the wisdom to know the difference."

Many of the ghosts are indeed things that cannot be changed, such as playbacks of old fights and arguments with your spouse. These playbacks can become bad thought habits, and should be guarded against. They can be replayed on your mental video machine both day and night. Such thought habits are destructive, in that they prevent relaxation, and they also cause frustration by endlessly repeating in your mind unresolvable issues. Review of such fights is pointless, and the playbacks are always accompanied by a nasty set of emotional reactions such as frustration and anger, also pointless, but habit-forming. These habits are like ruts or grooves; once you get into them, it is easier to stay there than to get out. You must teach yourself not to dwell on such things, to avoid the grooves, and establish a more useful thought pattern.

One way to achieve this is to pair up good and bad subjects. For example, whenever you start to replay the big fight scene of three years ago, consciously turn your thoughts to an especially nice memory, much closer to the present, which includes only people and places from your present life and is not at all connected to the subject of the harmful thought pattern. At first it is hard to stick to the new thought, but you can learn how to by practising. At the first twinge of an old and familiar painful thought pattern, teach your mind to trigger the newer, more pleasant pattern.

Teaching yourself new thought patterns doesn't mean that you shouldn't still confront the causes of the old ones, but only that you should not let them dominate your quiet moments, night or day. One of the most difficult things for most of us to learn during a lifetime, regardless of our circumstances, is the achievement of reliable peace of mind. With dedication and practice, you will be able to ensure regular times when your mind and heart are at rest. This is true even for "worry-warts." It is really a matter of deciding that life is too short to waste on mourning the past, or re-suffering past sorrows and mistakes. Sometimes it takes a jolt such as a divorce or a death, or what Gail Sheehy calls a "passage," to give us the incentive to live our own lives more fully. Certainly such determination is at least half the battle; once you have decided to live in the present rather than bemoaning the past or longing for the future, each day really does become full of soul-feeding events which you just couldn't see before.

The same thing holds true for friends and for new opportunities. While you are grieving and adjusting to the newness of life on your own, you are not receptive to what other people are offering, or even to the new opportunities for work and for friends which surround you. Once you have passed the initial crisis, however, less of your energy is used up by simply getting through the day and you become more aware of the external world, less vulnerable and progressively more alive.

BECOMING RESPONSIBLE

More important than assigning blame is the ability to accept the changed situation. It really doesn't matter very much whose fault it was, and the truth is that it is almost always the fault of both people. More important is acceptance that you are on your own now, and your behaviour should move you toward independence and acceptance of full responsibility for the way things are today. Failure to admit and accept that you were in part responsible for the failure of the relationship, even if only by sins of omission rather than commission, prevents you from growing in maturity. It is unrealistic to place the blame for a relationship between two people on one of them. Behaviour patterns don't happen in a vacuum; they develop in response to a set of consistent circumstances. That is, a dominant husband becomes more dominant because his wife doesn't exert her own opinion or defend her point of view. You just can't have it both ways; if you want someone else to make decisions for you and the other person does just that, then you can hardly blame the other person for playing a dominant or aggressive role within the relationship. By giving someone else the power to dominate you, you are giving that person the power, also, to reject you; you are choosing dependence. By habitually behaving in this way, you undermine your own ability to behave in a confident, independent fashion, either within the marriage or after its demise.

Women are not inherently weak and submissive; rather, they are trained to be so. Such behaviour is a perpetuation of childhood and militates against the achievement of maturity. In *I'm Okay, You're Okay*, Thomas Harris has analyzed the various levels of behaviour of which we are all capable. He pinpoints three levels of behaviour: child, parent, and adult. We all behave at times like children, wanting and accepting leadership from others. This is a characteristic of childhood which persists to some extent in all of us as adults. Many of us also behave like parents, even if we have not become biological parents at all. This sort of behaviour is typified by the rescuer, the person who looks after everything, who makes sure that everything is okay. Such people take responsibility for the behaviour of others and frequently prevent them from taking responsibility for themselves. They are often resented by other adults. To behave like an adult is the primary goal—to accept responsibility for your own behaviour and to treat others as if they, too, are themselves responsible for theirs.

Above all, permit yourself to change. You will not throw off all the undesirable habits that you identify all at once, but you will make progress. Remember to give yourself credit; do not expect it to come from others. After all, you are trying to be someone that you can like, first of all; the rest will follow, when you behave like someone who likes herself. (You can hardly expect others to like you if you don't.) What is right for you this week, or this month, or this year may not be right for you in the future. Learn to be yourself, and at the same time, accept that you will change. And try to conduct that change along pathways that suit you.

If the ideas and expectations embodied in the stereotypes were a major part of your marriage, then the new situation will offer freedom to both you and your ex-spouse, freedom to assess and change patterns which just don't work anymore. He will be free of the responsibility of providing most of the leadership and most or all of the income; he will be free of the expectations of success as a family man. You will be free to experiment with new and more creative ways of parenting, free to work, to redesign your daily life to suit your own needs and desires. Or will you really be free? The answer is, only if you help yourself to become so. It doesn't happen overnight, or in divorce court. But it can and should happen, or each of you will simply repeat the pattern of the past with someone else, and likely fail again.

A NEW DOMESTIC ORDER

Human beings really are creatures of habit; we find routine reassuring. Once we have a sense of order and predictability in our lives, we are able to do more things. We tend to seek order and routine in our lives, and divorce disrupts that sense of order upon which our psychological security is based. Although many routines in the household are indeed upset, it is very healthy and cleansing to get on with the creation of new routines, patterns, and traditions. Although it is quite normal to regret the passage of old routines and traditions, and to resent the circumstances that caused their demise, the sooner you get your home life organized, the better. Once you have established a new household routine, you will have a sense of security that comes not only from this restored predictability, but from the sense that you can indeed organize and run the household competently on your own.

During the first few weeks after the separation, your life is necessarily in a state of disorder. Where the household tasks were split before (regardless of how evenly or unevenly), you are now responsible for everything just when you feel least capable of taking on added responsibilities. Furthermore, you may not know how to do some of the tasks now before you. Of course you can take over the garbage detail, but you may feel strange with a hammer or a screwdriver in your hand. Paying the bills, budgeting, and maintaining the car may be just as strange to a traditional wife as doing the household repairs. The only way to deal with all these things is to run straight at them. Even if you hardly have the energy to get yourself out of bed in the morning, make some reasonable lists, set up a schedule and get at it. You will start to feel better as soon as the physical running of the house is organized because you are proving your competence and independence to yourself, even if you are still in an emotional tizzy. No matter how badly you feel, keep the physical plant running reasonably well.

Although this ordering of your life is very important to your own sanity, it is even more important if you have children. They, too, are upset, and things are even worse if the house is a mess, meals aren't on time, and their clothes are all in the laundry. They need to feel that life will go on, that they can still count on the parent they have to provide a home. Predictability is very important to children. If you can manage to create a sense of order and reliability, children don't feel that everything has stopped. They see that they will still eat and sleep and play in much the same way as before, and they are less frightened.

NEW PARENTING PATTERNS

This may be an ideal time to include children more than before in housekeeping tasks. Although it is a rare person that is enamoured of housework, it can be less unpleasant if it is shared, and if everyone does it for two hours on Saturday morning while the stereo plays some cheery music and you all stop for juice breaks together. It can even be fun, sometimes. Kids need to accept responsibility for the maintenance of the place they live in, and they will eventually have to maintain their own homes.

This is a great time to teach non-sexist skills, too. Get the girls and the boys to help you figure out how to unjam the vacuum. Teach the boys how to do their own mending. Get the girls to change the tires on the car. (By the way, kids will always agree that in a sexist household, boys and men always get the neatest jobs—it is more fun to wash the car than to clean the toilets!) If the kids help with the housework, you may have more energy and time left to spend with them.

Now that you are on your own, you may well find that you are a better parent, as a single parent, than you were during your marriage. You have more control over your time and your energy now, especially if your energy was drained by tension during the last part of your marriage. Now you are free to assess your role as a parent, to clarify your objectives, and then to get to work and achieve them. Here is your big chance to consciously determine what you really want to teach your children, while they are still at home. Are there experiences you have been meaning to share with them? Places you want to go with them? Memories you want to share with them? Then do it now. Time really does fly, especially when you are busy, as most single parents are. Make sure that they aren't all suddenly grown up one day, while you are left behind saying, "If only I had..."

At the same time, don't try to become Supermom. Kids from divorced families say that they don't want Mom to try desperately to please them, to compete with the absent parent, or even to become pals. "Just be yourself," they say. "Let's get on with living, make whatever changes we have to, and then get used to them. We don't want to live in a constant state of indecision and change. We don't even want to play much of a part in what happens—just tell us what we have to do, but don't bore us with the reasons—they only affect you, anyway. We can adjust to nearly anything, as long as we know what to expect."

Kids want and expect leadership from parents. To suddenly be left without leadership or to be expected to provide it themselves simply compounds an already difficult situation. Although kids may not have been aware of the amount of tension in the household during the marriage because it developed gradually, they certainly react when it is removed. Often they visibly relax once one parent has moved out. Even though the idea of separation and divorce is unpleasant and upsetting, they are less tense themselves without necessarily knowing the reason. The myth that you can protect the children from the effects of an unhappy marriage is just that, a myth. Even if the unhappiness is never verbally acknowledged to the kids, they are deeply affected by the tension of their parents. Adults who choose to stay together because of the children may not be doing them much of a favour if they are supplying two tense, irritable parents instead of one relaxed and happy parent.

> *"I am free now to make decisions for my kids, to try to be more consistent. Before, I would make decisions, and then my husband would come home and overrule them. Now the kids are learning finally to trust and respect me."*

NEW TRADITIONS

When a marriage dies, many of the special traditions die with it. Christmas celebrations, birthdays, Thanksgiving, and other family occasions will be different from now on. These are occasions that our society sees as "family times." All the advertising that takes place around Christmas time is directed at the stereotypical family, the family with both a mom and a dad in residence. Because so many good memories and high expectations are usually tied to such occasions, they are times which can prompt renewed sadness and grieving just when you think you have recovered.

Many women feel that anything less than an old-fashioned family Christmas will cheat the children. These women go to great lengths to recreate an atmosphere of the past when the family was a single unit, to the extent of inviting the divorced husband over for Christmas Day. Usually they succeed only in creating a day full of superficiality and tension, because such an attempt can only be false.

As with so many other things now, you have a chance to review your family traditions for special occasions. Better, perhaps, to recognize that things are indeed different, and create some new traditions. What are the customs and activities which you really value, and which ones have you been dying to get rid of for ages? Here is your big chance to make Christmas really enjoyable for everyone, even yourself.

The word "tradition" implies a long custom, but although there are common threads, new traditions are started much more often than we realize. For example, although many families have a Christmas tree year after year, the established times for putting it up and decorating it, even for opening gifts, may vary as family members grow up and their schedules change. Many young families carry on the traditions of their parents until they have their own children.

Then the traditions change, little by little, until the way that the young family celebrates Christmas has become unique to them. With separation or divorce, too, traditions must change; if they don't, the family is not facing and accepting the change.

How do you change such sacred traditions as Christmas? By letting everyone in the family become involved with the planning. Keep some of the special elements, of course, if you want to, but talk over other possible plans. If you don't like cooking, why not order a cooked turkey, or choose something else that is easier. Maybe you can share Christmas with a new group of friends and all contribute to the dinner, or, if you have always had a very social Christmas in the past, you may wish to have a quiet and relaxed day at home with just the children. Lots of women are delighted to do away with the big dinner and prefer to spend the day on the floor playing with all the kids' new games. Other families delight in the festivities of a big dinner with candles and linen and dress-up clothes. What you choose to do is limited only by your imagination, and it can change from one year to the next. Whatever you do, you will likely find that everyone is happier experimenting with new and different ways to celebrate family occasions than they are with the hollowness of a not quite perfect repetition of the past.

LOWER CHRISTMAS BUDGET

After separation and divorce, many families are living on a lower income than previously, because the same income must now provide for two homes. With a big reduction in the financial resources of the family, many women feel that they should make it up to the kids with gifts equally plentiful and expensive as before. This is yet another denial of reality and quite an unnecessary one. If you try to pretend that the scale of income is not diminished you are just increasing the pressure on yourself. You needn't make a big deal of telling the children, but you should definitely make sure that they know what to expect and what the budget will allow. Then, do your best to make the most of what you have. Here again a little imagination will help. Many inexpensive gifts are just as much fun as the newest toy on the market.

ALTERNATIVE GIFTS

You can supplement the tangible gifts with some intangibles. For example, you can give a child a visit to Mom's office; a walk in the country at the time the birds are nesting; a day of hiking together; three free invitations that they can give to friends to come to dinner with the family; and so on. Kids can give parents many special things, like doing the supper dishes for a week, doing the ironing, a sleep-in morning with breakfast in bed, and so on. The family can give friends dinner invitations or the promise of a winter picnic on a bright sunny day, babysitting services, or any other thing that can be similarly shared.

Then there are the presents that cost so little and mean so much: a magnet and some pieces of metal; a magnifying glass and lots of interesting little things to examine; an "anything" notebook filled with blank pages for writing secrets; remnants of lace and ribbons and scraps of material and a needle and thread for making doll clothes; an old broken motor for taking apart; a box of old, brightly coloured clothing with hats and scarves bought from the Salvation Army for making disguises; a length of fabric and a pattern with the promise of sewing lessons; wool and knitting needles and lessons from Mom; a set of inexpensive tools and a joint carpentry project.

These are the sorts of new customs and traditions that make a new kind of Christmas memorable. They help everyone to look to the future, rather than back to the past.

OTHER HIGH DAYS AND HOLIDAYS

There are often elements in the old patterns that kids would just as soon do without. For example, one family who always had a big roast for Sunday dinner stopped this pattern abruptly after the separation. One of the kids asked Mom on Saturday if they were still going to have one of those "round meats" every Sunday. Once she figured out that "round meats" were roasts, and all the formality that relates to such a dinner, they switched to spaghetti for awhile. They still have round meat now and again, sometimes even on Sunday, but it is no longer a tradition, and Sundays are more relaxing for everyone.

One of the more difficult holidays to endure for some people is New Year's Eve. For many people, this has always been an adult celebration, so it is difficult to find a substitute. After years of New Year's Eve parties, one woman chose to spend her first New Year's alone with a bottle of champagne and a steak and two huge picture books of Michelangelo's sculptures borrowed from the library for the occasion. It is still one of her best memories, many years and many New Year's Eves later.

If you have children, you may create a special celebration with them, or you may join together with several families. Rather than the awkward smooching at midnight, you may choose to adopt another custom, such as the Spanish custom of eating grapes, one for each chime of the midnight bells. If you manage to eat all twelve before the last chime, you will have good luck throughout the following year. Children like that sort of tradition. In fact, many adults are relieved to be free from the New Year's Eve social event and prefer to spend the evening quietly with family or friends or entirely alone.

Regardless of which traditions from the past you choose to retain, and which new traditions you start to enjoy, family holidays will still carry an emotional link to the past. This is true even if past Christmases were full of anger and tension. Traditional holidays go all the way back to our childhood, and each one is linked with the ones that have gone before. You cannot erase the past from your mind, and you should not aspire to do so. With time, however, you can add rich and happy memories to the strings of Christmases, Thanksgivings, and birthdays within your family's experiences.

NEW FRIENDS

Making friends as a single person again is both a frightening and a rewarding experience. It can be frightening because many women only made friends within their marriage as part of a couple. Often the friends were originally attracted to the husband because of his business, and the friendships between the wives developed secondarily. Friendship patterns change with separation and divorce as some of the old couple friends fade away, either because they choose to remain friends with your husband, or more often because they are uncomfortable with the idea of your separation. Also, you may choose yourself to leave some of the friends associated with the marriage behind as you assess your new life and your interests. Married women have some definite sources for friendships, such as their husbands' business associates, parents of children's friends, and neighbours. Single parents still have some of the same sources, but may also seek other single parents as friends. Although many of the same problems and joys of parenting exist for both married and single parents, it is nice to have someone in the same situation with whom to discuss the unique problems of single-parenting. Single mothers who return to the work force find that they have very little time for friends at all, and the friendships they have may centre around their job. Most jobs and most neighbourhoods now have a supply of single parents who can be fairly easily found. Most communities have single-parent associations, and all aspects of parenting are discussed at their regular meetings. Such associations are a good source of both friends and information.

It is time for you to reach out. Once you behave as if you are receptive to new friends, they will indeed appear. You must, however, find them yourself. Once you get over the initial hurt of separation you can begin to look outwards toward your community again. There are many people just as lonely as you are for a variety of reasons. Among these people are those with whom you have an interest in common. There really isn't any reason for you to sit at home feeling sorry for yourself because no one has called to invite you out. Do the calling yourself.

In every community there are some older people who are alone a lot, and who would appreciate your friendship. You may choose to buy a set of concert tickets together with such a friend and by doing something you will both enjoy, enrich both your lives. This may also be the time when you reach back into the past to friends whom you neglected during your marriage. Or you may choose to re-establish contact with friends whom your husband didn't like. Re-establishing contact is always risky because you may find that you have grown in opposite directions over the years, but you may also find someone who has matured into a valued and trusted friend.

Although many women feel abandoned once they have separated from their husbands, friends may actually be waiting for a sign that you are ready to re-emerge into society. Even though no one is calling you, there are many opportunities, both old and new, for friendship, once you are open to it again. You must simply force yourself to take advantage of a few of the opportunities, and then the rest will follow. Loneliness is usually self-imposed.

CHANGING NAMES

There are several options open to you when you end a marriage. You can return to your maiden name if you have been using a married name, or you can retain the name from your marriage. You must, however, register any change with the Bureau of Vital Statistics (federal government) and make sure that all your friends, relatives, and business connections are notified of the name change. The process costs about $25 and you will receive a change-of-name certificate which you must show when you need that sort of identification. It is a headache, but make sure that the house, the car, the insurance, your driver's licence, mortgage, paycheque, charge accounts, and utility accounts are all changed to your current name. In some cases a phone-call will do; in other cases, you will have to send a letter and a copy of the certificate. Check your list against the items in your budget book, and don't forget about your income tax, bank account, and family allowance, if you receive one.

Now then, which name should you choose? It is entirely up to you, but there are a few things to be considered. Changing your name is a big project, and you will undoubtedly miss notifying many people. People who want to contact you as they are passing through town will find it impossible, or at least more difficult. Your friends and business associates will take awhile to adjust to your new name. However, it is very important to some women to take this step in order to diminish the shadow of an unpleasant past, or to sever symbolically the dependency implied by a husband's surname. A less dramatic way of altering your own sense of identity is to begin using Ms with your married surname. This form of address, which no longer indicates whether or not you are married, is becoming very common.

Naming practices vary from one place to another. In North American society, women take their father's surname at birth and later the surname of a husband. In many other societies, children retain the names of both their father and their mother, in various patterns. For example, a Spanish woman who is called Ana Maria Garcia Martinez can be addressed in many ways, each equally acceptable. She can be called Doña Ana, Doña Ana Garcia (the last being her mother's name) or Señora Martinez (the last being her husband's name).

In North America, many women are now choosing to retain their maiden names after marriage, and to give their children both names, hyphenated. The question of which one comes first can usually be decided by the way the combination of names sounds best. If and when you choose to remarry, you may hyphenate your present name and your new spouse's name. By retaining your present name as the first word you don't lose your place in the telephone directory, and friends can still find you.

Although eyebrows may still be raised when a woman has a different name than her spouse, many women who had established careers before marriage prefer to retain their maiden names. Many women who have a different name than their partners find that they are treated with a little more individuality than are people who are known as "Mrs.," and that the inconvenience of frequent explanations is worth it.

"Ms" is now seen as a form of address quite regularly. However, we still don't really have the terminology to cover all situations in divorce and marriage. The most blatant example is the word "divorcee," which refers to a divorced woman. There is no equivalent word for a divorced man. We are beginning to replace the term "broken home" with the awkward "single-parent family." The latter doesn't have the negative connotations of the former, but it is still cumbersome.

The twentieth century has produced many new variations on the theme of the family, and many of those new versions are proving to be just as solid and stable as the old version which they are replacing. Perhaps the terminology will appear from the pen of a sensitive linguist, but more likely, we will become used to the jargon and accept that, just like orange juice, we are "blended" or "reconstituted" families.

CHILDREN'S NAMES

If you have children, your decision may be influenced by the wish to have the same name as they have. In this case, you either all retain the name of your ex-spouse, or everyone changes to your maiden name. Legally you cannot change the names of any children under the age of eighteen without their father's consent; and fathers never consent, because it appears like a negation of their fatherhood. Names are especially important to men because of the hangover from the outdated tradition of property and titles passing to the first-born son, and family lines being traced only through the father's side. Names are less important in this sense to women, who in North America always have the name of a man, either their father or husband. Until recently, women haven't had the same sense of ownership about their names.

If you or the children really want to change your surname, you can change yours legally, and simply start to use it as the children's last name as well. There is nothing illegal about using another name, as long as you use it consistently. When the child turns eighteen the process described previously for changing the name legally as well can be followed, with no parental approval necessary.

Kids find a name change a very big adjustment because they are asked to explain it endlessly. Usually, this is a time when they are making so many other major adjustments. Think twice before you ask them to change their identity, too.

NEW IDENTITY

For many women one of the most difficult aspects about divorce is the need to establish an independent identity. Many women have come to identify themselves so strongly as the wife of Mr. X that the loss of this identity is a serious blow. The role of wife is secure in our society. Although we think of it as a low-status position in terms of societal recognition, there is a definite sense of place accorded to a wife and an attendant set of privileges. In other words, the role of wife *is* an identity, and for many women it becomes their chief identity for many years. When this role is suddenly cancelled, the loss of identity is a serious issue which must be confronted. You no longer feel right describing yourself to yourself or others as Mrs. X, Mr. X's wife. Now you are just you. Unless, of course, you fall into the other trap and let yourself be Y's mother.

For women who have not worked outside the home, there may be a considerable loss of prestige in the community following separation and divorce. Having been part of the "couples" group in the neighbourhood, you suddenly have no reference group. The people that knew you as half of a couple are uncomfortable dealing with you alone and may avoid you for awhile. Suddenly, all the prestige and status built into the role of wife is gone, and you are really on your own. No more reflected glory, no more safety and security and protection; now the responsibility is all yours. If you choose to stay on in the same community as you occupied during your marriage, you may indeed sense this loss of prestige, and it may add to your deepening sense of loss. Our community structure is still based on the two-parent family, and it will take awhile for this to change. Meanwhile, you must be patient, because memories are very short, and soon you will be accepted as yourself and not either as a wife or a divorcee. But this exalted state will only be achieved by hard work on your part. To be accepted in a community you must be active in it or at least visible. Get out and attend various events so that you can put as many as possible uncomfortable debuts as a single person behind you quickly.

People will soon get used to your new status as a single person. Some people, in fact, may adjust too quickly. Lots of women are hurt by the sudden sexual advances that some of the men in the neighbourhood or at the office will make once they hear you are "on the loose." This, too, is just a stage that will quickly pass, unless you choose to prolong it. Community activities will go a long way toward helping you to establish your new identity as a single person, both in the minds of the people in the community and in your own mind. The more things you do successfully by yourself, the more confidence you gain. Each meeting or concert or errand that you attend or carry out successfully on your own is a feather in your cap and will give you the courage to keep on trying until you are sure of your own identity.

Often this new identity is just an older, more mature version of the person you remember being in the years before your marriage. It is pleasant when you discover that lots of the components of you, the independent you, are just beneath the surface of the personality of the married you.

BACK TO WORK

Closely related to the question of built-in prestige of the role of wife is the question of job status. For a woman who has successfully run a home for years, who has an established place in the community, getting a job is often a terrible comedown. From being in charge of a home and a family, you are suddenly an employee; from having your own empire at home, you are suddenly just one of the people in the office, one of the employees in the company. Most women who return to the work force after raising a family, or after several years away, never regain the job level that they had achieved before they left the workplace for marriage. There are many reasons for this, such as age, lack of recent work experience, and lowered self-esteem, which can cause lowered work productivity. Whatever the reasons, there is a message in this observation for women. Returning to the work force can indeed be successfully achieved, but it is seldom easy.

It is even more difficult if you must do your job-hunting while you are still recovering from the big blow to your self-confidence that often results from separation and divorce. The first thing you have to do, in any case, is to decide what sort of job you are looking for. You may have some training from earlier years which will provide a field to which you can return, or you may be starting from scratch.

WHERE TO START

If you are starting from scratch, you must assess your own skills fairly and realistically. Most women tend to underrate their own abilities, or else they unrealistically want to start somewhere near the top of the ladder because that's where their contemporaries, who have been working all along, happen to be. Both extremes must be avoided. To be realistic, you need some paper, a pencil, and an hour or so. First, write down all of your educational achievements. This includes high school, university, and any extra courses in any field. Often, during the years at home there have been non-credit courses in crafts, in child care, in exercise, or in other special interests. Think carefully, and write them all down. Next, write down all the clubs, organizations, and associations you have belonged to over the years: all of them, whether you were a Brownie leader, a hockey mom, a member of the community league executive, a hospital volunteer, or anything else. Put dates next to these; you need the year and an estimate of the length of your involvement and the positions you held—president, secretary, committee chair, fundraiser, and so on. Next, prepare a similar list of any paid employment you have ever held.

Now, on another sheet of paper, write a list of the kind of jobs you think you would like to have, and another list of the ones you think you would be qualified for, if these are markedly different. Put this aside, and return to the record of things you have already done. You may find a pattern there that reflects your real interests and skills, and this pattern may not coincide with what you think you want to do. Look carefully at the lists of clubs and courses. Have you gained some special leadership skills, some specialized knowledge? Have you become so skilled in a handicraft that you could teach it? Are there any possibilities in these lists that could be turned into paying jobs? So often women don't count their community and extracurricular experiences when they are considering returning to the job market, but it is through such activities that women do become community leaders. Such women are much better prepared to make the jump back into the job market than they think they are.

If you weren't a secretary, odds are that you were a nurse or a teacher. You may wish to requalify in your field. Check into the requirements. Sometimes there are grants available to cover such refresher courses; if not, you may have to take another job until you can afford the time and money to return to your profession. Or, you may decide that it is time to develop another skill or interest, and you will start on something else entirely.

Having made all these lists, you are now ready to let them simmer in your mind for a little while and track down a few possibilities. If any of your past activities has potential, make a few phone-calls and find out. Can you teach an exercise class? Will the community league sponsor you to teach art classes to senior citizens? Can you get a job at the day-care centre? There is no need to make a final decision yet. You are just gathering information. You must also have several cups of coffee over the job section of the daily newspaper with a red pen in your hand marking both the jobs that you think you could do and the salaries they pay. But remember, this can be depressing!

After a few days of this, with a bit more realistic information, you can match the jobs that you know of which you think you could do with your minimum salary requirement. (This is derived from your budget.) You determine your minimum salary requirement by subtracting the total amount of money that comes into your hands from all sources each month from the total amount of your bare bones budget. That is what you must earn, if possible, and anything above and beyond that is gravy.

The next thing you do is make a list of all the job possibilities you have uncovered from all sources which meet your minimum salary requirement. Your list should include the title of the position, the name, address, and phone number of the company, and the name of the contact person or personnel director, if you have it.

The next step is writing a résumé, but before we turn to that, we must consider what to do if the last section didn't suit you, and you have not come out with a nice list of potential jobs. If you do not have much in the way of education, clubs, and courses to write down, and you haven't held a job for more years than you want to think about, and you really haven't the faintest idea what sort of job you could take, then you need a little more help. Career counselling is available in all cities. Most universities have career counselling offices, and usually you needn't be a student or even a potential student to utilize their services. You can also call the federal employment offices who will know where such services exist if they don't indeed provide them. Women's Centres often have career counselling and courses on returning to work. Many community organizations offer similar courses from time to time. If you aren't sure where you are going to fit, career counselling may help.

If you are lucky enough to be in a community that offers a course for women returning to work, grab it. These courses may be concentrated in a weekend seminar, or they may be one night a week for a month or two. They cover many useful subjects such as applying for a job, interview techniques, résumé writing, wardrobe choice, and job etiquette. Some include assertiveness training and communication skills. These courses really help you to regain your confidence, because they provide very tangible advice. They teach survival skills for a woman in the work force, and they provide both professional advisers and a source of other women who are at about the same stage as you are. The organizations which sponsor these courses usually provide babysitting service for the times of the classes and often can help you to find day-care service for when you do start back to work. Such courses are often free, or very inexpensive. If you can't afford to take one but want to, ask if there are any grants or scholarships for people like yourself who need the course but can't afford it. Such courses are sometimes connected to career counselling services, too.

Even with all this information, some women still can't make a decision and get started. Your first job, however, doesn't need to be exactly right for you. It will be a place to start and will provide experience and contacts which will help you to make other job selections in the future.

What is important now is to begin somewhere. One woman who was in her mid-thirties when her marriage ended had dreams of becoming a counsellor for disturbed children. With no experience and an incomplete high school education, no money and four kids, this wasn't possible. She took what she called a "non-think job" in a chicken-packing plant for the first two years. She wanted a job that paid the bills, but left her time and energy at the end of the day to spend with her kids. Once the family had settled into a routine again, and the separation was a thing of the past, she was able to return to her dream of counselling. She began doing volunteer work first, to meet some of the people working in this field in her city, and then began to take in foster children. Later on she returned to school part-time until she completed the training she needed. She knew that she didn't have to make her final career choice at the beginning when she was still not sure what the future would hold. She took things step by step, and she still thinks that she owes much of her regained self-confidence to the experience and friendships from the chicken-processing factory.

This is a good way for many women to begin. Regardless of the type of job you take at first, you will gain experience, and you will earn the money that will give you the confidence you need to go on to something else. Being paid real money, often for the first time ever, is a source of deep satisfaction for most women, regardless of the type of job they have.

WRITING A RÉSUMÉ

When you apply for a job, you usually are requested to submit a résumé or a summary of your educational and job experience. There are many books available on the subject, and there are professional firms that will prepare your résumé for you. Most people can do it for themselves.

Your résumé will influence the attitude of the person who reads it, who may interview you and who may eventually hire you. If you set yourself up as a woman, mother of three children, with no previous job experience, who is desperately in need of a job at the age of thirty-four, you will be treated as such. You will have lost control of your job interview before you even arrive. Try to sort out what needs to be said and what doesn't. It is no longer necessary to state your age, sex, religion, race, or marital status on a job application form, although many forms still ask for this information. Most women feel that their marital status and whether or not they have children are facts which are not relevant to a prospective employer. Since your sex is not necessarily obvious until you are called for an interview, many women prefer to leave that information out, too. Similarly, your age is reasonably obvious at the time of the interview, and if you are called for an interview, your age is less likely to be held against you anyway. Try not to make an issue of this sort of thing; be as tactful as you can.

When a woman is returning to the work force after an absence of several years, things like age, children, and the fact that she is divorcing her husband, are very high in her consciousness. It is hard for such a woman to believe that these things are not important to a prospective employer. Many women feel that they should apologize for their lack of experience; this is further exaggerated by the low sense of self-esteem which often follows the end of a marriage. Whatever your secret fears about your ability, they should remain secrets, at least during the job interview. Don't put yourself in the position of asking the interviewer to employ you as a favour, despite your shortcomings. This is a good way to talk yourself out of a job. Instead, think carefully about the sort of person you would likely hire for the position, then present yourself calmly and confidently in the best light you can, even if your tummy is really filled with butterflies.

Things like age, divorce, dependants, and experience, or lack thereof, are very important items to you, but they should not influence the hiring procedure. Some interviewers have worked out their biases about working with women, with working mothers, and so on, but many have not, so it is better not to jeopardize your chances. Although current human rights legislation prohibits discrimination on the basis of age or sex, many employers are still influenced by the old stereotypes that women are unreliable; they get pregnant, or married, or have to stay home with sick children, or get sick more often than men. The average length of time people of either sex stay in a job these days is between two and three years, so the stereotype doesn't hold much water. Either both men and women are unreliable or women are equally as reliable as men. In fact they are often more so, because they need the job so badly.

Discrimination is a matter of attitude and not of legislation. Hiring an employee remains, in the final analysis, a personal decision on the part of the person who is doing the hiring. Most hiring is still done by men, and many men (and women) are still not comfortable working with women, particularly in the more senior positions. It is only common sense to present yourself in the most objective, businesslike fashion possible. Your experience as wife and mother is not considered relevant, and is often held against you. You want the prospective employer to see you as a capable person who will do the job well and whose maturity underlines her ability to prevent her personal life from unduly interfering with her job.

The first step towards creating this impression is a résumé, also called a "curriculum vitae." Two examples are included in this chapter. If you pay someone else to write it for you, make sure that the attitude of this person is also fair and non-sexist, especially if it is a man. Try to select someone who has a lot of experience in preparing résumés for women and, if possible, find out from other women just how helpful the résumé was in getting them the first interview and ultimately, the job.

A well-written résumé should get you to an interview. You may wish to rearrange your résumé when applying for various jobs, highlighting the skills and experience most relevant for each. If you happen to have a lot of work experience, education, and so on, you should prepare a one-page summary résumé and append the rest. The attention of the prospective reader must be caught on page 1, not page 6, which may never be read, anyway.

If you are applying for a job by mail, your résumé should be accompanied by a one-page covering letter. The letter complements the résumé by focusing on just one or two highlights in your career which, in your opinion, make you an especially desirable candidate for the job. Make sure that your letter opens with a statement of which position you are seeking; the company may be trying to fill many positions at the same time.

If you have done your list-making faithfully and accurately, you already have the raw material for your résumé. We are including a sample résumé here, but format is really a matter of choice. In any case, your name, address, and phone number should be at the top of the front page, where it can be easily found when the company wants to phone for an interview. You'd be surprised how many good candidates have never heard about a job for which they applied, because they simply forgot to include their address and phone number.

The next section may be either your education or your job history. This is up to you, and it depends both on which is most impressive, and which is most relevant to the job for which you are applying. In either case, begin with the more recent item, and work backwards; your highest level of education or your most recent job is of more interest to a prospective employer than your high-school career. Be sure to include both credit and non-credit courses and seminars in your education section. Even apparently irrelevant classes and workshops may be important because they imply an interest in learning. After you have listed the work and education sections, highlight your volunteer and community activities, with the most relevant at the top again. Make sure that you include the positions you held, as well as the organization; being president of the minor hockey parents' association is a responsible position which provides valuable leadership experience.

For most people, writing a résumé is difficult at first. The reason is that it is hard to assess yourself objectively, and it is against a woman's upbringing in humility and self-effacement to consciously go about presenting herself in the best possible light. If you are uncomfortable with this, give it a try, anyway. If you are unhappy with the results, get a friend with some work experience, preferably someone who has done some interviewing and hiring, to have a look at it. Such friends may have useful suggestions.

Résumé

Theresa M. Fisher
c/o General Delivery
Simmonds, Alberta
T0C 7P0

Phone: 737-4892

Education

In 1972, I completed an intermediate typing course at Northern Alberta Institute of Technology.

    Typing speed: 55 words/min.
    Typing theory: 90%

I took a matriculation program in high school and graduated with a high school diploma from Ardrossan High School in June, 1969.

Employment

August 16, 1985, to August 30, 1985:

> Pe Ben Industries Company Ltd.
> 17th Street & 45th Avenue
> Edmonton, Alberta
> T6C 4G3
>
> Employed for a short term as a Receptionist-Switchboard Operator.

June 14, 1985, to July 19, 1985:

> Smith & Company
> Barristers & Solicitors
> 274 Parkville Ave.
> 8170-50 Street
> Edmonton, Alberta
> T6B 9E1
>
> Employed part-time as a Receptionist/Typist, aiding the legal secretary with her work.

April 22, 1985, to June 14, 1985:

> Simmonds Historical Society
> General Delivery
> Simmonds, Alberta
> T0C 7P0
>
> Position: Researcher Clerk
>
> Duties: To help set up a museum, archives, and historical display in the new Simmonds Community Hall. This was a Canada Manpower Project.

October, 1976, to March, 1977:

> Physical Plant Department
> General Services Building
> University of Alberta
>
> Position: Receptionist/Clerk Typist II
>
> Duties: This position entailed: being a receptionist—dealing with the public, typing of correspondence for four area supervisors, use of rotary phone and paging systems, filing and other general office duties. My typing speed at that time was 60 words a minute.

February, 1973, to October, 1976:

> Vehicle Pool Division
> Physical Plant Department
> University of Alberta
>
> Position: Clerk Typist II
>
> Duties: This position entailed: typing of correspondence for the Manager, typing quotations for vehicle purchases, processing of vehicle maintenance work orders, handling a small petty cash, helping with the yearly inventory, filing, and other general office duties.

July, 1969, to February, 1973:

> Accounts Payable Department
> University of Alberta
>
> Position: File Clerk
>
> Duties: Filing

Office Equipment

Over the years I have gained experience in the use of the following office equipment: postage machine, calculator, dictaphone, IBM Selectric typewriter, Canon 350 electronic typewriter, Xerox, Canon and 3M photocopiers, telex (tape-type) and 3M computerized telex, rotary phone and paging systems, 37 line SG1 (PABX) switchboard, two-way radio system and some use of the IBM-PC computer (Multi-Mate) system.

Volunteer Work

Since 1978, I have been actively involved in the organization and operation of the Simmonds Winter Indoor Playground. Briefly, this is a miniature playground operating out of a community centre, which allows mothers with children 5 years and under a place for these children to socialize and test their motor skills, during the cold winter months, when play is not possible out of doors. It also offers mothers a place to have coffee and get acquainted with their neighbors.

References

Business:
Elizabeth Smith, L.L.B. —Smith and Jones
 Barristers & Solicitors
 1584 Stoney Plain Road
 Edmonton, Alberta
 Phone: 438-2211

Nancy Davies —Ethical Consultants
 3641-47a Street
 Edmonton, Alberta
 T6F 4X2
 Phone: 438-1804

Tim Peters —Administrative Manager
 Physical Plant Department
 420-J General Services Bldg.
 Univ. of Alberta, T6G 2H1
 Phone: 432-4261

Personal:
May Potter —Co-ordinator—Family Living Skills, Simmonds
 Family and Community Services
 205 Horseshoe Avenue
 Simmonds, Alberta
 T8H 1C8
 Phone: 465-9908

The following résumé was prepared by a woman in her early forties who has returned to university and is seeking a job while she is studying. She hopes that the job she gets this summer will prove to be a source of permanent employment when she completes her studies next spring.

February 20, 1986

Marilyn P. Saunders
230 Smith Ridge
Appledale, Alberta
T0B 1K0

Telephone: (403) 443-2612
Social Insurance Number: 256 587 990

Education

1985–1986:	Full-time student in the Faculty of Library Science (University of Alberta)
1958–1962:	Faculty of Education (University of Alberta) majoring in English. (B. Ed., 1962)

Professional Experience

1985 (Feb. 1 to Aug. 1):	Legal Secretary at the law firm of Smith & Co., Edmonton, AB. Was offered the position of secretary/receptionist in a two-lawyer office for a period of six months. Responsible for general secretarial duties, reorganizing files, and assisting with a move to new premises.
1983–1985:	Chair, Member Relations Committee, Appledale Co-operative Association Ltd.
1978–1985:	Director, Briarpatch Farm Ltd., Ardrossan, AB
1977–1982:	Newsletter Editor, Alberta Association of Commercial Rabbit Producers
1981:	Contract with Alberta Agriculture to write a monograph: *Raising Meat Rabbits in Alberta*—an Alberta Agriculture (1983) publication. (Currently being reissued by Agriculture Canada)

1978:	Contract with Alberta College, Edmonton, to produce 75th Anniversary Homecoming Celebration. Responsible for planning and executing all celebrations, advertising, and public relations as well as locating the alumni and co-ordinating their activities pertinent to the event.
1964–1968:	English Instructor, Alberta College (Department Head: 1967–1968)
1962–1964:	High School Teacher, County of Camrose

Community Service

1983–1985:	Member of the Board of Directors of the Appledale Band Parents' Association
1979–1985:	4H Club Leader
1980–1981:	Represented Northern Alberta Co-operatives on the Women's Participation Committee in the Co-operative System (Saskatoon)
1980–1981:	Executive Secretary, Strathcona County Information and Volunteer Referral Centre
1976–1978:	Secretary-Treasurer, Poplar District, Girl Guides of Canada
1974–1976:	Appledale School Advisory Committee, Early Childhood Education (President 1975–1976)

Interests and Activities

Travel:	1965: Spent 9 weeks in the Yukon, Alaska, and northern British Columbia.
	1966–1967: During a 6-month leave of absence from Alberta College, travelled throughout Great Britain and western Europe.
Sports:	Mountain hiking, cross-country skiing, swimming.

Other: Reading, knitting, doing word puzzles.

Familiarity with the use of the IBM-PC microcomputer, especially with the Multimate software program for word-processing.

The first time you see a résumé of your own experience, it can be quite a shock. Many women have done much more than they give themselves credit for, and are surprised at how impressive their résumé actually looks. A résumé is really just a carefully organized list; your covering letter of application completes the package.

Once you have received a phone-call or letter arranging for an interview, don't panic. If you can, select a time that is convenient to you, so that you won't be too rushed and rattled when you arrive for the interview. Select your clothing well ahead. It is more important that it is comfortable and suitable than it is that it's fashionable. It is risky to wear a new outfit that you aren't sure of; better to wear a dress or a suit that you know looks good on you and that is comfortable to wear. Your clothing shouldn't be flashy; rather, it should be understated and businesslike, suitable for the job for which you are applying.

THE JOB INTERVIEW

Take a couple of extra copies of your résumé and the covering letter along with you to the interview, even if you have already sent them in with the job application form. Often the original got lost in the company files, and the interviewer doesn't have it. If you can supply another copy, you save time, both for the interviewer and yourself. You will also save yourself the trouble of having to recount your history from memory when you are already a bit nervous. This way you may not forget the most relevant thing you have done until you are on your way home.

During the interview, try not to babble. Many people cover their nervousness by talking more than usual. They feel obliged to fill all the silences with words. Although this is a very useful technique at cocktail parties, try to avoid doing this at a job interview. Instead, respond as briefly, but as completely, as you can to the questions the interviewer asks. Don't let yourself ramble too much with extra information unless it is really something you think will make a difference. It is a good idea to practise a few things at home first. Make sure that you have rehearsed a response to questions that you find unfair. For example, if you are asked about your marital status, you should be able to calmly and firmly reply, "I don't think that is relevant." Similarly, you should have rehearsed a response to a question like, "Tell me about yourself," which does not mean what it seems to. You will need a reply that describes one or two bits of experience in your past which are related to your interest in the job. Another typical question is, "Why do you want to work for this company?" Do not talk about the nice people that you think work there; instead, explain why you believe that this particular job will help to further your career. These questions are often called "icebreakers," and they are enough to freeze up your mind for the whole interview if you are not careful. Keep your replies brief and calm. When you come to the end, stop. This is obvious, but many interviewers prolong the silence to see if you will add anything further. Do not succumb to the feeling that you must fill every silence.

Don't attempt to control the interview; make sure that you are in control of your part, but do not try to direct all the conversation. If you appear too aggressive, you may not get the job. The interviewer must feel at the end of the interview that you are someone with whom he or she would like to work; there should be a relaxed and professional relationship between you by the end of the session.

It is up to the interviewer to extract the necessary information from you; however, some people are more skilled than others at doing this. If, towards the end of the interview, you really feel that an important piece of information has been missed, supply it. But remember, the decision to hire you will be based on many things: your résumé, your interview ability, your past experience, the personal reaction of the interviewer to you, and your standing in relation to the other applicants. Some of these factors you can control; some you cannot. You will seldom get the first job for which you apply, so you will likely have several opportunities to practise your interview skills. With a bit of experience in interviews, your confidence will increase.

There are some big hurdles to be overcome by women who return to the work force after a long absence. Your co-workers will not likely remember your inexperience for very long, and soon you will find that you are expected to know as much as someone who has been employed for the fifteen years that you were working at home with the kids. Frightening though this may be, you will probably learn quickly, and soon the gap will not be very wide, as you become familiar with your job and the company. Meanwhile, you will learn how to say, "I'm sorry I don't know how to do that yet, but I will find out." Older women find it easier than younger people to admit that they don't have all the answers.

In many offices and factories, you may find that you will be among the older employees, but not necessarily among the most senior. It is difficult to adjust to being supervised by someone much younger than yourself. It is also difficult to compete for jobs or promotions with people who are much younger than you. After awhile, age will not seem so important. Once you have managed to get back into the job market, you discover that people are usually more interested in ability and experience than in age.

On the positive side, many women find that their age works to their advantage because other employees assume that the years were indeed filled with relevant experience and treat them with more respect than their younger colleagues. This attitude reflects our childhood teaching to look up to an older person—and makes age an advantage to some of us.

The job of wife and mother teaches many skills that are directly applicable to most jobs. You have learned to plan ahead so that the house is equipped with all the necessary supplies. You have learned to plan for long-term maintenance of your home and to work within a budget. Long-range planning and budgeting are important elements of the business world. You may also have picked up some accounting skills.

You haven't really forgotten how to learn—you have had to learn about a whole new set of problems for all the various developmental levels that your kids have passed through. You have learned flexibility—you can adjust to the lightning changes in the moods of a teenager! You have also learned that everyone, including you, makes mistakes, and that they are usually correctable. You really have been gaining a lot of relevant experience at home. You have organizational skills that will help you in your job. You have a lot of experience with planning and compromising; with interpersonal communication; with co-ordination of various people and activities; with supervision; and even with failure. All these things add up to a level of maturity and wisdom which will go a long way towards turning you very quickly into a real asset to any company. Most important, you probably have a highly developed level of common sense and possibly even a sense of humour.

GUILT

One of the myths that were discussed earlier in the book is the myth that a woman's place is in the home. We are now living in a society where well over fifty per cent of married women work outside the home and still contribute adequately to their families.

The myth, however, still influences our behaviour. We apologize for being a working wife, and more for being a working mother, and still more for being a working, divorced mother. Time after time, however, the myth is proven to be wrong in real life. Working women do not raise a higher percentage of delinquent kids. In fact, working mothers feel that they are more in touch with the world with which their children are learning to cope. Mothers who go back to work after a few years at home often find that the time they spend with their children is more meaningful now that they have less of it. Whereas before much of the time spent at home was also spent by the television set with the kids, now they make a point of spending time talking and listening to each child. Part of this reaction may indeed be a response to a sense of guilt, but part is also a result of the growing assurance that you can indeed do both things well. The guilt of the working wife and mother is outdated; guilt should only accrue to a mother if she is not actually doing a good job of mothering, and we now know that this does not necessarily have anything to do with whether or not a mother works outside the home.

ALTERNATIVES TO FULL-TIME EMPLOYMENT

Returning to full-time employment may not be appropriate for you at the time of your separation. You may have small children that you prefer to raise yourself until school age, avoiding day-care and baby-sitters. You may need some recovery time for yourself, or you may want to do things a little more gradually. Financial pressures may make such choices impossible for some women, but everyone should consider some of the other choices of work patterns that are available.

WORKING AT HOME

If you happen to have some antiquated skills in typing that you can dust off, rent a typewriter or a word processor and practise. You may find a brush-up course near where you live. You can begin by putting a notice up on university bulletin boards to type essays and theses at home. Any bookstore will sell you a guide to the standard format for typing such papers. Find out what the current price per hour or per page is, and select your price.

If you are not ready for full-time employment and have no leftover skills that you can think of, you may consider part-time employment. Remember, though, that part-time employment, whether in or outside the home, tends to grow and grow to fill all the time available but with a part-time salary.

CHILD-CARE WORKER

Many women with and without children prefer to work at home. Women have already been trained as child-care workers by virtue of growing up as girls in this society. Thus it is logical for many women to turn to the field of child care as a source of employment. You can put an ad in the local paper and start with the people that answer your ad. Or you can join a government-sponsored program if there is one in your community. There are many different kinds of programs.

Another option is to provide day care for under-school-age children whose parents work. This is usually an all-day job, but sometimes it is just for a few days a week. Most communities maintain a registry of approved homes. This is also arranged through the city or provincial social services department. The registry may or may not help you to do your advertising. Accrediting outfits are not always placement agencies as well. The major advantage to being associated with an approved program is credibility. Some programs also provide subsidies to parents with low incomes for day care, so you may feel that your income, in turn, is more secure if you are receiving your fees from an organized program.

Yet another version of child care is the after-school program. These are beginning to appear in more and more communities. There are variations on the routine with some programs providing supervision of kids early in the morning until school begins, some providing hot lunches, and some including supervised play between the time that school is over in the afternoon and the parents' jobs end at suppertime. This sort of work in your own home may suit your need to spend time with your own small children while earning money and getting some job experience.

BACK TO SCHOOL?

An increasing number of women are choosing to go to technical college or university in order to prepare for a full-time career in a specialized field. Such "mature students," as they are usually called by the administration of the institutions, tend to do extremely well in the courses they choose. (The term "mature," by the way, is not meant to recognize your superior wisdom, but only to distinguish you from the eighteen-year-olds.) If you have the time, the energy, and the money to return to school, you will likely find it very difficult at first until you develop good study habits. After this hurdle, however, most of us mature students float to somewhere near the top of our classes. The reasons for this are many: we aren't desperately worried about getting a date for the "hop" on Friday night; we are not being rushed by a fraternity; we actually do our assignments and hand them in on time; we are there because we see studying as a means to a specific end—a job, a salary, and independence. (These characteristics do fit the occasional eighteen-year-old, too, and such kids are also near the top of the class.) Teachers find that "mature" students are a positive delight, because they take the time to prepare the reading for the daily seminar discussions, and do their assignments on time. Older people have a lot more life experience from which to draw in class discussions than eighteen-year-olds. Although it is a bit of a shock to both you and the professor at first when you discover that you are indeed old enough to be his or her mother, your relationship may soon become one of mutual respect rather than the more formal teacher/student relationship that is common with younger students. The biggest benefit of all, though, is the excitement of finding that you do indeed have the ability to think about intangible ideas that are not directly related to dusting and diapers.

Most educational institutions have widely varied financial-assistance programs which should be investigated well in advance of registration. There may be a grant or a scholarship that will suit you. Some scholarships require that you have attended university the previous year and achieved a certain average. Thus you pay your own way for the first year, working toward a scholarship for the rest of your studies. Alternatively you may choose to take out a student loan. Usually these have better repayment terms than you will ever get from a bank. You apply for these through the university student-loan office.

Some couples design a divorce agreement which includes financial support to cover the necessary years of re-training for the wife. These couples feel that it is now the woman's turn to develop a career, since she was at home providing support or sometimes at work providing the financial support which enabled the husband to advance his career. In such cases, the financial support ends as soon as the education is completed, and the woman begins working in her new career.

Of all the possibilities for entering or returning to the work-place, you must choose the right one for you. If your first choice isn't exactly right, you can change jobs later on. Most people are capable of doing more than one type of job satisfactorily. It is simply a matter of honest assessment of your personal skills, abilities, and interests, and your ability to get started. If you really try to fit yourself into an entirely unsuitable job and fail, all you can do is reassess the situation, perhaps seek some job counselling, and start again. Your ultimate goal is a job that you enjoy, one that pays fairly and one in which your skills are recognized and respected. It may take a few jobs and a few years to get there.

VOLUNTEERISM

Volunteerism is highly underrated as a source of valuable and satisfying experience. Volunteer jobs often are very similar to paid positions, but they have many additional advantages. First of all, your hours are usually much more flexible than in a paid job, and part-time work is easy to arrange. In fact, most volunteer positions are part-time. Secondly, you can often advance much more rapidly in a volunteer position than you can in a paid position. Finally, a volunteer job provides useful contacts in your field of interest without the obligations that go with business contacts.

Many companies and organizations are beginning to look at volunteer organizations as training grounds for valuable employees. Some executives realize that a woman who has been president of a voluntary association or who has served on policy-making boards has already had a great deal of decision-making experience. She can move into a responsible job with little or no formal preparation.

Women are beginning to recognize that volunteerism is a good way to develop their skills and to play an important role in the community. Volunteerism is both more demanding and more forgiving than paid employment. If you become involved in an important community project, you may find yourself working eighteen-hour days, but you have more choice over which hours, and you can quit if you want to without the repercussions of quitting a paid job.

Volunteer jobs are often more demanding of you as a whole person. For example, a paid job is usually somewhat delineated by a job description and various traditional expectations. A volunteer job can grow as fast or faster than you can, offering much more challenge than you expected and taking as much of your knowledge, skill, and patience as you are willing to donate. Failure is tolerated more easily from volunteer projects than from those carried out by hired employees, but generally there is a higher sense of mutual commitment and good will.

Volunteer positions exist in every community. They can accommodate almost any interest and any amount of time and energy. You can spend one afternoon every two weeks visiting a lonely senior citizen in hospital, or you can be a full-time secretary or executive, all on a volunteer basis. You can have a position with almost no responsibility or you can have one with a great deal of responsibility, or you can work your way up. Many communities now operate volunteer placement offices where you can find the volunteer position which suits your interests, your time, and your skills.

Volunteer work is a good way to gradually get back into circulation if you have been out for a long time. Once you know that you can do a volunteer job well without much supervision or pressure, you will have more confidence in applying for a paying job. For many women, volunteer work provides a link back into the community and new friends, as well as a chance to broaden their thinking about things outside the home. A volunteer job can also help you to instill a regular routine into your life as you learn to meet outside deadlines.

Once you do manage to begin doing something away from home, your perspective will change; your own problems and loneliness will recede into the proper framework of the broader world, and you will be able to be more objective about your future. If you want to do volunteer work, but have little money to spare, you may find that some volunteer jobs do pay expenses, or small honoraria. If the price of a babysitter or bus fare is keeping you from applying for a volunteer position in your community, ask if such costs can be covered.

References

Harris, Thomas A., *I'm Okay, You're Okay*. New York: Avon Books, 1967.

A do-it-yourself psychology book which offers a useful paradigm for understanding and improving relationships.

Mungall, Constance, *Changing Your Name in Canada: How to Do It Legally*. Vancouver: International Self-Counsel Press, 1977.

Pogrebin, Letty Cottin, *Growing Up Free: Raising Your Child in the Eighties*. Toronto: McGraw-Hill Ryerson, 1980.

A comprehensive guide which up-dates old theories and adds some new ones, especially about television and violence, and non-sexist child-raising.

Pogrebin, Letty Cottin (ed.), *Stories for Free Children*. New York: Ms. Foundation for Education and Communication, 1982.

Excellent selection of stories for children of all ages. Beautifully illustrated. Pleasant for adults to read to children.

Rubin, Lillian B., *Women of a Certain Age: The Midlife Search for Self*. New York: Harper Colophon Books, 1979.

A very readable study of the process of seeking a personal identity apart from husband and children.

Scott, Niki, *The Working Woman: A Handbook*. Kansas City: Sheed, Andrews and McMeel, 1977.

Lots of informal advice on work-related issues such as selecting a day-care program, dressing for work, taking more courses, and so on.

Sheehy, Gail, *Passages: Predictable Crises of Adult Life*. Toronto: Bantam, 1977.

A review of the various stages of adulthood as experienced by both men and women. Includes careful analysis and useful advice.

CHAPTER SEVEN

Dating and Remarriage

Sooner or later you will likely take another look at the opposite sex and begin dating again. Some people wait a long time before they feel they are ready for this step, and others prefer to avoid it altogether and remain on their own. Living alone is quite acceptable nowadays—the word "spinster" and its implications of incompleteness or manlessness are quite outdated. For some women, dating just sort of happens on its own, and for others it takes a conscious effort. This can depend not only on you and your personality, but also on your location and life patterns. There are many problems associated with dating for some women. For example, you may be afraid to date because you are concerned about the effect it will have on your children. Or you may feel a bit silly dating like a teenager again. Some women have had almost no dating experience as teenagers, having married one of their first boyfriends, and are scared to death about starting now.

REBOUND

The first opportunities for other relationships with men usually come at the time of the break-up of the marriage. This can happen even before the actual separation, when you are so unhappy and lonely that you find a friend nearby who is kind and comforting. The same thing can happen just after the separation, too, when you are very vulnerable, lonely, and a bit confused. These relationships can be very helpful, and go a long way towards pulling you through the tough times. There are dangers, too, however. If you slide from one marriage into another with no time on your own in between, you are likely to repeat the same patterns as before, and you will drastically reduce your chances of learning from the failure of your first marriage.

Both men and women are especially vulnerable just after the

break-up of a marriage. Often such people are drawn together into what can be a potentially dangerous rebound situation. Beware of falling into a long-term relationship too quickly, however good it seems. Both of you need some time alone to rethink the roles of the past marriage in order to avoid similar mistakes in the next.

Whether one or both of you has recently emerged from a marriage that failed, there is still another danger to be avoided in the event that the relationship becomes a lasting one. If one person is comforting and the other being comforted, it is possible that this pattern of dependency will last throughout the relationship. Crisis dependency is one thing, but a permanently unequal relationship with one person doing all the giving is not very rewarding for either person. Once begun, such patterns are hard to change. Alternatively, relationships can also be very rewarding, and blossom into deep friendships based on the shared understanding you have of each other's past experience. Just be sure that you understand the dynamics of what you are doing.

BEGINNING TO DATE

The most important benefit of dating is the lift it gives to your ego. After the battering your self-confidence often takes at the end of a marriage, it is uplifting to find that someone actually thinks you are attractive and/or interesting. Furthermore, it is quite a revelation to some women that they can still respond as they once did to a new romantic situation. Although it may be strange and even a bit awkward to feel fluttery and nervous again, to wonder what to wear and what to say after so many years, it is also very enjoyable.

But what if you want to be dating, and don't know how to begin? There are many, many alternatives nowadays that didn't exist even twenty years ago. Now that the stigma of being divorced has faded for women, it is quite acceptable to actively seek male friends. Something that many women don't realize is that there are already lots of men nearby that they haven't really noticed before: men in the neighbourhood, at work, in various associations. You must be reasonably selective, however, because most of the men in a suburban neighbourhood or community league are likely to be married. Still, if you become active in a parent-teacher association, you will find that there are single dads there, too. The same is true of children's sports activities; there are single fathers in minor hockey associations and soccer leagues and so on.

Going still further afield, you may choose to become involved in supporting a local political candidate. Political campaigns are fun and will lead you to new friends of both sexes. You can take up a new sport, such as golf, tennis, or racquet-ball; various groups and associations serve different age groups in different towns and cities. Check if you can to see which ones are frequented by single people.

Most larger towns now have singles clubs. Their activities can vary widely to include organized meetings and seminars, regular dances and parties. To find out where they are, watch the newspaper or ask your other single friends. There are often singles bars, particular bars in a town or city that are known as good places to meet other single people. The grapevine will tell you where these are. If you find such places intimidating on your own, get a friend to go along with you.

There are many dating agencies that will match you with someone with compatible interests. They usually provide five or ten dates for a fee, but their methods vary widely. You have nothing to lose by phoning to find out, or even visiting the office. Make sure that the charge for the service is reasonable.

Many local newspapers are now sponsoring columns for advertising for the kind of friend you prefer. If you want to try this, get a postal box through the newspaper, or some other neutral way of keeping your address or phone number from getting into the paper to protect yourself from cranks and more dangerous sorts.

A more personal way of meeting people is to set up your own singles club, either with a group of ten or so single friends, or by advertising and accepting the first twenty that respond. Then, once you have a list of people, hold a dinner party for which everyone contributes either money, or food, or both. Take turns holding it in homes, or else reserve a few tables in a restaurant and have everyone pay his or her own way. Holding such parties every month or so at a local restaurant is less trouble, but it may be less expensive if they are held at someone's home. You might want to try pot luck, with everyone bringing a special dish; or you can vary the pattern, using a different approach each time. What is important is the opportunity for mixing beforehand over a round of cocktails. Make it clear that it is compulsory to circulate. The places at the tables should have been labelled beforehand so that people who do not know each other sit side by side. In creating a singles group it is wise to start with certain similarities. Select people who are at approximately the same income, social, and educational level, and within a ten-year age span. The organizer should receive confirmation from those who are attending a week or so in advance so that vacancies, if there are too many, can be filled, or the party cancelled, if necessary. Such groups can be lots of fun and can be the source of new romances or the base of a new group of good friends with similar interests, or both.

Blind dates arranged by friends are another way of meeting people. The advantage of this is that you can still be in the company of your friends. The disadvantage is that if you don't like the date, you may inadvertently hurt the feelings of your well-intentioned friends when you refuse to date the person again. Still, many nice friendships have started on blind dates, and chances are good that your friends will select someone with some of the same interests as you have. Just take along your sense of humour, and try not to be hurt if your friends match you up with a creep. Maybe it is the only single male they know, and they really thought they were doing you a favour by giving you a chance to get out.

Nothing will ever happen if you stay home; you must go out in order to meet people, even if it is hard to do at first. Get involved in things outside your home, and soon you will have some friends with whom to share whichever activities you choose.

Dating the second time around is much more fun and much more relaxed than it was when you were a teenager. Of course, you will be nervous sometimes, but the feelings are much less violent than the teenage terror, and your sense of humour is usually much closer to the surface. If you are just getting back into circulation after ten years of diapers and cookbooks and women's magazines, you would do well to make a point of watching the news on TV and reading the newspapers, if you don't already. You might try reading a few of the current bestsellers to find out what the current topics of social conversation might be. Men are no longer solely interested in sports and the stock market, if indeed they ever were. There are now many men who are running a home on their own, with or without children, who are sincerely interested in child care and cooking, with whom it is fun to exchange ideas.

GOSSIP

Whether you choose to date or not, and whether you date a lot or a little, there will likely be gossip about your dating career either in the office or in your neighbourhood or both. Gossip is a natural phenomenon, and it is not necessarily based on fact. Sometimes rumours are circulated by unhappy wives in your neighbourhood who find some comfort in having you as a scapegoat for their unhappiness, even if you have only said hello to their husbands once a year at the community dance.

If you develop a friendly working relationship with an associate, you may find that it is commonly believed that you also sleep together. The rumours will persist, and you must be aware of this possibility. You cannot guard against them, even with the most chaste behaviour, because your actions usually have nothing to do with the rumours. You may never even know about them, in which case you are lucky. Try to shield yourself from the gossip about you—it will only make you self-conscious.

If someone does tell you what people are saying about you, make sure you handle it properly, that is, casually. Do not let yourself be upset or defensive. The best thing to do is to laugh, if you can. If you treat the rumours as unimportant, others may do so, too. If you provide a reportable reaction, you will simply feed the rumour mill. The whole thing is very much like the sort of rumours that girls in grade seven and eight pass around about each other. They are often vicious, even if they have a grain of truth in them.

It is important to keep such rumours from spoiling your working relationships, your community activities, or indeed, your romances. Do not explain or defend, and do not let yourself become guilty and self-conscious. Realize that such rumours take place for almost every divorced woman (and man!) and that their power lies in their ability to hold you back, to make you self-conscious enough that you will not venture any further in personal relationships. The better you are at your job, or the more visible you are in the community, the more likely this is to happen to you. And most women who have had this experience will laugh and tell you that they could never have had the time or the energy to have carried on even half the affairs that they were reported to have had.

Even though you must take the rumours and allusions with a grain of salt, you must also guard your reputation. If you are dating someone in the office, you needn't sneak around, meeting in obscure bars in neighbouring towns; but you needn't spend every coffee break and lunch hour together, either. It is all a matter of common sense, but it is also useful to remember that others are watching, and if they can make up juicy rumours when nothing is happening, they can develop entire scenarios when they have a little fact upon which to build. Whatever you choose to do is up to you, but you are not invisible, especially when you are in love. You may not mind if people are aware of your romantic life. If you do, try to see it as others may see it, and avoid creating embarrassing predicaments for yourself, your friend, or your associates at work. This is sometimes very difficult to do because perfectly sane and competent adults can act like irresponsible teenagers when they are in love. Falling in love really is grand, but a woman aspiring to greater things in the business world cannot afford to appear foolish or unreliable. The rule is: date responsibly.

PRACTICE RELATIONSHIPS

Dating is a great opportunity to experiment with new patterns of behaviour. If you were very submissive during your marriage, now is the time to try being more aggressive; if you were a fishwife during your marriage, now is the time to practise biting your tongue. Assess your own behaviour carefully, and try to change any of the bad patterns which persist from your first marriage. These patterns will not change in a vacuum, despite your best intentions. They will only change with real practice in real relationships.

Dating provides you with an opportunity to assess what you want in a relationship; in fact, you should carefully consider whether you want a romantic relationship at all. Try not to let infatuation and sexual attraction stop you from taking this opportunity to assess yourself and your requirements for a good relationship; otherwise, you may find yourself involved in another marriage or long-term arrangement without having had time to grow or change at all.

One way to gather your wits about you is to get out your pencil and paper again. Make a list of all the characteristics you would like to have in the ideal man. Keep this list handy, and when you feel that you are getting very attached to someone, get out the list to see if you are close to your standards or not. Of course, you will never meet your ideal man; instead, you will find men with many positive characteristics that you never thought of, and others with a few surprising negatives. Remember, most of these characteristics are not immediately evident. When we first meet someone, we often see a lot of what we want to see, plus some of what they want us to see. It takes a lot more time to discover what the other person is really like and then what you are like together.

Take the time to find out before you become too involved; once you have moved in together it is hard and very painful to split up again. Remember, even if the man comes close to being your ideal, it takes two to make a relationship, and you still may not bring out the best in each other in close quarters. You will both change over time. Be sure that your commitment to each other is realistic and allow lots of room for growing and changing for both of you. This is especially important if you are trying to effect major changes in your pattern of living. If you are just starting back to work, the person you need to bolster your self-confidence during the first tentative weeks and months may not be the person that you want when you have become a confident, competent working woman. If you are changing a lot, let your relationships and friends expand and change, too. Make sure you are as aware of each other's personal and professional goals as possible so that they can be incorporated into the relationship over time.

SEX

Let's return to the concept of responsible dating and examine the implications for sexual behaviour. Here again, it is a time for learning and for assessing your own behaviour, values, biases, and expectations. For many couples, an unsatisfactory sexual relationship was one of the many problems that led to divorce. It may not have been acknowledged as such, but marital problems are usually reflected in the sexual relationship, anyway, since sex is such a basic mirror of our emotions. If the marriage ended with the last husband having extra-marital affairs, a woman may understandably have some doubts about her own sexual ability—and desirability.

An aversion to sex is often the result of sexual problems in a marriage, but more often such problems are overlaid with traditional Victorian ideas about sex. There are a number of myths connected with sex in our society, and these must be confronted before a really satisfying sexual relationship can be experienced. First of all, sex is not dirty, and sex-related words are not swear-words unless they are used in a smutty context. Still, society has taught us for generations that sex is dirty, and it is categorized with the words related to excretion of waste products from the body. Although we do not necessarily suggest that you radically alter your vocabulary, it is wise to take a close look at your attitude to sex-related words. Perhaps your reaction to them is connected to the fact that you aren't comfortable with conversations which discuss sexual topics, let alone the actual act itself. Victorian inhibitions, along with a lack of self-confidence, combine to make a discouraging complex of attitudes.

SELF-ACCEPTANCE

The first step in overcoming such inhibitions is to learn to accept your own body. We have talked a lot about self-confidence, and confidence in your own appearance is an important part of that. Take a long, hard look at yourself in the mirror, both with and without clothes on, and get used to the way you really look. This is hard to do in a society that promotes youth and artificial beauty as strongly as ours does, but it is an essential part of learning to like and accept yourself. If you don't like what you see, think carefully about whether what you want to look like is possible, or is even right for your personality. Appearance is important, but not in the way the television ads imply. You are most confident when you feel and look the best you can. It is not important to compete with the teeny-boppers. Women's figures are incidental, and only important if obesity, alcohol or drug abuse, or illness limits their ability to live fully. It is important that you recognize that the women who are truly beautiful come in many shapes and sizes. What makes them beautiful is their self-acceptance, their competence in interpersonal relationships, their philosophy.

Your appearance reflects your state of mind. If you are happy, rested, and healthy you look your best. If you are tired and strained it shows in your eyes, your face, and your posture. Your goal should be to be as healthy and happy as you can most of the time, and this will ensure that you also look your best most of the time.

It takes a special effort to stay healthy and look your best when you are under a lot of stress. A regular exercise program, whether you work alone at home three or four hours a week or join a group, is a big step towards both physical and mental health. Regular exercise causes you to sleep better and gives you an outlet for some of the stress.

Adjusting your diet to exclude the junk foods and synthetic foods that give you extra calories but few vitamins and minerals will not only improve your energy level, but probably help your budget too. Just replacing sugar-loaded cereals with whole grain ones, white bread with 100 per cent whole wheat, and cutting out ketchup, sugar, potato chips, and soft drinks will make a difference.

You might also want to try a new hair-style or some new make-up. Go to one of the cosmetic studios which offer free demonstrations and experiment with new colours. Find a new hair-style in a magazine and cut it out. Get a hairdresser to do it for you. Try to pick one that doesn't require a lot of work every day, one that complements the life of controlled freedom that you are beginning to lead.

LOVE AFFAIRS

There are many harmful myths associated with a woman's role in intercourse, such as the Victorian belief that women shouldn't play an active part during intercourse. When combined with the myth of the vaginal orgasm, this can prevent you from ever achieving sexual fulfillment. You must, in any case, become comfortable with your own appearance and acceptance of your body. If you were still undressing in the bathroom at the end of your marriage, it is time you learned to accept yourself.

You must learn to accept responsibility for your own body, even while making love. This can be exceptionally difficult if you still harbour the notion that masturbation is bad. Contrary to what you may have heard from your parents, masturbation does not make hair grow on your hands, does not prevent you from enjoying sex as an adult, does not make you pregnant, does not cause a rash, is not a sin, does not show on your face the next morning, and does not cause you to go blind. In fact, masturbation is pleasant and relaxing, and provides useful knowledge about your own body which will help you to enjoy orgasms when you have intercourse. Masturbation is an integral part of the sexual act, and if you are uncomfortable with it, or believe you cannot achieve orgasm, you may need a bit of practice in the privacy of your own room when you are alone and relaxed.

If your concerns about sex seriously interfere with your enjoyment of intercourse, you may be well advised to see a counsellor before you carry your hang-ups into another relationship. If you have seldom or never had an orgasm or are not sure if you have (then you haven't), you should find out why before you cheat yourself and your next partner out of the richness of an enjoyable sexual relationship. Get busy and read some books so that you can expand your repertoire and learn to enjoy sex more fully next time. It is now quite acceptable to go to a sexual counsellor. There are many books on the market which offer advice about sexual problems. There are also a variety of ways of making love, most of which are fine if done in a suitable place and in such a way that no one is hurt.

The important thing to remember is that you are responsible for your own sexual response. It is unfair to expect your partner to figure it all out without a word or a reaction from you, and still manage to make the bells ring and the lights flash. A sexual relationship is a joint undertaking; you both take part in increasing each other's pleasure and ensuring your own. You must be able to indicate which parts of your body are sensitive to sexual stimulation. You must be prepared to experiment, to enjoy sex each time, without the tremendous pressure of having to perform and without the notion that it was a failure if you both didn't have an orgasm. It is time to relax and enjoy sex as part of an adult relationship in which you both participate. Here again is a good place for your sense of humour. You should be able to laugh at yourself, even in bed. And lots of funny things happen there which can be devastating if you don't laugh.

Female orgasm is the result of friction of the clitoris. Sustained friction causes increased blood flow to the vulva, and secretion of a lubricant. The friction also stimulates the nerve endings of the clitoris such that it achieves an erection. The stimulation builds to a climax which gives way to an overwhelming sense of release. Orgasm may be difficult to achieve under stress—though it is very healthy to relieve stress in this way. Some people produce very little natural lubricant, and secretion declines with aging. Colourless, odourless, tasteless, harmless lubricants such as KY jelly are available at every drugstore.

Clitoral stimulation can be achieved many ways, depending on the anatomy of the couple and the particular set of inhibitions. Some women can achieve orgasm from intercourse without manual stimulation because the clitoris is situated closer to the vaginal opening. Most women require manual stimulation during foreplay. For some couples this may include oral stimulation and vibrators. Unless there is a physical deformity, everyone can have orgasms. Once you take full responsibility for your own sexuality, you will be free to experiment until you discover the key to your own release and enjoyment.

SEX BY DEFAULT

Women have been taught that their role in sex is submission, that they should not initiate sex but that they should submit to their husbands, if they want sex. This idea has spoiled many marriages, and hurt many men and women. Most men do not want full responsibility for sex; they have had this responsibility for a long time, and it has led to a very one-sided experience and a lot of frustrated women.

For women who still believe that their role is to submit, there are many potential problems once the marriage has ended. One of these is "sex by default." If you have never learned to say "no" to your husband—and an honest "no," not an excuse—then you will have serious difficulty learning to say "no" to anyone else. You may be a sitting duck for anyone who comes along and takes you out; old family friend, co-worker, or date. Often when circumstances find you alone with a man, there is the possibility of a sexual encounter. The reasons for this may exist because you truly have come to like each other, because there is a strong sexual attraction which is mutual, or because he feels that you are fair game. Men have been taught that sexually aggressive behaviour is expected of them, and this puts them in the same trap as the submissive role does for women. Such trained behaviour patterns can mask the beginnings of a good relationship. Learn to handle sexual advances honestly and calmly. You must learn to say "no," nicely and firmly. It is not his fault if you just don't have the courage to say "no"; nor can he read your mind. Our conditioned submissiveness can often override the desire to be assertive and say no. But make sure that when you say "no," you really mean it and are not flirting.

If you decide to say "yes," do it clearly and consciously; don't permit yourself to submit if you are at all unsure of the man, your feelings, or the situation. Whenever you have sex, make sure that you learn to accept the responsibility for your own actions and decisions.

Rape occurs often in our society, and it is in part a result of the dominant/submissive tradition of men feeling that sexual gratification is an uncontrollable need and that satisfaction is their right. The courts are having a hard time defining rape. For many male judges, rape can still be explained either in terms of the physical need of the male or the sexually exciting behaviour or dress of the woman. This problem vanishes if we believe that both men and women are responsible for their own behaviour, sexual and otherwise, and that no one has the right to force unwanted sex on anyone else, under any circumstances. It will take many more careful and responsible court judgements, however, before society overcomes the myth that rape is really somehow the fault of the woman.

Returning to the problem of how to say "no," you have lots of choices. You can say "No, thank you" and leave the room; you can say

"No, not now...later," if you really mean later; or you can say, "No, this isn't right for me. I don't want a sexual relationship with you. I'm sorry. Let's go out for coffee." (Or for a walk, or back to work, or whatever else you can think of.) This is much easier to say than it is to do, but practise a bit in your mind so that you will be prepared for such situations when they do arise.

For some women, the problem is not saying "no." It is learning to say "yes" when they really want to but are still blocked by bad experiences, memories, and fears of the past. The best idea is always to try to be honest with yourself and the other person. If you want to develop a sexual relationship but you need more time, say so. This means that you will also at some time in the future have to find the courage to say, "Now." Initiating intercourse is also very difficult for many women who have lived a life of sexual submission, and still find sex somewhat distasteful. Whether you learn to say "yes" or "no," the consequence of acknowledging and being true to your own feelings vastly improves your self-confidence and self-esteem. You will really be proud of yourself. And if you make a mistake, face it, and think it through so you won't do it again. The only good thing about some mistakes is that we learn from them!

AN AFFAIR WITH A MARRIED MAN

The concept of "mistress" is almost completely outdated now, although there are still a few women who are financially dependent upon one man in return for sexual favours. Most women prefer to remain financially independent from the men with whom they have affairs until such time as the relationship becomes a serious commitment to live together.

A relationship with someone who is married to someone else creates a unique set of complications. First of all, if your marriage ended with your husband being involved with another woman, you will carry a great deal of guilt through the relationship if you see yourself now as the "other woman." The idea of the other woman being responsible for the end of a marriage is actually another myth, but it will live for a long time, because it is so much more comfortable for many women to blame the failure of their marriage on another person outside the marriage and thus never have to face their own responsibility in the marriage. In many marriages, affairs occur just before the end. Usually an affair is yet another sign of an already seriously disintegrating partnership, or at least the sign of the maladjustment of one of the partners; seldom is it the only cause for marriage breakdown. Still, the accusations and the resultant guilt persist.

If you are having an affair with a married man, the feeling of guilt can also stem from the reality that you are living a deception; that your relationship exists without the knowledge of the man's wife, and certainly without the approval of society. Both the idea of being dishonest, and the knowledge that you are going against the values of your society can add to your discomfort and exert stress on the relationship.

The price of an affair with a married man is high. You cannot exercise equal control of the relationship; he alone can decide when he can leave his family to be with you. You cannot mix with a normal circle of friends socially. You are seldom free to initiate meetings, and often you are not even able to phone him. Over time these things can lead to resentment. You must ask yourself if such an arrangement is really a perpetuation of the pattern of submission of your marriage. What can you learn from this sort of relationship? With so little control in the relationship, how can you increase your sense of independence or freedom? You will once again be in a relationship where the man has all the power, and by being part of the relationship, you are acquiescing to his dominance. You cannot expect him to do much work on the relationship, because he is well aware that it is temporary and secondary, and regardless of how he explains his marriage, he is still committed to it or he wouldn't still be there.

Finally, he will not likely leave his wife and family to spend the rest of his life with you, but even if he does, will the relationship seem as glamorous and desirable without the mystique of the love affair? There are certain advantages to such an affair, such as the assurance of a lover without the responsibility of building a life together. Perhaps the inaccessibility of the lover translates into more freedom than other relationships allow. Perhaps the absence of hope for the long-term future postpones making any decisions about your own life.

DATING AND CHILDREN

Dating is a normal thing to do after your marriage has ended. It is good for you and for the children because it helps to focus your mind on the present and not on futile regrets and "if-onlies" from the past.

As with so many other things, it will likely take less time for your children to adjust to the idea of your dating than it does for you. There can be some added benefits for your children if they do meet the occasional date or if they are included in some of your outings in that they get to know a wider circle of adults after whom they can pattern their behaviour.

The best policy, as always, is honesty. Tell your children that you will be dating, if you think you are ready to start. Do not ask their permission; just tell them in a simple, straightforward, and unemotional way. Then get on with it. Do not ask their approval of your dates. You are free to choose your own friends. You needn't introduce them at all, if you prefer. But do not subject yourself to the doubts and guilt of dating without your children's knowledge. The guilt will interfere with your enjoyment of the friendship, and will also interfere with your relationship with your children. They will lose their trust in you if they suspect that you are dating secretly, and if you do this chances are that someone else will tell them before you do. Nothing is gained by keeping your dating a secret, because shielding children from this locks them away from what you are really thinking and doing, what you are becoming, and also prevents them from adjusting to reality, and getting used to the idea that things have indeed changed. Further, deception on your part simply reinforces your own insecurity and guilt, as well as the inevitable erosion of the kids' trust in you. The exposure that children have to their parents' dating also gives them a chance to compare the new partners with their own dad or mum, as well as to compare the various dates with each other, and to consider one of them, eventually, as a possible stepparent. This kind of thinking is not harmful to kids, but good for them.

If your relationship includes sex, you will be wise to find some place other than your home for those special times. There are several reasons for this. One is that you will be far more relaxed if you are not worried about whether or not one of the kids is going to pop in on you. Another reason is that it is not good for the kids to find a different man in bed with Mummy every so often. Instead, you can get a sitter and spend weekends away together now and again. Of course, tell the children where you are going and with whom. There is no need to deny that you are sleeping with your friend in response to a direct question from your teenaged daughter. Neither is it necessary to hit them over the head with the fact that you are enjoying a sexual relationship. They have the right to know that you are going out and perhaps even with whom. The nature of your relationship is your own business until such time as you suspect it will be permanent, at which point you should prepare the kids for the idea of a new stepfather.

TELLING YOUR PARENTS

Your parents may have difficulty accepting the fact that you are dating, too. This is true only if they did not really accept the fact that the marriage has ended. Nevertheless, your attitude must be much the same as it is with your children. Be honest; do not ask for permission, but inform them of your decision, and try to help them with their acceptance of the fact that you are dating or that you are going to live with someone else. You can try to help them to accept your decision, but you are not responsible for their feelings or for their reactions. It is hard, sometimes, for parents to learn to treat even their grown-up children as adults. Nevertheless, whether or not you are still treated as a child, it is up to you to behave as an adult, openly and honestly.

PERMANENT RELATIONSHIPS

Before making such a drastic decision, it is a good idea to spend awhile letting your friend become acquainted with your children. Here again, this is not to seek their approval, although it is to be hoped that they will all get along well. It is simply a chance for them to become comfortable with the idea, and for you to watch them all together. You may find that he is good with your children for short periods of time, but not so patient after a couple of hours. Make sure that they all spend some time together without you, too, so they can develop their own relationships with each other without your obvious concern and potential intervention. All of you should have had plenty of time to adjust to each other before you begin to live together. You should be very sure, too, that this will be a long-term relationship, because there is a lot of work to be done by everyone in getting used to each other, and it would be a shame if it were all in vain. This is especially true if you are also combining two groups of children.

LIVE-IN

If you decide to live together without getting married, don't be afraid to say so. Live-in relationships are quite common and becoming more so since many people, both men and women, are reluctant to make the legal commitment again until the relationship has stood the test of time. Some people simply prefer not to marry, although their emotional relationship involves the same commitment as a marriage.

The main advantage to living common law is that termination does not require the expense and red tape of divorce. The major disadvantage is that there may be little or no protection for the surviving spouse in the event of death of the other. In some provinces a common law spouse is legally a "stranger," and has no right to the estate unless there is proof of individual purchase of each material asset of the relationship. Even a will can be successfully contested by legal relatives, and the bequest to a common-law spouse overridden. In other provinces, for example Ontario, the couple is deemed married in the eyes of the law if they have lived together for several years, and especially if they have children. The law varies from place to place because Common Law and Wills are both under provincial jurisdiction. It is important to check into this carefully if you are living with someone, or planning to.

In case of a live-in relationship with kids, make sure you supply them with the answers they need to minimize their embarrassment with other kids. Make sure that you have discussed all their questions and doubts carefully so that they understand that you are happy with the relationship. Explain that they may encounter criticism because you choose not to be married, but that this is based on an old-fashioned idea that being married is the only way to have a loving relationship. Marriage is still the most common way, but no longer the only common one. Don't wait until your kids tell you about such questions; prepare them beforehand because they will likely be too embarrassed to tell you after it happens.

It is best not to compound the problem with dishonesty. Pretending that you are married or permitting the children to pretend is an unnecessary deception and prevents all of you from living the situation as it really is and relaxing and enjoying the relationship that you have chosen to build. In this case, as with dating, if you treat the explanation in a matter-of-fact way, it will likely be accepted in the same way. If not, deal in an accepting and understanding way with whatever questions and emotions are raised by the child, but do not permit the child to think for a minute that he or she has the power to stop the relationship or to choose your friends for you.

You should include kids in some of the planning and their feelings should be respected and discussed. But you are solely responsible for the major decisions in your life, just as they will be for theirs. No child should grow up with the burden that you didn't date, or didn't remarry, or gave up an important relationship for "the sake of the children." Such an attitude breeds resentment on both sides. These are your choices and your decisions, and you are unfair if you blame your children for your choice to live alone.

Avoiding new relationships because of the children is akin to prolonging an unhappy marriage "because of the children." In both cases the children will likely disclaim responsibility as they get older, and feel more pity for your inability to make a more mature choice for yourself. In neither case are they likely to thank you. Neither a lonely, unhappy mother nor a tense and argumentative set of parents provides a good environment for a child. Many kids would argue that a well-adjusted single parent, a stepparent, or a divorce, are all alternatives which are preferable to the stagnation of the perpetually unhappy family.

Life is unpredictable, fortunately. Thus, even though you can categorically state that you will never be interested in men again, let alone another long-term relationship like marriage, time and circumstances may alter your resolve. Although such things are seldom carefully planned, your next relationship will be easier for you if you take enough time beforehand to get to know and like yourself. Your choice of partner is less likely to be the first one that comes along, if you have taken the time to develop your self-confidence and discover what your essential values really are.

Although the idea of approaching a second marriage in a rather scientific way sounds a bit cold, it is not. Once you decide that you really understand a lot about the relationship, and that you want it, you can relax and watch it take shape, knowing that both of you are trying your best. It is easier to talk things over habitually once you are living together if you begin the relationship on the basis of openness and honesty. If you have assessed the bad habits and behaviours and the situations which triggered them in your first marriage, you are more likely to recognize and stop them when they interfere in your new relationship.

Before you decide to spend the rest of your life with another person, think very carefully about the match between your two sets of values. Sometimes opposites are complementary; sometimes they are not. Make sure that you share the values which are most important to you. For example, if he is a city person and you want to live the casual life of the country, can you see a way to accommodate each other before you make your commitment? There are many basic differences that can be anticipated and thoroughly discussed, and they should be. Love does not conquer all your differences, though it helps. In fact, if the differences are fundamental, they may never be entirely accommodated or resolved. Look very carefully at your own values and decide for yourself what the values of the other person are, both through discussion and observation. This time, take the time to enter into the relationship with your eyes open. If you do this and have a reasonable level of self-confidence, your chances of creating a rich and lasting relationship are very high.

There are many ghosts from the past which will have the power to disrupt your new relationship if you let them. If you are still grieving over the past, if your past husband can still upset you enough that it affects your new relationship and your ability to cope with the present, then you are not yet ready to make a sincere commitment to someone else. You must have accepted your past and taken control of your own feelings about it before you can contribute your fair share to a new relationship. When upsetting things from your past life do occur, you should be able to deal with them with a minimum amount of fuss and without a prolonged interruption in your present activities. If a comment from your past husband can still throw you into a tailspin or cause you to cry all night or prevent you from concentration on your job, then you still have some work to do.

You must accept the past history of your mate, honestly and without too much agonizing over his past loves. Although it is perhaps easier to dispense with them all in your mind as evil, grasping, ugly, unpleasant women, this is not a very mature solution. It also gives rise to a basic contradiction: if his past women were so bad, how come he selected you? Don't spend any time on that one, either. If you do, it is time to get back to working on your own self-confidence. You are each part of the other's continuing life pattern. This includes the past, the present, and the future. Get on with making the present as complete and rich as you can. This cannot be achieved if you are still preoccupied with the past.

Second marriages seem to work better because both people have made a double commitment to permit each other to grow and to work on the marriage, too. Second marriages often have more flexibility, partly because they are based on a more mature sense of commitment.

Your commitment to your first marriage was of a different nature—you couldn't really know what went into making a good marriage, but you were determined to try. This time you have a much clearer idea of the components of a good marriage, and you have a much clearer understanding of yourself. Such maturity leads to a successful and rewarding relationship for both people.

Once you have developed this confidence, you will not be thrown by the inevitable comparisons that second marriages encounter. If friends have known you in previous relationships, of course they will compare. For example, friends of your new husband will be comparing you with the previous wife, just as your friends will be comparing your new mate with your previous one. This is not harmful, since they all usually wish you well. Try not to prolong this sort of discussion, if indeed it ever reaches the point of discussion. Your goal is to live in the present, over which you have some control.

In your new relationship, the important thing to nurture and preserve is your independence. Marriage does not mean that you must become dependent on someone else for decision-making, nor does it mean that you must make all the concessions in developing a suitable life-style for both of you. Rather, independence means making sure that there is room for you both to continue to develop your own interests and your own personalities along the paths you have chosen, while living together and sharing a close friendship of equals. Marriage can encompass two independent, mature people with varied interests and busy, satisfying lives, if it is based upon mutual respect, the sincere wish to try to understand each other, and a joint commitment to make the marriage work.

If the relationship is built upon a solid foundation of trust, you can take time to be alone and time to see some of your friends on your own. You can have time to read by yourself, time to rest if you are tired, and time to work overtime if you want to, because there is no doubt that any of these things can threaten the relationship. If you can be sure of trust and mutual respect, you have the framework for a rich and enduring relationship.

References

Alvarez, A., *Life After Marriage: Love in an Age of Divorce*. Toronto: Bantam Books, 1983.

A very literate collection of reflections and experiences associated with divorce. The author is sensitive, insightful, and amusing.

Cowan, Connell, and Melvin Kinder, *Smart Women, Foolish Choices: Finding the Right Men, Avoiding the Wrong Ones*. New York: Signet, 1985.

A short book with a few pointers; written by two male psychologists. Worth a quick read.

Steinem, Gloria, *Outrageous Acts and Everyday Rebellions*. Toronto: Holt, Rinehart & Winston, 1983.

A collection of some of Steinem's best articles about women and their experiences as they discover the problems and challenges inherent in womanhood.

Stenson, Janet Sinberg, *Now I Have a Stepparent and It's Kind of Confusing: A Book That Explains Remarriage to Young Children*. New York: Avon, 1979.

EPILOGUE

You cannot leave the past behind you, but you can outgrow it, much like shedding a snake's skin reveals a new creature, yet retains all the essential characteristics of the old. Once you have learned to take care of yourself, you are in a much better position to help other people to learn to do the same. You are a better friend, mother, wife—and you are a good companion for yourself. The paradox is that once you have learned to live alone, you are better prepared to live with others. Once you are comfortable with yourself, you can afford to be flexible, to accept other people as themselves and to learn from them. You can explore various possibilities for your own personality and life pattern and adopt those which suit you best. You can accept that life is a process of change.

You are no longer bound by the rigid expectations of society; you are a growing and changing person who is thoroughly enjoying life, who experiences all that life offers, willingly and fully. Once you have learned to weigh and assess ideas in the light of your own values, you will always make better choices for yourself. You are a whole person who is capable of coping with whatever life has in store. You can look after yourself.

NOTE RE APPENDICES

Appendix I contains a representative sample of forms used under the old Divorce Act, and Appendix II contains examples of forms for the new Divorce Act, 1985.

Forms from the old Act have been included here for several reasons. First of all, many readers will have begun their divorce proceedings under the old Act, or be attempting to alter or adjust judgments made under the old Act. Furthermore, most of these examples are documents that were actually filed in real cases; the forms are, for the most part, filled in, so that the reader can get a sense of how such forms would read.

The forms for the new Divorce Act, 1985 are indicative of what the process will be like from now on. The forms are much simpler, clearly stated, and easy to follow. As discussed earlier in the book, it is now possible to obtain a divorce without either of the spouses or their lawyers attending in court. See the example of the Divorce Judgment (Without Oral Evidence) in Appendix II.

Finally, the reader is asked to remember that most of these forms are taken from the Alberta Rules, and that forms and procedures may vary slightly from one province to another. These are, of course, selected forms. There are many others.

APPENDIX I

Forms From the Old Divorce Act

Separation Agreement Checklist/211
Petition for Divorce and Custody/215
Affidavit of Service/222
Standard Form for Budget Affidavit/223
Affidavit for Interim Custody of Children and a Restraining Order/227
Restraining Order/231

Separation Agreement Checklist

1. PARTIES

    Full names including all given or christian names of:
    (a) Husband.
    (b) Wife.

2. RECITALS OR BACKGROUND

    (a) Intention to live apart by reason of irreconcilable differences.
    (b) Marriage:
        (i) Date
        (ii) Place
    (c) Children:
        (iii) Full Names
        (iv) Birthdates
    (d) Any pending litigation.

3. CONSIDERATION

    (a) The premises.
    (b) Mutual covenants in the agreement.
    (c) Other consideration including settlement of pecuniary or property issues in any pending litigation.

4. SEPARATION

    (a) Separation:
        (i) has occurred
        (ii) will occur on signing of agreement
    (b) Nature:
        (iii) permanent
        (iv) temporary—date of expiration
    (c) Each spouse to be free from control of other as though unmarried.

5. NON-MOLESTATION

    Neither spouse to molest or annoy the other or compel the other to cohabit.

6. CUSTODY

    (a) To the husband.
    (b) To the wife.
    (c) Joint or divided custody spelling out where the child shall live—attempt to create two homes for child instead of one.

7. ACCESS

    (a) Reasonable.
    (b) Weekly or Monthly or other:
        (i) day(s)
        (ii) hour(s)
        (iii) place(s)
    (c) Christmas and New Year.
    (d) Birthdays.
    (e) School holidays.
    (f) Summer.
    (g) Within City, Province or Country.
    (h) Whether access not to be exercised in presence of girl friend or certain parties.
    (i) Passport facilities.
    (j) Notice.
    (k) Other communication, e.g., letter and telephone.
    (l) Should access be made essence of agreement so that if non-custodial party deprived of access, obligation to make any payments ceases?

8. OTHER PROVISIONS FOR THE CHILDREN
   (a) Education—e.g., special schools.
   (b) Religious training.
   (c) Prohibition against either spouse removing child from jurisdiction.
   (d) Special health treatment.

9. FINANCIAL SUPPORT

   A. FOR DEPENDENT SPOUSE:
   (a) Term—
       (i) joint lives, or
       (ii) life of dependent spouse (payments binding on estate)
       (iii) until unchaste (dum sole et casta)
       (iv) until divorce
       (v) until remarried
       (vi) until lives with another man.
   (b) Quantum—
       (i) Incidence of Income Tax
       (ii) Method of payment:
           (1) a lump sum
           (2) periodic sums
           (3) lump sum plus periodic sum
           (4) annuity.
   (c) Dates payable.
   (d) Manner and place
       (i) direct
       (ii) other, e.g., into banking account.
   (e) Security to ensure payment, e.g., mortgage.
   (f) Whether binding upon estate.

   B. FOR THE CHILDREN:
   (a) Term—during life of payer or continuing against estate—until
       (i) child 16 and ceases school attendance; or
       (ii) ceases to reside with dependent spouse; or
       (iii) reaches 21 years; or
       (iv) marries; or
       (v) dies.
   (b) For other provisions, see sub-paragraph A above.

10. VARIATION CLAUSE
    (a) Subject matter:
        (i) custody
        (ii) access
        (iii) child support
        (iv) inter-spousal support.
    (b) Kinds or types of variation clauses
        (i) Arbitration upon material change in circumstances
            — Definition of material change
            — Notice of desire to vary
            — Time before arbitration invoked
            — Appeal from Arbitrator to Judge in Court of Appeal
            — Agreement binding until varied.
        (ii) Arbitration conditional upon happening of some certain event, e.g., wife stops work.
        (iii) Variation dependent upon income level:
            (1) fixed percentage of net or gross;
            (2) fixed percentage of net or gross over certain amount;
            (3) fixed reduction if wife earns more than certain amount;
            (4) fixed increase if wife fails to earn certain amount.
        (iv) Variation tied to cost of living.

(v) Variation in fixed amount upon happening of certain events
— retirement
— incapacity to work.

11. OTHER FINANCIAL OBLIGATIONS

(a) Medical insurance for:
(i) children and wife
(ii) children.
(b) Regular dental care.
(c) Special orthodontic expenses.
(d) School and university tuition.
(e) Mortgage payment.
(f) Other.

12. ESTATE

Undertaking to maintain will leaving fixed portion to spouse or children. How can family be protected against testator divesting himself of all property so that he dies without leaving any estate to be distributed?

13. PERSONAL PROPERTY

(a) Already divided.
(b) Division according to list scheduled to agreement.
(c) Other arrangement.
Consider among other items:
(i) household goods, furniture and appliances
(ii) stocks, bonds and promissory notes
(iii) banking accounts
(iv) automobiles and boats

14. REAL PROPERTY

(a) Matrimonial Home:
(i) apartment or house?
(ii) owned or rented? In whose name?
(iii) what disposition of lease or of ownership?
(iv) transfer from one spouse to the other
(v) sale and equal or other division of proceeds
(vi) wife and children to remain in occupation for definite term
(vii) who to assume mortgage, insurance and taxes until term of occupation expires?
(b) Disposition of other real property, e.g., cottage or chalet.

15. FAMILY BUSINESS

(a) Does either spouse own a business in which the other has an interest?
(b) Resignation as officer or director
(c) Disposition of stock holdings
(d) Disposition of claim against company as creditor.

16. INSURANCE

(a) Life Insurance:
(i) Is insurance to benefit wife, children or both wife and children?
(ii) Is coverage to terminate upon termination of husband's obligation to provide support, e.g., upon remarriage of wife, or upon children reaching 18 or 21?
(iii) Is there to be an irrevocable appointment of beneficiary?
(iv) Who is to own policies?
(v) If relying upon existing policies, what are the particulars of the policies, giving:
(a) number of policy;
(b) face value of policy;
(c) name of insurance company.

 (vi) Are policies in good standing or are premiums owing?

 (b) Insurance on Personal Property:
  (i) Which items of personal property are insured, and against what risks?
  (ii) In whose name is the insurance?
  (iii) Are the policies in good standing or are premiums owing?
  (iv) Are any of the policies to be transferred?
  (v) Is new policy to be taken out for insurance against
   (1) fire?
   (2) theft?
   (3) other?

17. EXISTING AND FUTURE DEBTS

 (a) Does either spouse owe money to the other?
 (b) Is there a promissory note or evidence that a debt was created (distinguish gifts)?
 (c) Is debt to be repaid or cancelled?
 (d) Are the husband and wife jointly liable on any obligation such as a bank loan or mortgage?
 (e) If so, what disposition is to be made when the obligation matures?
 (f) If husband is to assume it, should he undertake to indemnify wife?
 (g) Each spouse to pay his or her own debts incurred after date of agreement.
 (h) Wife to indemnify husband for debts incurred after the agreement which he obliged to pay on her behalf.

18. DOWER

Bar of dower and power of attorney
 (a) Delivered with agreement.
 (b) Will deliver when required.

19. PENDING LITIGATION

Disposition of pending
 (a) claims for support in family division and in actions for alimony;
 (b) applications for custody and child-maintenance;
 (c) applications for partition or sale of property;
 (d) claims in any other litigation not disposed of.

20. RELEASES

 (a) mutual release of all claims excepting those arising out of agreement
 (b) release of right to administer estate
 (c) release of rights under Dependants' Relief Act and Devaluation of Estates Act.

21. SUBSEQUENT DIVORCE

 (a) Agreement not to amount to condonation.
 (b) Agreement to survive divorce.

22. FURTHER ASSURANCES

Undertaking to do all things necessary to carry out terms.

23. LEGAL FEES

Is husband to pay wife's legal fees?

24. INDEPENDENT LEGAL ADVICE

Acknowledgement that each party independently advised.

Petition for Divorce & Custody

FORM F.D. 1—PETITION

(Complete where applicable—omit pages that are not applicable)

No.

IN THE QUEEN'S BENCH
FAMILY DIVISION

WINNIPEG CENTRE

(Centre)

BETWEEN:

(also known as   ),
Petitioner

— and —

Respondent.

PETITION

TO THIS HONOURABLE COURT:

1. I hereby seek an order for the following relief:

   ☒ Divorce   ☐ Maintenance for myself

   ☒ Custody   ☐ Access   ☒ Maintenance for children

   ☐ Declaration of parentage   ☒ Non-cohabitation

   ☐ Exclusive occupancy of family home   ☒ Prohibition

   ☒ Financial disclosure   ☒ Non-molestation
                                              ☐ Partition or Sale

   ☒ Division of Marital Property.   equal ☒   unequal ☐ *
   ☒ Other (specify)—Payment of Loan   ☒ Costs
   by Respondent or discharge of Petitioner's vehicle as security for loan.

I ask that my petition be heard at ___Winnipeg Centre_____

*state reasons in paragraph 2.

2. A. My grounds for seeking a divorce or other relief are:

   Pursuant to Section 3 (d) of the Divorce Act, (Canada);

   Pursuant to the Family Maintenance Act;

   Pursuant to the Marital Property Act.

   B. The facts upon which my Petition is based are:

   The Respondent has treated the Petitioner with physical and mental cruelty so as to render cohabitation intolerable. By reason thereof the parties have been living separate and apart since February, 1984.

3. Reconciliation:

   There ~~is~~ (is not) a possibility of reconciliation or resumption of cohabitation.

4. Particulars of Relationship:

   A. Date of marriage January 17, 1966

   B. Place of marriage

   C. Surname of wife before marriage

   D. Maiden surname of wife

   E. Marital status of spouses at time of marriage

   _____unmarried_____ Wife _____ummarried_____ Husband

   F. ~~I am not married to the respondent and my cohabitation with the respondent commenced on~~

   G. My cohabitation with the respondent ceased ~~on~~ in February, 1984.

   H. I was born at .... on
   .... February .... 8 ...., 19..44
                    (Month)   (Day)

   I. The respondent was born at .. Vancouver, British Columbia ....
   on............... May .... 26 ...., 19..44
                    (Month)   (Day)

5. A. My address is:

   B. My spouse's address is: unknown

   C. I am domiciled in Canada.

   D. I have (the ~~Resondent has~~) been ordinarily resident in Manitoba since.... 1980

   and have actually resided in the said Province for at least 10 months of that period.

6. Children

    A. The names and dates of birth of the children in respect of whom relief is claimed are:

    born December 12, 1968

    born May 9, 1973

    B. I claim custody of:

    C. ~~I claim access to:~~

7. Separation Agreements or Orders

    The dates of all written or oral agreements or orders are:

    Oral agreement to separate approximately February 15, 1984 and oral agreement for him to be permitted to occupy basement as his separate residence from February, 1984 until his posting in Edmonton July 9, 1984. Oral agreement November 6, 1984 that the Respondent would pay $300.00 a month maintenance for the children and custody of the children to the wife.

8. Employment

    A. My employer's name and address:

    Winnipeg, Manitoba

    B. My gross monthly income is:

    $2,500.00

    My net monthly income is:

    $1,759.60

    C. I am paid each:

    month

    D. The "total income" declared on my last income tax return (1983) was $22,960.00   year

    E. The name and address of the respondent's employer is:

    Edmonton, Alberta

    F. The respondent's gross monthly income is: approximately $2,500.00 a month

    The respondent's net monthly income is: approximately $1,750.00 a month net

G. The respondent is paid twice a month

9. Particulars of my financial situation are shown on Schedule A.

10. ~~A. The legal description of real property in respect of which partition or sale is sought:~~

   ~~B. The municipal address of the above described property is:~~

   ~~C. The property is registered in the name(s) of:~~

   ~~D. The market value of the property is.~~

   ~~E. Particulars of registered encumbrances are:~~

11. Declaration of Petitioner.

   I have read and understand this Petition. Those statements contained therein of which I have personal knowledge are true, and those of which I do not have personal knowledge, I believe to be true.

   DATED at ..Winnipeg, Manitoba.. , this ..20th.. day of ..November......... 19 84.

   _____
   signature of Petitioner

   _____
   address of petitioner

Statement of Solicitor (If Petition seeks a divorce).

I, ... the solicitor for ....(also known as................).... , the Petitioner herein, certify to this Court that I have complied with the requirements of section 7 of The Divorce Act (Canada).

DATED at ..Winnipeg, Manitoba.. , this ..20th.. day of ..November......... 19 84.

_____
signature of solicitor

_____
address of solicitor

Schedule A
FORM F.D. 1—PETITION

SCHEDULE A
FINANCIAL STATEMENT OF _____
(also known as   )

1. Monthly Income

Income

Total gross income from all sources	$ 2,500.00
Family Allowance	$ 57.00
Tenants or Boarders	$ —
Pension (specify)	
	$ —
Workers Compensation	$ —
Public Assistance	$ —
Investments	$ —
Other (specify)	$
Total income from all sources A	$ 2,557.00
Net (Take Home Income A–B)	$ 1,863.15
Total gross income for last calendar year	$ 22,960.00

Deductions

Income tax	$ 616.37
Union Dues	$ —
Unemployment insurance	$ 42.36
Pension Plans	$ —
Canada Pension Plan	$ 11.35
Payroll Savings Plans	$
Other (specify) blue cross	$ 23.77
Total deductions B	$ 693.85

2. Actual Monthly Expenses

Food Groceries and household supplies	$ 300.00	SUB-TOTAL	$ 1,683.50
Meals outside the home	$ 50.00	Transportation Public Transit taxis, etc.	$ 5.00
Clothing	$ 100.00	Car operation Gas and oil	$ 80.00
Laundry and Dry cleaning	$ 25.00	Insurance and license	$ 42.91
Housing	$	Maintenance	$ 15.00
Rent or Mortgage	$ 773.00	Life Insurance (can't afford)	$
Taxes	$ 133.00	Education and recreation	
Home insurance	$ 28.00	School fees, books, etc.	$ 37.50
Heat	$ 50.00	Music lessons, hockey, etc.	$ 100.00
Water	$ 10.00		
Hydro	$ 50.00	Newspapers, publications, stationery	$
Phone	$ 7.50		
Cable T.V.	$ 7.00	Entertainment, recreation	$ 50.00
Repairs and maintenance	$ 20.00	Alcohol, tobacco	$ 50.00
Other (specify)	$	Vacation (can't afford)	$

Health and Medical		Personal care	
Insurance	$ _____	Hairdresser, barber	$ 20.00
Drugs	$ 5.00	Toilet articles	
Dental Care	$ 5.00	(Hairspray, soap, etc.)	$ 10.00
Hearing Aid and		Babysitting, day care	$ _____
Batteries	$ 30.00	Children's allowances,	
SUB-TOTAL	$ 1,683.50	gifts	$ 20.00
		Support payments to other relatives	$ _____
		Savings for the future R.R.S.P. (excluding payroll deductions)	$ 25.00
SUMMARY		Miscellaneous	$ 20.00
Net monthly income	$ 1,863.15	Loan Payment	$ 337.00
Present monthly expenses	$ 2,495.91		
Balance	$ -632.76	TOTAL:	$2,495.91

Schedule A
FORM F.D. 1—PETITION

SCHEDULE A
Assets and Debts

Whether shareable or not

3. Assets

	Present value	Value at date of separation (if marital property in issue)
Real Estate (Market value)	$85,000.00	$ N/A
Car (Market value)	$ 9,000.00	$ 9,000.00
Year 1983		
Make Cougar		
Bank accounts and Cash on Hand	NIL	NIL
R.R.S.P.	$ 300.00	$ 100.00
R.H.O.S.P.	NIL	NIL
Furniture, appliances, etc.	$ 5,000.00	$ 4,500.00
Stocks and Bonds	NIL	NIL
Money on Loan to others	NIL	NIL
Life Insurance (Cash value)	NIL	NIL
Pension Plans	NIL	NIL
Other (specify)	NIL	$ 7,500.00 German currency
*alleged to be non-shareable TOTAL	$99,000.00	$21,000.00

4. Debts

	Present Amount Outstanding	Amount Outstanding At Date of Separation (if marital property in issue)	Present Monthly Payments
Bank Loans in husband's name but secured by car	$11,786.88	$12,000.00	$ 337.00
Mortgage	64,000.00	NIL	773.00
Finance Companies	—	NIL	
Department Stores	3,000.00	NIL	
Credit Cards	—	NIL	
	—	NIL	
Other (specify)			
TOTAL:	$78,786.88	$12,000.00/ approx.	$1,100.00

*alleged to be non-shareable

Affidavit of Service

403 783

AFFIDAVIT OF SERVICE
(Personal Service)

IN THE COURT OF QUEEN'S BENCH OF ALBERTA

JUDICIAL DISTRICT OF EDMONTON　　　　　　　　　　No. 54919.

BETWEEN

    also known as　　　　　　　　　　　　　　　　　~~Plaintiff~~
    　　　　　　　　　　　　　　　　　　　　　　　Petitioner/
    　　　　　　　　　　　　　　　　　　　　　　　Applicant

and

    　　　　　　　　　　　　　　　　　　　　　　　~~Defendant~~
    　　　　　　　　　　　　　　　　　　　　　　　Respondent

I,　　　　　　　　　　　　　　　　　　　　　　of Edmonton,
in the Province of Alberta,　　　Process Server　　, MAKE OATH AND SAY:
1. THAT I DID on　　　　the　　29　　day of　　October,　　A.D. 1984,
personally serve
the above named　　Respondent　　　　　　　with a true copy(ies) of the
original　Notice of Motion and Order　　　　　　　　in this action
which (is ~~are~~) hereunto annexed and marked as "EXHIBIT(S)"　　"A" and "B",
respectively,
to this my AFFIDAVIT, by delivering the said copy(ies) to and leaving the same with
　　　　　　　　　　　　　　　　　　　　　　　the said　Respondent

at

2. THAT AT THE TIME of such service the said
admitted to me that (he, ~~she~~) was the　Respondent　　named in the within action.
3. THAT TO EFFECT such service I necessarily travelled　14 kms.

SWORN before me_____)
　　　　　　　　　　　PRINT NAME
at　Edmonton,　　　　　　　　　　　)
in the Province of Alberta　　　　　　　)　_____
this　30th　　day of　October　　　　)
A.D. 19　84.　　　　　　　　　　　　)

_____

A Commissioner for Oaths for Alberta

Standard Form for Budget Affidavit

IN THE COURT OF QUEEN'S BENCH OF ALBERTA
JUDICIAL DISTRICT OF EDMONTON

BETWEEN:

- And -

AFFIDAVIT

I,   , of the   of   ,
in the Province of Alberta, MAKE OATH AND SAY:

1. THAT I am the   in the within action and, as such, have a personal knowledge of the matters hereinafter deposed to except where stated to be on information and belief.

2. THAT the particulars of my present financial situation are accurately set out below, to the best of my knowledge and belief.

3. THAT my income from all sources is listed below:

INCOME			
CATEGORY	WEEKLY	MONTHLY	YEARLY
Salary or Wages			
Commissions			
Mileage Allowance (re employment)			
Family Allowance			
Unemployment Insurance			
Worker's Compensation			
Public Assistance			
Pension			
Dividends			
Interest			

INCOME (Continued)

CATEGORY	WEEKLY	MONTHLY	YEARLY
Rental Income .... Support From Others (list below): 1. 2. 3.			
TOTALS:	$	(a) $	$

Weekly Total:	$ _____	× 4.33	=	(b)	$ _____ monthly
Yearly Total:	$ _____	÷ 12	=	(c)	$ _____ monthly
Total Monthly Income	(a) + (b) + (c)		=		$ _____ monthly

4. THAT my current expenses are as set out below:

EXPENSES			
CATEGORY	WEEKLY	MONTHLY	YEARLY
Rent or Mortgage Payment .... Common Expense Charges .... Property Tax .... Property Insurance .... Electricity .... Water .... Gas .... Cable T.V. .... Telephone .... Repairs and Maintenance .... Food .... Clothing .... Laundry .... Alberta Health Care Plan .... Medicine .... Dental Care .... Dues .... Unemployment Insurance .... Pension Contributions .... Income Tax .... Taxis and Public Transit			

EXPENSES (Continued)

CATEGORY	WEEKLY	MONTHLY	YEARLY

Car Insurance ....
 Gas and Oil ....
 Car Servicing and Repairs ....
 Parking ....
 Life Insurance ....
 Entertainment ....
 Recreation ....
 Grooming ....
 Vacation ....
 Gifts ....
 Day Care ....
 Babysitting ....
 Support For Others ....
 Debt Payments (list below):
   1.
   2.
   3.
   4.
 	
 Others (list below):
   1.
   2.
   3.			

TOTALS:	$	(a) $	$

Weekly Total: $ _____   × 4.33   =   (b) $ _____ monthly

Yearly Total: $ _____   ÷ 12   =   (c) $ _____ monthly

Total Monthly Expenses   (a) + (b) + (c)   = $ _____ monthly

5.   THAT I have debts outstanding at the present time, the particulars of which are as set out below:

DEBTS		
CATEGORY	PARTICULARS	AMOUNT
	TOTAL DEBTS:	

6. THAT my assets at the present time are as set out below:

ASSETS		
CATEGORY	PARTICULARS	MARKET VALUE
	TOTAL ASSETS:	

7. THAT a summary of my present financial situation is as set out below:

<table>
<tr><td>Total Monthly Income:
(minus)
Total Monthly Expenses:
SURPLUS -or- DEFICIT:</td><td></td><td>Total Assets:
(minus)
Total Debts:
NET WORTH:</td><td></td></tr>
</table>

Affidavit for Interim Custody and a Restraining Order

IN THE COURT OF QUEEN'S BENCH OF ALBERTA
JUDICIAL DISTRICT OF EDMONTON

BETWEEN:

also known as

Petitioner

– and –

Respondent

AFFIDAVIT

I, also known as ,
MAKE OATH AND SAY:

1. THAT I am the Petitioner in this action and as such have a personal knowledge of the matters deposed except where stated to be on information and belief.

2. THAT I married the Respondent in Regina, Saskatchewan September 30, 1967 when I was sixteen years old, to escape a bad home situation.

3. THAT the Respondent drinks very heavily, and when drunk is both verbally abusive and violent.

4. THAT I have on more than one occasion called the police and had them remove his rifle from the house because I was afraid that he was going to use it on myself or the children.

5. THAT when the Respondent thought I was going to leave him he said that he would kill the children and myself and then commit suicide. He once held a gun to my neck and threatened me but a friend had previously taken the bullets from the gun.

6. THAT there are three children of the marriage, born January 9, 1972; born September 20, 1978 and born December 3, 1979, all girls.

7. THAT the Respondent is obsessed with pornography, and brings to the house pornographic videotapes which he watches and unless I intervene he would let the small children watch also.

8. THAT he has a friend with whom he generally watches these films, and this friend has attacked me, torn my clothes and on one occasion come into my bedroom partially undressed and I had to fight him off. That the Respondent has ignored my distress and calls for help on these occasions.

9. THAT the Respondent has tried to force me to do things that he has seen in these sexually explicit films, which horrified me.

10. THAT our twelve-year-old daughter has suffered abuse from this man and is having counselling from the Child Development Centre, and will require counselling for a long time. She kept running from home and was placed in a Foster Home for a while for her protection.

11. THAT our six-year-old daughter had a birthday and the Respondent and his male friend came and were kissing the little girls full on the mouth and the little girls were very upset by the whole scene.

12. THAT he steals and has stolen property in the house—yet he has held fingers over the lit burner of the stove threatening to burn her for taking something.

13. THAT the girls and myself are presently at a Shelter where we are safe, but we are going to be setting up a home for ourselves and are afraid of being found by the Respondent, who has repeatedly threatened us.

14. THAT the three girls do not wish to see or hear from the Respondent.

15. THAT the Respondent and I are owners of the property at   and he is still living in this house.

16. THAT I do not want to live there ever again, but I want to have sufficient furniture, and household goods to set up my home with the girls, and will still leave him some furniture.

17. THAT my clothing and the children's clothing is still in the house and we need these clothes.

18. THAT when I spoke to the Respondent about collecting any belongings from the house he said that he would smash everything before I could get it, including my fishtanks and china, dishes and other belongings, while the Sherriff was at the door.

19. THAT I have attached to this Affidavit a List described as Appendix "A" in which I have listed the furniture and household equipment that I would like and I have listed in Appendix "B" the furniture and household equipment I would leave with the Respondent, which is more valuable.

20. THAT I make this Affidavit in support of an application for Interim Custody of the Children of the Marriage, a Restraining Order Restraining the Respondent from molesting or harming myself or the children, and an Order granting me possession of the personal goods and other items listed on Appendix "A" and provision for a Police

Officer from the City of Edmonton Police Force to accompany me to pick up these articles.

SWORN BEFORE ME at the
City of Edmonton in the
Province of Alberta this
24th day of October,
1984.

_____

A COMMISSIONER FOR OATHS
IN AND FOR THE PROVINCE
OF ALBERTA.

COMMISSION EXPIRES—SEPT 4/87

APPENDIX "A"

Clothes of
Children's clothes
Children's bedroom furniture
Quilt
Lamps
Spice racks and spices
Baking equipment (muffin pans, cake pans, stainless steel bowls)
Couch and chair given by girlfriend
Bookshelves and books
Fish tanks (4), equipment and fish
Coffee table, china cabinet and contents
Bar set, wine glasses, etc.
Cassette tapes
Lawn chairs
Gas barbeque
Large 21" color T.V.
Children's bicycles
Popcorn maker
Toaster
Mixer
Food processor
Vacuum cleaner
Electric frypan

APPENDIX "B"

Washer/dryer
Fridge, stove
Rifle
Mechanic's tools
Kitchen table and chairs
Couch and chair
Master bedroom suite
Freezer
Small T.V.
V.H.S. video machine
Stereo
Pots, pans, cutlery, dishes
Sheets, pillowcases, blankets
Rototiller

Restraining Order

IN THE COURT OF QUEEN'S BENCH OF ALBERTA
JUDICIAL DISTRICT OF EDMONTON

BETWEEN:

    also known as   Petitioner

- and -

                                                Respondent

BEFORE THE HONOURABLE)	ON MONDAY, THE 17th DAY
)	
LAW COURTS BUILDING)	OF DECEMBER, A.D., 1984
EDMONTON, ALBERTA)	

ORDER

UPON THE APPLICATION of the Petitioner herein; AND UPON HEARING READ the pleadings; AND UPON HEARING Counsel for the Petitioner and Counsel for the Respondent; IT IS HEREBY ORDERED AND ADJUDGED:

1. THAT the Respondent,   , is hereby restrained from entering those premises at which the Petitioner and the infant children reside in the City of Edmonton, in the Province of Alberta, and from using the telephone to call the Petitioner.

2. THAT the Respondent,   , be and he is specifically restrained from interfering with or molesting the Petitioner or her children, either at the residence of the Petitioner or at the children's school or elsewhere in the City of Edmonton, or elsewhere in the Province of Alberta.

3. THAT upon it appearing to a Police Officer having jurisdiction in the Province of Alberta that the Respondent is in breach of any of the terms of the within Order then and in such event the Police Officer shall forthwith arrest the Respondent, restrain him, and bring him, at the earliest possible time, before a Judge of the Court of Queen's Bench of Alberta to show cause why he should not be committed for civil contempt.

4. THAT the Respondent shall have leave to apply to amend, vary or strike out the within Order upon seven (7) days clear notice.

JUSTICE OF THE COURT OF QUEEN'S BENCH OF ALBERTA

APPROVED AS TO FORM AND CONTENT:

Solicitor for the Respondent

ENTERED THIS   DAY
OF JANUARY, A.D., 1985.

CLERK OF THE COURT

APPENDIX II

Forms From the New Divorce Act, 1985

Petition for Divorce/234
    Appendix A – Financial Statement/237
    Appendix B – Debts/239
Notice to Respondent/240
Request for Divorce (Without Oral Hearing)/241
Divorce Judgment (Without Oral Evidence)/242
Request for a Certificate of Divorce/244
Certificate of Divorce/245

Petition for Divorce

IN THE COURT OF QUEEN'S BENCH OF ALBERTA
JUDICIAL DISTRICT OF _____

BETWEEN:

_____

Petitioner

- and -

_____

Respondent

PETITION FOR DIVORCE

To this Honourable Court:

1. The petitioner applies for a Divorce Judgment and the following relief:

   (a) ___ Custody;
   (b) ___ Access;
   (c) ___ Support for children in the amount of $ _____ per month or _____ ;
   (d) ___ Support for myself in the amount of $ _____ per month or _____ ;
   (e) ___ Non-Molestation Order;
   (f) ___ Costs.

2. The petitioner's grounds for seeking a divorce are that there has been a breakdown of the marriage by _____

(Provide those grounds set out under section 8(2) of the Divorce Act, 1985 (Canada) as are applicable.)

3. (1) There is no possibility of reconciliation.

   (2) The following efforts to reconcile have been made:

4. There has been no collusion in relation to this Petition for Divorce and, if the Petition is under section 8(2)(b) of the *Divorce Act*, there has been no condonation or connivance on the part of the petitioner in the bringing of this Petition.

   (If otherwise give particulars and the facts that justify the granting of the Divorce Judgment notwithstanding.)

5. Particulars of the petitioner's marriage are as follows:
   (a) date of marriage was _____;
   (b) place of marriage was _____;
   (c) the petitioner's surname before this marriage was _____;
   (d) the respondent's surname before this marriage was _____;
   (e) the parties marital status at time of marriage was
       (petitioner) _____, (respondent) _____;
   (f) the petitioner was born at _____
       on _____, 19 _____;
            (month)   (day)
   (g) the respondent spouse was born at _____
       on _____, 19 _____;
            (month)   (day)
   (h) the petitioner ceased cohabiting with the respondent on _____

6. (1) The petitioner's address is _____;
   (2) The respondent's address is _____;
   (3) The petitioner (or the respondent) have been ordinarily resident in the Province of Alberta for at least one year immediately preceding the date of this Petition.

7. Particulars regarding the children of the parties are as follows:
   (a) the names and dates of birth of all of the children are:
       _____;
       _____;
       _____;
   (b) the petitioner claims custody of:
       _____;
       _____;
       _____;
   (c) the petitioner proposes the following access arrangements:

   (d) the following financial arrangements for the support of the children have been made:

   OR

   (d) the petitioner proposes the following financial arrangements having regard to the relief claimed:

8. The particulars of all written or oral agreements between the petitioner and the respondent affecting the support of the petitioner, the support of the children and custody or access to the children, as the case may be, are as follows:

9. The particulars of all court proceedings regarding the marriage, support of the parties or children and custody of or access to the children, as the case may be, are as follows:

10. Particulars regarding the parties' employment
    (a) with respect to the petitioner are as follows:
        (i) the name and address of the petitioner's employer is
        _____ ;
        (ii) the petitioner's gross income is
        _____ ;
        (iii) the petitioner is paid every _____ ;
        (iv) the total income declared on the petitioner's last income tax return in 19 _____ was $ _____ and the petitioner's net taxable income was $ _____ ;
    (b) with respect to the respondent, so far as is known to the petitioner, are as follows:
        (i) the name and address of the respondent's employer is
        _____ ;
        (ii) the respondent's gross income is
        _____ ;
        (iii) the respondent is paid every _____ ;
        (iv) the total income declared on the respondent's last income tax return in 19 _____ was $ _____ and the respondent's net taxable income was $ _____ .

11. Particulars of the petitioner's financial situation are shown on Appendices A and B.

_____
Petitioner or Solicitor for
the Petitioner whose address is

_____
and whose address for service is

_____

Statement of Solicitor

I, _____ , the solicitor for the Petitioner _____ , the Petitioner herein, certify to this Court that I have complied with the requirements of section 9 of the *Divorce Act, 1985* (Canada).

DATED AT _____ , in the Province of Alberta, this _____ day of _____ 19 _____ .

_____
Signature of Solicitor

_____
Address of Solicitor

Issued out of the office of the
Clerk of the Court of Queen's
Bench of Alberta, Judicial District
of _____ at _____ , in the
Province of Alberta, this _____ day of
_____ at _____ 19 _____

_____
Clerk of the Court of
Queen's Bench of Alberta.

APPENDIX A
FINANCIAL STATEMENT

1. MONTHLY INCOME

INCOME:		DEDUCTIONS:	
Total gross income from all sources	$ _____	Income Tax	$ _____
Family Allowance	$ _____	Union Dues	$ _____
Pension (specify)		Unemployment Insurance	$ _____
		Pension Plans	$ _____
		Canada Pension Plan	$ _____
	$ _____	Payroll Savings Plan	$ _____
Workers Compensation	$ _____	Other	
Public Assistance	$ _____	(Specify)	$ _____
Investments	$ _____		
Other (specify)	$ _____		
A. Total income from all sources	$ _____	B. Total deductions	$ _____

Net (Take home)
Income (A minus B) $ _____
Total gross income for
    last calendar year $ _____

2. ACTUAL MONTHLY EXPENSES

Food, groceries and household supplies	$ _____	SUB-TOTAL	$ _____
Meals outside the home	$ _____	Transportation, public transit and taxis, etc.	$ _____
Clothing	$ _____	Car operation	
Laundry and dry cleaning	$ _____	Gas and oil	$ _____
Housing	$ _____	Insurance and license	$ _____
Rent or		Maintenance	$ _____
Mortgage	$ _____	Life insurance	$ _____
Taxes	$ _____	Education and Recreation	
Home insurance	$ _____	School fees	$ _____
Utilities	$ _____	Books, etc.	$ _____
Repairs and Main.	$ _____	Music lessons, hockey, etc.	$ _____
		Newspapers, publications, stationery	$ _____
Other (specify)	$ _____	Entertainment, recreation	$ _____
		Alcohol, tobacco	$ _____
		Vacation	$ _____
Health & medical insurance	$ _____	Personal care hairdresser, barber	$ _____
Drugs	$ _____	Toilet articles (hairspray, soap, etc.)	$ _____
Dental care	$ _____	Babysitting, day care	$ _____
SUB-TOTAL	$ _____	Children's allowance, gifts	$ _____
		Support payments to other relatives	$ _____
		Savings for future (excluding payroll deductions)	$ _____
		Miscellaneous	$ _____
		TOTAL	$ _____

3. SUMMARY

Net monthly income $ _____
Present monthly expenses $ _____
Balance $ _____

APPENDIX B
DEBTS

	Present Amount Outstanding	Arrears, if any	Present Monthly Payments
Bank loans	$	$	$
Mortgage			
Finance companies			
Department stores			
Credit cards			
Other (specify)			
TOTAL			

Notice to Respondent

IN THE COURT OF QUEEN'S BENCH OF ALBERTA
JUDICIAL DISTRICT OF _____

NOTICE TO RESPONDENT

TO:

(the respondent)

AN APPLICATION HAS BEEN MADE FOR A DIVORCE JUDGMENT. The details are set out in the attached Petition for Divorce.

1. IF YOU DISPUTE ANY OF THE CLAIMS or IF YOU WISH TO MAKE ANY CLAIM YOURSELF, YOU MUST FILE AN ANSWER at the court office shown on the Petition for Divorce within the following times:

    (a) if you were served in Alberta, within 15 days from the date of service;

    (b) if you were served elsewhere in Canada, within 40 days from the date of service:

    (c) if served elsewhere than that referred to in clause (a) or (b), within the time indicated on the Order for Service.

2. IF YOU DO NOT FILE

    (a) AN ANSWER, or

    (b) DEMAND OF NOTICE requiring that notice of any application to be made in this action be given to you,

and unless you serve a copy of that Answer or Demand of Notice on the petitioner at the address for service given in the Petition for Divorce you are not entitled to notice of any further proceedings and an order may be made in your absence and enforced against you.

DATED AT _____ , in the Province of Alberta, this _____ day of _____ , 19 _____ .

Clerk of the Court of
Queen's Bench of Alberta

Request for Divorce

IN THE COURT OF QUEEN'S BENCH OF ALBERTA
JUDICIAL DISTRICT OF _____

BETWEEN:

_____
Petitioner

- and -

_____
Respondent.

REQUEST FOR DIVORCE
(WITHOUT ORAL HEARING)

TO THE CLERK OF THE COURT:

1. I request that this action be set for hearing as an undefended divorce to be considered pursuant to Rule 568 on the basis of affidavit evidence.

2. Service of the Petition for Divorce on my spouse was effected by _____ on the _____ day of _____ 19 ____ , (or as indicated in the affidavit of service).

3. The affidavit evidence to be considered with my Petition for Divorce has been filed and is attached hereto.

4. The respondent has not filed an Answer or a Demand of Notice (or has filed a Demand of Notice but has consented to this request by consent endorsed hereon).

5. The respondent's address is _____ .
6. The respondent's solicitor's address is _____ .
7. The petitioner's address is _____ .
8. The petitioner's solicitor's address is _____ .

DATED at _____ , in the Province of Alberta, this _____ day of _____ , 19 _____ .

_____
Petitioner or Solicitor

AR 117/86

Divorce Judgment

IN THE COURT OF QUEEN'S BENCH OF ALBERTA
JUDICIAL DISTRICT OF _____

BETWEEN

_____
Petitioner

- and -

_____
Respondent.

Before the Honourable   At _____ in
_____   the Province of Alberta,
Judge of the Court of   on the _____ day
Queen's Bench of Alberta   of _____ , 19 ____ .

DIVORCE JUDGMENT
(WITHOUT ORAL EVIDENCE)

The Petition for Divorce coming on before the Court this day, and upon reading the pleadings, and the affidavits of _____.

IT IS ADJUDGED:

That the Court renders a judgment of divorce this _____ day of _____ , 19 ____ between Petitioner and Respondent, who were married at the _____ of _____ , in the Province of _____ , the divorce to be effective on the 31st day after the day that this judgment is rendered, unless this judgment is appealed before that 31st day.

OR

the divorce to be effective on _____ day of _____ , 19 ____ , the Court

    (a)   being of the opinion that by reason of special circumstances it is in the public interest for the divorce to take effect earlier than the 31st day, and

(b) being advised that the parties to this divorce proceeding have agreed and undertake that no appeal from this judgment shall be taken, or if an appeal from this judgment was taken, it has been abandoned.

LET THIS JUDGMENT ISSUE:

_____
JUDGE OF THE COURT OF
QUEEN'S BENCH OF ALBERTA

_____
Clerk

ENTERED at _____ in the Province of Alberta this _____ day of _____ 19 _____ .

_____
Clerk of the Court

Request for Certificate of Divorce

IN THE COURT OF QUEEN'S BENCH OF ALBERTA
JUDICIAL DISTRICT OF _____

BETWEEN:

_____
Petitioner

- and -

_____
Respondent.

REQUEST FOR A CERTIFICATE OF DIVORCE

I, _____ of the _____ of _____ in the _____ do hereby request that a Certificate of Divorce be issued.

DATED at _____, in the Province of Alberta, this _____ day of _____ 19 ____ .

_____

Certificate of Divorce

IN THE COURT OF QUEEN'S BENCH OF ALBERTA
JUDICIAL DISTRICT OF _____

CERTIFICATE OF DIVORCE

    This is to certify that the marriage of _____ and _____ that was solemnized on the _____ day of _____ 19 _____ was dissolved by a judgment that became effective on the _____ day of _____, 19 _____ .

    DATED at _____, in the Province of Alberta, this _____ day of _____, 19 _____ .

                                                  Clerk of the Court of
                                                 Queen's Bench of Alberta